Language Contact and Composite Structures in New Ireland

SIL International
Publications in Language Use
and Education
Number 4

Publications in Language Use and Education is a serial publication of SIL International. The series began as a venue for works covering a broad range of topics in sociolinguistics and has been expanded to include a broad range of topics in education, including mother tongue literacy multilingual education, and informal education. While most volumes are authored by members of SIL, suitable works by others will also form part of the series.

Series Editors

Gloria E. Kindell
Graduate Institute
of Applied Linguistics

Stephen L. Walter
Graduate Institute
of Applied Linguistics

Volume Editor

Rhonda Hartell Jones

Production Staff

Bonnie Brown, Managing Editor
Karoline Fisher, Compositor
Hazel Shorey, Graphic Artist

Language Contact and Composite Structures in New Ireland

Rebecca Sue Jenkins

SIL International
Dallas, Texas

© 2005 by SIL International
Library of Congress Catalog No: 2004110936
ISBN: 1-55671-156-5
ISSN: 1545-0074

Printed in the United States of America

All rights reserved. No part of this publication may be reproduced, stored in a retrieval system, or transmitted in any form or by any means—electronic, mechanical, photocopy, recording, or otherwise—without the express permission of the SIL International, with the exception of brief excerpts in journal articles or reviews.

Copies of this and other publications of the SIL International may be obtained from

International Academic Bookstore
SIL International
7500 W. Camp Wisdom Road
Dallas, TX 75236-5699

Voice: 972-708-7404
Fax: 972-708-7363
Email: academic_books@sil.org
Internet: http://www.ethnologue.com

Contents

List of Maps, Tables, and Figures ix
    Maps. ix
    Tables ix
    Figures x

Acknowledgements. xi

Abbreviations and Symbols xiii

Introduction. xv

1 The Linguistic Situation in Papua New Guinea 1
    Unique Language Situation 1
    Language and Culture 4
    National Language Policy 7
        Historical development 7
        Current policy 9
    The Languages of New Ireland 10
    Tigak and the Austronesian Language Family. 12
    Language Contact Phenomena in New Ireland 14
        Bilingualism 18
        Diglossia 20
        Dialect gradation, codeswitching, and borrowings 22
        Language shift, attrition, and death. 35
    Predictions: Papua New Guinea's Linguistic Future 53

2 A Review of Literature on Language Contact Phenomena ... 63
Language Contact and Language Change: General ... 64
Bilingualism and Diglossia ... 65
Codeswitching and Borrowing ... 67
Language Shift, Attrition, and Death ... 69
Pidgins and Creoles ... 71
    General references ... 71
    Theories of pidgin/creole formation ... 72
Psycholinguistic Research on Language Processing ... 74
    Models of language processing ... 74
    Levels of language processing ... 76
    The mental lexicon and morpheme types ... 77

3 Theory, Methodology, and Hypotheses ... 79
Models ... 80
    The Matrix Language Frame (MLF) model ... 80
    Characteristics of the matrix language ... 80
The Abstract Level Model ... 82
    Language production models: Psycholinguistic and linguistic background ... 82
    The levels of the language production process ... 84
The 4-M Model ... 87
    Background to morpheme typing ... 87
    The four morpheme types ... 88
    The matrix language determination of morpheme types ... 91
Beyond Codeswitching: The Extension of the MLF and Related Models ... 94
Methodology ... 96
Hypotheses ... 97
    Hypotheses about the matrix language ... 98
    Hypotheses about morpheme types in Tok Pisin ... 99
    Hypotheses about constituent types in Tok Pisin ... 100

4 Tigak, a Typical Austronesian Language ... 103
Tigak Phonology, Syllable Structure, and Stress ... 104
    Phonological characteristics ... 104
    Syllable structure ... 105
    Stress ... 106
Tigak Word Order ... 106
Tigak Word Categories ... 108
The Tigak Noun Phrase (NP) ... 110
    Articles ... 111

Complex noun phrases	112
The Tigak Pronominal System	113
The Tigak Verb Phrase	114
The verb phrase and the equative clause	114
Transitive and intransitive verbs	116
Serial and compound verbs	119
Tense, mood, and aspect	120
Prepositions	121
Possession	122
Subordinate Clauses	123
Discourse Characteristics	126

5 Is Tok Pisin an Austronesian Language? 129

Sociolinguistic and Historical Background of Tok Pisin	131
The Extended MLF Model for Pidgin Formation Applied to Tok Pisin	137
The composite matrix language of Tok Pisin	140
Constituent and morpheme types in Tok Pisin	146
Austronesian Features of Tok Pisin	153
Phonology, syllable structure, and stress	153
Word order	154
Word categories	160
The noun phrase	160
The pronominal system	162
The verb phrase	164
Prepositions	176
Possession	178
Subordinate clauses	180
Discourse characteristics	184
Summary of Austronesian features in Tok Pisin	184

6 Convergence and Renewed Influence 189

Tigak Convergence to Tok Pisin	190
Convergence at different levels of abstract structure	191
Discourse convergence	199
Pragmatic convergence	200
Tok Pisin Convergence to English	200
Lexical borrowing	201
Numbers and noun constructions	201
Negative questions	202
Tense marking and participant reference	203
Tigak Convergence to English	203
Tense marking and participant reference	203

    Plural marking and number distinctions 204
    Possessives 204

7 Conclusion 207
    The Interrelationships of Language Contact Phenomena
      in New Ireland 208
    Tok Pisin: Its Development and Its Future 209
    Findings and Conclusions. 212

**Appendix 1: Examples of Shared Lexical Items in Austronesian
    Languages** 217

**Appendix 2: A Comparison of Austronesian Grammatical
    Structures** 219

References 231

List of Maps, Tables, and Figures

Maps

Map 1.1. Main towns of Papua New Guinea 3
Map 1.2. Distribution of languages in Papua New Guinea 5
Map 1.3. Location of the Meso-Melanesian cluster
and its subgroups 11
Map 1.4. Lavongai-Nalik chain of New Ireland 13
Map 1.5. Northern New Ireland languages 15
Map 1.6. Tigak Islands 17
Map 1.7. Tigak dialects 25
Map 1.8. Tungag and Tigak. 27
Map 1.9. Kavieng, capital of New Ireland Province 39
Map 1.10. Nalik language area 41
Map 1.11. Kuot language area 47
Map 1.12. Sumuna. 50

Tables

Table 3.1. Examples of the four morpheme types 90
Table 4.1. Tigak independent pronouns 113
Table 5.1. Tok Pisin pronouns 163
Table 5.2. Tigak independent pronouns 163

Table 5.3. Correspondence of Tok Pisin to Austronesian
   pronominal system 185
Table 5.4. Correspondence of Tok Pisin to Austronesian
   VP word order 186
Table 5.5. Correspondence of Tok Pisin to Austronesian
   NP word order 187

Figures

Figure 3.1. Abstract levels in language production. 84
Figure 3.2. Feature-based classification of morphemes
   in the 4-M model. 88

Acknowledgements

I would like to acknowledge each person who has had a part in this study, but there are far too many to mention by name. Special appreciation goes to Carol Myers-Scotton for all the extra miles she has gone to enable me to complete this task in the limited periods of time I have had in the United States. She has directed courses of study that I otherwise would have missed. She has encouraged me, prodded me, corrected me, and directed me in my writing. Most of all, she has inspired me with her own extraordinary intellectual accomplishments and prolific level of production while always maintaining personal contact with and interest in her students.

I am also grateful to the other members of my thesis committee from which this book derives: Dorothy Disterheft, Bruce Pearson, and Elizabeth Joiner. Thank you for your patience with a "long distance" student. The linguistics faculty at the University of South Carolina deserves more than thanks.

Thanks are also due to my friends and colleagues who have encouraged me, prayed for me, and supported me through the entire process. Their interest has kept me going and helped me to keep the goal in sight.

My greatest debt is to my family. My husband and children have willingly taken on extra burdens in order for me to pursue my studies. They have given of their time and their energy that I might use my time and energy in this effort. Thanks for having faith in me and patience with me. I would not have made it without you!

Abbreviations and Symbols

-	morpheme boundary	EXC	exclusive
.	syllable boundary	FUT	future
1, 2, 3	first, second, third persons	GEN	genitive
		H	high
ASP	aspect	HAB	habitual
AN	Austronesian	INC	inclusive
ADJ	adjective	IndQnt	indefinite quantifier
ADV	adverb	INT	intensifier
AGR	agreement	INSTR	instrument
ART	article	IRR	irrealis
CML	composite matrix language	LIG	ligature
		L	low
COMP	complementizer	L1	first language
CONT	continuative	L2	second language
CP	complement phrase	LOC	locative
CS	codeswitch(ing)	LWC	language of wider communication
Cs	causative		
DEM	demonstrative	MA	motion away
Dl	dual number	MT	motion toward (aspect marker)
DNG	Dutch New Guinea		
DO	direct object	MT	modern Tigak
EAPE	Eastern Australian Pidgin English	ML	matrix language
		MLF	matrix language frame
EL	embedded language	MOD	modifier
EQP	equative phrase	MPE	Melanesian Pidgin English

N	noun	S	subject
NAN	non-Austronesian	SADV	sentence adverb
NEG	negative	SAGR	subject agreement
NIP	New Ireland Province	SG	singular
NP	noun phrase	SIL	SIL International
OB	object	SLA	second language acquisition
OBAGR	object agreement		
OBP	object of preposition	s.o.	someone
P/C	pidgin(s) and creole(s)	SOV	subject, object, verb word order
PCOMP	predicate complement		
PL	plural	s.t.	something
PM	predicate marker	ST	standard Tigak
PNG	Papua New Guinea	SVO	subject, verb, object word order
POS	possessor		
PRE-V	pre-verb	TMA	tense, mood, aspect
PRF	perfective	TP	Tok Pisin
PRN	pronoun	TR	trial (number)
PST	past	TZ	transitive suffix
QLD	Queensland	V	verb
QNT	Quantifier	VI	intransive verb
RDP	reduplication	VR	valence reducer
RECP	reciprocal	VT	transitive verb
REFL	reflexive		

Tigak and languages other than Tok Pisin (TP) in the examples are in italics. Tok Pisin is in bold.

Introduction

My interest in language contact phenomena developed slowly, as my studies in sociolinguistics became more relevant to my linguistic research in Papua New Guinea. When I began my sociolinguistic studies my husband and I had been working among the Tigak people of New Ireland for over ten years (1986–1999) with SIL International.[1] The Tigak language is an Austronesian language indigenous to New Ireland, one of the regions of Papua New Guinea from which many of the early speakers of the pidgin/creole language Tok Pisin came. In this study I will use Tigak as the example of a typical Austronesian language to demonstrate the Austronesian source for many of the conceptual and structural characteristics of Tok Pisin which come from multiple sources. Most of the subjects are native speakers of Tigak.[2] For comparative purposes, some subjects are native speakers of other Papua New Guinea languages who also speak Tigak and/or Tok Pisin. The survey data were gathered from speakers in each village of the Tigak language area in a natural setting as my husband and I lived on Ungan Island from 1987 to 1996. Extensive material was also gathered from Tigaks living in the town of Kavieng and the surrounding villages during eight months of 1996. At other times I worked with Tigak speakers in the towns of Lae, Rabaul, Port Moresby, and Ukarumpa.

[1] SIL International, formerly known as the Summer Institute of Linguistics.
[2] The corpus of our recorded data from New Ireland contains speech samples from 131 named or identified subjects. Of these subjects, nine do not speak Tigak. Other recorded samples could not be attributed to a specific speaker. Tok Pisin data are from various sources including non-Austronesian L1 speakers such as gardeners, carpenters, housemaids, store clerks, waiters, public vehicle drivers, preachers, police and other civil servants, and politicians.

Although Tigak is among the larger language groups of Papua New Guinea in terms of number of speakers, it is still a small language group by world standards with a population of approximately 10,000. The Tigak people are ideally situated for a study in language contact living on the northwestern tip of the island of New Ireland and on numerous smaller islands surrounding that tip (see map 1.4 in chapter 1). Because all the language groups of New Ireland are small, they are in immediate contact with other languages. Five different indigenous languages are spoken in the territory contiguous to Tigak territory (see map 1.5 in chapter 1). The provincial capital of New Ireland is Kavieng, located in the center of the Tigak language area on traditional Tigak ground. Because it is now the provincial capital and houses the government offices and many business headquarters for New Ireland, Kavieng is populated by speakers of all twenty languages indigenous to New Ireland, as well as by speakers of numerous languages indigenous to other areas of Papua New Guinea, speakers of English, and speakers of Tok Pisin (a pidgin/creole language developed primarily within Papua New Guinea). Thus, the Tigak people have contact with more different languages than any other language group in New Ireland, possibly more than the population of any area in Papua New Guinea except the National Capital District surrounding Port Moresby.

Most Papua New Guineans are multilingual, and the Tigaks are no exception. The population as a whole, however, exhibits a wide range of linguistic competence. Some monolingual Tigaks still live on the more inaccessible islands, but few Tigaks are completely monolingual. Most seemingly monolingual speakers of Tigak could be called at least passively bilingual because they usually do understand the nearest other indigenous language or Tok Pisin, even if they speak only Tigak. Most of the island dwellers do speak Tok Pisin, and the more educated ones also speak English and sometimes one or two other indigenous languages. The Tigaks on the mainland of New Ireland use Tok Pisin in more domains than the island Tigaks because they have easier access to Kavieng, where Tok Pisin is the primary means of interethnic communication. Within Kavieng there are young Tigaks who do not speak the Tigak language, but who speak only Tok Pisin and English. Within fifty miles of Kavieng there is a dying Papuan language, an Austronesian language with at most five living speakers, and many languages exhibiting varying degrees of convergence to Tok Pisin and/or English.

Studying and speaking an Austronesian language and Tok Pisin and being surrounded by numerous examples of language contact phenomena, I became interested in how these phenomena affected each other and in how they could be explained. Some of the sociolinguistics principles I studied were not applicable to the situations I observed, and many theoretical approaches were contradictory to each other. This lack of explanatory theory spurred me to look more closely at the data available in New Ireland and at the theories covering the contact phenomena I observed, hence this study. In particular, I was struck by the semantic and morphosyntactic parallels between Tok Pisin and Tigak, an Austronesian language. The diversity of theories concerning pidgin/creole formation and the lack of explanatory power in them focused my attention on the relationship of the languages involved in the development of Tok Pisin and the mechanisms producing this contact variety.

Language contact theories have in the past often focused on one phenomenon at a time and have succeeded only in describing the phenomenon under consideration. The development of pidgins and creoles has, in particular, been an area of widely diverse (and often strongly defended) theories. The theories range from early monogenisists like Taylor and Whinnom (as reported in Holm 1988a) through modern relexificationists such as Lefebvre (1986, 1993, 1996, and 1997); from simplificationists represented by Voerhoeve (1971), Ferguson (1971), Ferguson and DeBose (1977), Le Page (1977), Koefoed (1979), and Hatch (1983) to universalists such as Kay and Sankoff (1974), Givón (1979b), and Bickerton (1981, 1999); from superstratists represented by Chaudenson (1977) to substratists such as Schuchardt (edited by Gilbert 1980), Alleyne (1986), Thomason (1980), Rickford and McWhorter (1997), and Siegel (1998). Others, exemplified by Slobin (1983), Mufwene (1986), Myers-Scotton (2001), and Winford (2003), acknowledge that the actual process of pidgin/creole formation involves aspects of many of these positions. There are certainly universal principles involved in any language production, whether universal patterns of simplification or innate language creation faculties; and all the languages in a contact situation, whether substrate or superstrate, will have some effect on the resulting language contact variety. The problem is in articulating a theory that is more than descriptive. It is also preferable for a theory to apply across the board to language contact phenomena rather than to only one phenomenon.

The primary purpose of this study is to demonstrate the connection between Tok Pisin and the Austronesian substratum, using Tigak as an example of a typical Austronesian language. I will establish this connection by extrapolating principles from a set of explanatory theories (the Matrix Language Frame, Abstract Level, and 4-M models) and applying them to the development of Tok Pisin, demonstrating its parallels to the Austronesian substrate. I will argue that the direction of influence for the morphosyntactic frame of Tok Pisin first went in one direction, from the Austronesian substrate languages to the developing pidgin/creole, but that the direction of influence has now reversed, with Tok Pisin influencing the indigenous languages. The motivation for applying these theories is the semantic and structural similarity between Tok Pisin and the Austronesian substrate languages of most of the early speakers of Tok Pisin. I will demonstrate how Tigak and other Austronesian languages contributed to the grammatical frame of Tok Pisin, but how Tok Pisin is now framing Tigak (and other indigenous languages) through convergence. As a secondary purpose of this study I will also discuss other language contact phenomena in New Ireland, especially those phenomena involving contact with Tok Pisin, in order to demonstrate the current widespread influence of Tok Pisin on the other languages of New Ireland, in addition to Tigak.

Among the common linguistic terms encountered in the literature, some of the most common are model, theory, and hypothesis. These concepts are also among the most misunderstood and misused within the linguistic community. At more than one major linguistics institute or conference I have heard linguists criticizing a particular theory or model because it does not exactly represent every linguistic detail under consideration. (All the while the same critics ignore the shortcomings of their own pet theories.) In the context of a study based so heavily on theoretical constructs as this present study, I believe we would do well to consider what a model is and what purpose it serves in linguistics. A primary source for the following comments is Fromkin (1968). In addition I rely on my own understanding of theoretical constructs formed during years of study and teaching in the fields of mathematics and the physical sciences.

First, the terms model and theory may be used interchangeably to represent abstract conceptions. The term hypothesis is generally used to represent a specific and limited idea within a model or theory. It is a prediction of a particular outcome under particular conditions. Thus, a model may contain or be based upon many hypotheses. In a more unrestricted sense, hypothesis is also used as a synonym for a model or theory. In contrast to the usual mathematical sense of a model as a formal abstract system that may or may not have a relationship to physical reality, in the present study the term model is used in the sense of a representation of a physical reality. The physical reality under consideration here is that of language production and its relationship to language contact phenomena. Although representing a physical reality, a model need not be a literal description. Its function or purpose is to help us visualize an abstract process to lead us to a better understanding of the physical phenomena it produces. A model or theory relates the conceptual to the empirical.

Fromkin (1968:53–54) states six "general requirements of a model of performance" in the field of linguistics. These six requirements are listed below.

1. It must be based on the physical data of speech performance.
2. It must describe the phenomena of interest.
3. It must predict events; which predictions are confirmed by further experiments.
4. It must suggest certain causal relationships...providing an explanation.
5 It must be consistent; it must not present contradictory explanations.
6. It must be testable; i.e., it must be disprovable.

It is clear that any model not based on any one of these six conditions would be of limited (if any) use in developing an accurate understanding of the phenomena in question. I will be using the extended Matrix Language Frame (MLF) and the related Abstract Level and 4-M models in this study to analyze language contact phenomena observed in New Ireland of Papua New Guinea using actual speech data I collected there. The data relate to languages that are in contact with each other and the resulting contact phenomena produced by that contact. I will use these models to make predictions (or hypotheses) concerning outcomes of various contact situations and to suggest the causal relationships that explain, in a consistent way, how or why the conditions produce the given outcomes. This application of these models to the language contacts phenomena observed in New Ireland is a means of testing the theories to either prove or disprove them. Such testing is an important process in the development of any theory, for it produces the refinements that clarify and improve the theory. A theory is initially developed with a limited body of data, but it is modified and refined as it is tested against larger and more diverse bodies of data.

The linguistic situation in Papua New Guinea is presented in chapter 1, including a general description of the languages and culture in Papua New Guinea, the language policies (past and present), the number and types of languages spoken in New Ireland Province, and the relationship of Tigak to the larger Austronesian language family. I describe different language contact phenomena that are currently observable in New Ireland Province in accordance with my secondary purpose stated above. Although Tigak is the Austronesian language presented and discussed in detail in this study, other languages (both Austronesian and Papuan) of New Ireland are discussed in relationship to the types of contact phenomena represented in each case. I will show that most of these contact phenomena are related to the influence of Tok Pisin on the vernacular languages of New Ireland. The normal conditions of multilingualism and diglossia common throughout the province are described. The degree and types of dialect variation, codeswitching, and borrowing are illustrated primarily from Tigak data. Other phenomena, such as language shift among urban dwellers, convergence, attrition, and language death, are illustrated with Tigak, Nalik, Kuot, and Sumuna, respectively. I conclude the chapter with my predictions about the linguistic future of Papua New Guinea.

I will review the literature related to the language contact phenomena discussed in this study in chapter 2. This review will include psycholinguistic research on language production and processing and general linguistic theory that has influenced the theories related to language contact. The sociolinguistic literature will include the topics of bilingualism, diglossia, codeswitching, borrowing, second language acquisition (SLA), language shift and attrition, and pidgin/creole formation.

Chapter 3 will present the theoretical framework for this study. The basic tenets of the MLF model and the characteristics of a matrix language will be described. The Abstract Level model will be presented with a review of the linguistic and psycholinguistic background to language production models followed by a description of the levels involved in the language production process. The 4-M model is introduced with a summary of the background of morpheme typing, followed by a description of each of the four morpheme types. This section closes with a discussion of how the matrix language determines what morpheme types are used under various contact conditions. The chapter concludes with a discussion of the extension of the MLF model to language contact applications other than the original application to codeswitching.

In chapter 4, I will present the subjects (the speakers of various Papua New Guinea languages) and the methodology of my data collection and study. The specific hypotheses that I am proposing within the theoretical framework of this study are presented, including those hypotheses related to the composite matrix language, to the morpheme types that occur in Tok Pisin from each contributing language, through the constituent types in Tok Pisin.

I present the Tigak language of New Ireland in chapter 5 by giving a basic grammatical description of this Austronesian language. The purpose of this grammatical analysis of Tigak is to provide a point of comparison for the language contact phenomena that follow, especially concerning the Austronesian characteristics of Tok Pisin.

The primary purpose of the study, the application of the Abstract Level model and related theories to the development of a pidgin/creole, is presented in chapter 6 with the case of Tok Pisin. I give a sociolinguistic and historical background for Tok Pisin, followed by the specific descriptions of the composite matrix language, the constituent types, and the morpheme types found in the language. The chapter focuses on a point-by-point comparison of Tok Pisin grammatical structure with that of the Austronesian representative, Tigak. In each case the source and means of the development of the particular construction is discussed based on principles of the MLF, Abstract Level, and 4-M models.

The reverse process from the formation of Tok Pisin, the convergence of Tigak to Tok Pisin, and the convergence of both Tigak and Tok Pisin to English, is described in chapter 7. This convergence is also explained within the theoretical framework of this study.

Chapter 8 summarizes the interrelationships of the language contact phenomena of New Ireland and the past development and the future of Tok Pisin. It concludes with a review of the hypotheses proposed and the findings of the study related to those hypotheses.

1

The Linguistic Situation in Papua New Guinea

Unique Language Situation

The uniqueness of the Papua New Guinean language situation is not in its language diversity, but in the magnitude of the number of distinct languages. It is the most linguistically heterogeneous nation in the world, and the language contact phenomena are no different in Papua New Guinea from those in other multilingual nations. Lingua francas have developed (Tok Pisin and Hiri Motu among others), a foreign language has been imposed on the country (English), and hundreds of indigenous languages exist within a few hours walk of each other. Clyne defines BILINGUALISM or MULTILINGUALISM as simply the use of more than one language (1997:301). Most Papua New Guineans know more than one language, and many are multilingual, knowing at least one vernacular language (often more) and Tok Pisin and English (see the fuller discussion of bilingualism in New Ireland below).

In 1982 the United Nations University in Tokyo hosted a workshop focusing on the problems encountered in the modern world concerning (primarily unwritten) minority languages. The first question participants were asked to consider was

> Are there any conflicts between the rights of ethnic and linguistic minorities to use and preserve their language and the desire of centralized states to establish a national language as a universal means of communication and administration? If so, can such conflicts be

resolved without sacrificing the interests of minority groups? (Coulmas 1984b:ix)

This question implies a dichotomy in a situation that is much more complex than the simple opposition between an individual's right to use a particular language and a government's right to simplify its administrative functions. Language and economics are closely tied, so language policy and national development are interrelated in any multilingual country. However, national development is not solely dependent upon or determined by a government's desires and plans. Eastman (1983) states emphatically that for economic development to occur a multilingual nation must use some language of wider communication to replace the different vernaculars. The linguistic and developmental situation in Papua New Guinea supports this conclusion. I will be discussing the linguistic situation in northwestern New Ireland, focusing on the linguistic behavior of the Tigak-speaking people of New Ireland Province, but also including language contact phenomena evidenced among other language groups surrounding the Tigaks. Among the factors discussed will be language choices and the reasons behind those choices, such as the factors mentioned above: government policies, education, economics, and an individual's right to choose his/her language. First, however, I will discuss the linguistic situation of Papua New Guinea as a whole.

Souter (1963) called Papua New Guinea the "last unknown." This is still an accurate description of Papua New Guinea. It is a young nation struggling to enter the modern world without the experience, education, technology, infrastructure, or developed resources to hold its own among world powers. The linguistic diversity of this small nation magnifies the problems of education and the development of national unity. Every Papua New Guinean is a member of a linguistic minority. Most Papua New Guineans feel the tension between the desire (for themselves or their children) to improve their socioeconomic status, which means using a lingua franca or a language of wider communication (LWC), and the desire to maintain their vernacular language, vernacular in the sense of a native or indigenous language that is usually unwritten or nonstandardized. Pool claims that "a country that is linguistically highly heterogeneous is always underdeveloped" (1972:213), and that in fact, the linguistic diversity itself prevents political and economic development (p. 214). Papua New Guinea is the extreme example of both characteristics: the most linguistically heterogeneous and the most underdeveloped country on earth today. The pull toward the use of a lingua franca or of a LWC is the result of imposed governmental policies and the desires of individuals for economic upward mobility.

Air Niugini, the national airline, advertises Papua New Guinea as "The Land of the Unexpected." One is never prepared for the reality of the diversity of this beautiful land. The nation of Papua New Guinea occupies the eastern half of the island of New Guinea (located between the equator and Australia) and thousands of smaller islands to the north, east, and south. It is a land of rugged mountains still being formed by the fastest-rising land on the globe, of vast stretches of ocean surrounding sandy atolls and volcanic peaks, of grasslands and swamps and tropical rainforests. These geographic features have contributed to the linguistic diversity of this nation and are a factor in current language maintenance.

Map 1.1. Main towns of Papua New Guinea (Todd 1984:156, map 7)

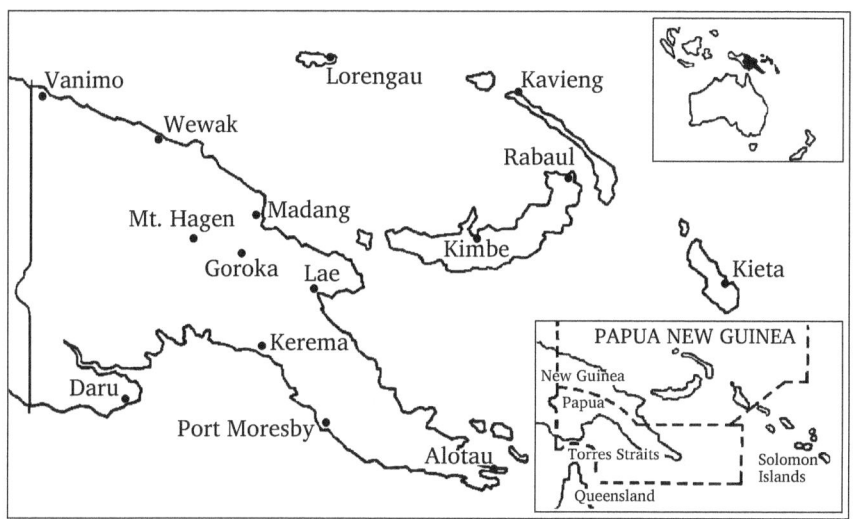

There is no written historical record of Papua New Guinea before European ships accidentally sailed near the western end of the island in the 1500s. No lasting contact was made until the last half of the nineteenth century. By the mid-1800s missionaries and traders were arriving at islands to the east of New Guinea (including New Ireland), and by the end of the century New Guinea and the surrounding islands were divided among the Dutch, the Germans, and the British. The Germans were motivated by the economic potential of the area and the British by the strategic location. Both powers, however, accomplished their ambitions in their own way without consideration for or consultation with the local population (Waiko 1993). After World War I the League of Nations placed both the former British territory of Papua and the former German territory of New Guinea under the administration of Australia, which maintained them as two separate territories. Only after World War II (in 1949) did Australia merge the two territories into a single administrative unit. In 1975 the Territory of Papua and New Guinea became the new independent nation of Papua New Guinea.

Language and Culture

Wurm calls the New Guinea area one of the "linguistically most complex and diverse areas in the world" (1975:3) which he estimates could have up to 1,000 distinct languages. Sankoff (1980b:8) uses Wurm's 1960 estimate of 700 distinct languages in Papua New Guinea, and Romaine (1992:9) still uses the estimate of 700 to 750 languages. Waters (1997) supervised a statistical review of recent available databases and listed 837 distinct languages within the nation of Papua New Guinea. With a population of only four million and about one fifth of the world's total languages, Papua New Guinea does have the highest rate of language diversity of any nation in the world. With this great diversity of languages Papua New Guinea is a multilingual nation in Edward's social multilingual sense (1994:55). It is also multilingual in his sense of individual multilingualism because most of the inhabitants speak more than one language.

All of Papua New Guinea's languages are "minority" languages in terms of the number of speakers compared to the total population since no single language is spoken by a majority of the total population. None of its languages forms a strong majority in either of two of the senses Bamgbose (1984:21) describes. That is, no single language is spoken by the majority of people in the nation or in any one province of the nation. Neither is a single indigenous language spoken by an overwhelmingly larger number of people than any other language in the country. Taken together, however, these minority languages do form a majority in Bamgbose's third sense of majority, in that everyone in Papua New Guinea speaks a minority language. In fact, most languages of Papua New Guinea have fewer than 1,000 speakers (Kulick 1992:1), although a half dozen approach or exceed 100,000 speakers.

The indigenous languages of Papua New Guinea are divided between two large and very different language families, the Austronesian and Papuan (or non-Austronesian) languages.[3] The Austronesian speakers are believed to be

---

[3]Non-Austronesian is probably a better label as there is disagreement concerning the classification of many so-called Papuan languages. The label "Papuan" implies that these languages belong to a single language family. Such a relationship among them is not definite, but rather is highly contested by some linguists.

the more recent arrivals and are concentrated on the islands and the coastal regions of the mainland. Tigak, the primary Austronesian example in this study, is spoken on the island of New Ireland (in the area surrounding Kavieng on map 1.1). Characteristics of Austronesian languages will be discussed in chapter 5 in connection with Tigak and in chapter 6 in connection with Tok Pisin. The Papuan languages are concentrated on the mainland, especially in the interior. Enga, the largest language group in Papua New Guinea with 150,000 speakers, is a Papuan language spoken in the highlands of the interior of the island of New Guinea itself. In contrast to Austronesian languages, these non-Austronesian languages "show no common pattern, and very little common vocabulary." In addition they have "no affiliation outside the islands" (Capell 1969:21).

Map 1.2. Distribution of languages in Papua New Guinea
(Todd 1984:159, map 8)

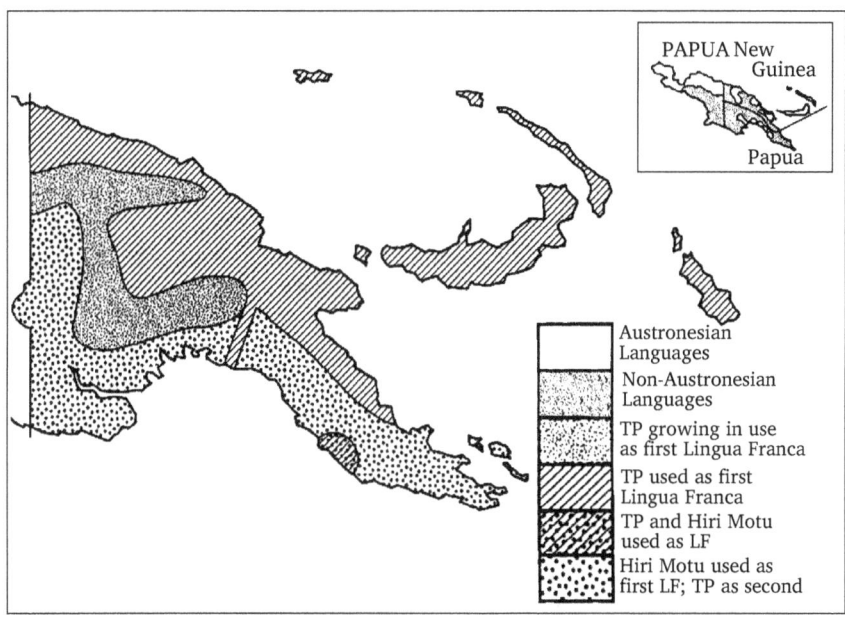

Although there is great language diversity in Papua New Guinea, the cultural diversity is much less, and the differences are often very subtle. All of Papua New Guinea is basically a tribal culture with a subsistence economy. Loyalty is directed to one's own clan. Each member of the extended family (the clan) has responsibilities and privileges based on age, gender, and accomplishments, and each member shares in the resources of the entire group. Except for those living in the middle of the territory of one of the half dozen largest language groups, all Papua New Guineans are in contact with speakers of other languages. Traditionally, there has been much fighting between language groups (usually over land) and even within language groups between clans. Depending on the particular trade relations between the language groups, some linguistic borrowing has occurred, but the languages have remained distinct. The distinction between languages (and even dialects in neighboring villages) is recognized and often emphasized. In fact, one theory for the large number of languages in Papua New Guinea is that "New Guinea communities have purposely fostered linguistic diversity because they have seen language as a highly salient marker of group identity" (Kulick 1992:2). The culture, however, is egalitarian, and the vernacular languages are all accepted as equal in status, theoretically at least. In practice, some languages are deemed to be more useful and prestigious than other languages. This point will be demonstrated many times below.

Traditional government was by consensus under the direction of "big men," the name given to those local leaders who could exert the most influence. Although wealth in the form of land, pigs, and other traditional artifacts was one factor in establishing big men, language also played a part. Bilingualism has always been widespread because of the close proximity of speakers of different languages, but a man who spoke more languages well increased his status because of the trade and negotiation advantages this skill gave him. Because of the trade possibilities, the languages that served as lingua francas did attain somewhat higher status in the geographical areas in which they were used. It is still true that the modern lingua francas (Tok Pisin, English, and Hiri Motu) are the languages with greater prestige in direct proportion to their usefulness as languages of wider communication. Sankoff notes that in precolonial Papua New Guinea "[l]anguage was viewed as being essentially pragmatic" (1980b:12). It still is.

Under colonial rule, the means of advancement for a Papua New Guinean was through language. Positions of authority over other Papua New Guineans and jobs paying cash were given to those who knew Tok Pisin, Hiri Motu, or English. English was the official language under the Australian administration, and Tok Pisin and Hiri Motu were used as national or, at least, regional languages. Tok Pisin is a pidgin/creole which has adopted much English vocabulary, as well as that of other European and indigenous languages, but which has an Austronesian grammatical structure (cf. Reesink 1987 for examples of Papuan substrate patterns). Tok Pisin originated on the islands and coastal regions where there was early contact with Europeans. It developed and is still used primarily in the northern and eastern (or New Guinean) parts of the nation which were under German and Dutch control, although its use and influence are spreading. Tok Pisin, in fact, has more speakers than any single indigenous language in the South Pacific. Hiri Motu is a pidgin based on Motu, an indigenous Austronesian language. It is used primarily in the southern area around the capital district which was under British and Australian control. Only in the Milne Bay area has English been used as a lingua franca instead of Tok Pisin or Hiri Motu. Figures for 1971 indicated that Tok Pisin was the most widely spoken lingua franca with approximately 45 percent of the population over age ten speaking it and only 9 percent speaking Hiri Motu (Sankoff 1980b:20). About 25 percent of this same population spoke English. (The 45 percent Tok Pisin speakers and the 25 percent English speakers were not disjoint groups, but did overlap. The Tok Pisin speakers who had a high school education or better would also have spoken English. Some of the English speakers did not speak Tok Pisin. The same is true today.) The illiteracy rate given in the 1971 figures was 70 percent (Baldwin 1978:18), so even many bilinguals did not read or write. Romaine (1992:87) gives census figures from 1980 that are the same as the 1971 figures, except that the percentage of English speakers had dropped by 1980 to 22 percent. Today the percentage of English speakers is still probably between 20 and 25 percent, but I would speculate that Tok Pisin is gaining speakers and that Hiri Motu is slowly losing speakers as more and more Tok Pisin speakers settle in the National Capital District area.

National Language Policy

Historical development

Eastman says "language planning is necessarily future-oriented" (1983:3). Unfortunately, in Papua New Guinea language policy has changed more often than the political administration; thus, no long-term language planning has taken place. For Eastman, language planning includes both language policy and language choice, but choice must come before policy (1983:12). In Papua New Guinea whatever language planning has been done has primarily been limited to language choice. Until the 1950s the administrative powers in Papua New Guinea maintained a laissez-faire attitude toward language use. As long as there were some intermediaries who spoke a lingua franca who could interpret commands to the people and as long as Christian missions were providing education, the government did not specify any language for a particular function. Up until that time, most education was conducted (by nongovernment agencies) in the vernaculars for the local primary schools and in either Tok Pisin or one of the regional vernacular languages for higher level schools.

Cooper's definition of language planning is "deliberate efforts to influence the behavior of others with respect to the acquisition, structure, or functional allocation of their language codes" (1989:45). In the 1960s Australia began an attempt to plan Papua New Guinean society through a westernization program which required English as the language of education. The stated purpose for the use of English was to prepare Papua New Guinea for independence (Litteral 1995a); however, the actual motivation was the convenience of the expatriate administration which had no materials in the vernacular languages and no teachers trained to use the vernaculars (see Huddleston (1980:10–11) for a discussion of the advantages and disadvantages of education in a national language). The policy was made and implemented from Australia with no Papua New Guinean consultation. Expatriate teachers were the rule. Funds were denied to missions and other nongovernment providers of education who did not comply with the policy. Most of the vernacular education that had previously been provided at the primary school level ended for a time. This policy of providing instruction in English only was a direct reflection of Australia's internal policy toward language, which for decades had been a policy of assimilation (Ozolins 1993:1).

As independence approached in the 1970s, the educational authority was moved to Papua New Guinea, but the control remained concentrated in one centralized National Executive Council. Although recommendations were made for the use of vernaculars and Tok Pisin in schools, English was still specified as the language of instruction. Local administration of schools, however, was slowly turned over to Papua New Guinean citizens, and more and more teachers were citizens, especially in the primary schools. All teachers were supposed to know English and use it as the language of instruction; however, many knew English only as a school subject they had studied but never used. Teachers were often assigned to schools outside their own language area, so they did not know the local vernacular of the students. Because of this situation, much teaching was actually conducted in Tok Pisin. In 1979 the North Solomons Provincial Government voted to begin vernacular preschools the following year. The idea of more local control spread during the 1980s, as did the call for more vernacular education, especially during the early years of primary school. In 1988 Parliament funded and appointed the National Literacy Committee, which promptly recommended a national language policy encouraging vernacular education. This policy is slowly being implemented.

Current policy

Papua New Guinea falls into Eastman's a-modal type nation with regard to choosing a national language (1983:12–14) because it must unite a multilingual conglomerate with no written tradition and no dominant indigenous language into a political entity.[4] Because of its peculiar composition of hundreds of minority languages with none dominant, no indigenous language has developed into a widespread lingua franca. English is encouraged as the language of wider communication (LWC), with Tok Pisin also widely accepted and encouraged as a national language. Since Papua New Guinea is an independent, self-governing, geographic territory, its language policy is not motivated by nationism as defined by Fishman (1972a:4–5). Papua New Guinea is already a nation in the political sense. Rather, its language policy is motivated by Fishman's nationalism. Its language practices are attempts to hold many language groups together as one national entity.

As is the case in many countries, what is official and what is practiced in Papua New Guinea is not always the same. Kloss (1966:135) observes that

> Three seems to be the maximum number of languages which can be placed on equal footing as official languages of the nation...Actually, the Swiss example shows that even a trilingual administration is not too workable a proposition.

The Papua New Guinea situation also supports this observation. At present, there seems to be no legitimate official language policy. From various sources one learns that either English is the one official language and Tok Pisin and Hiri Motu are national languages (Litteral 1995b:1), or that English, Tok Pisin, and Hiri Motu are all three official languages (Romaine 1992:19). The latter is, in fact, actual practice. These three languages are all used in the House of Parliament (with simultaneous translation provided); however, most of the public discussion from the floor is carried out in Tok Pisin. Government documents and signs may be in English only or in English plus one or both of the pidgins/creoles. Currently, English is the language of the educated elite in Papua New Guinea. It is spoken in all areas of the country, but only by those who have remained in school beyond the primary school level (grade 6). All indigenous languages are acceptable and permitted wherever understood. This policy of tolerance also follows the lead of Australia, which reversed its previous English only policy in 1978. The Australian National Policy on Languages enacted in 1987 and still in effect promotes making English

---

[4]The a-modal nation contrasts with Eastman's uni-modal nation, in which there is a literary tradition in some indigenous language as well as a LWC, and with her multi-modal nation, in which there are multiple languages with a literary tradition.

available to all citizens, while supporting indigenous languages as well (Ozolins 1993:250).

During the decade of the 1990s, education reform in Papua New Guinea placed vernacular education within the formal education system for the first three years of school. The responsibility and initiative for a **tok ples skul** 'talk place school' (a school conducted in the language of one's homeplace) rests with the local community. The community is responsible for providing funds to pay preschool teachers, for classroom space, for the selection of teachers, and for the preparation of vernacular materials. The provincial government is responsible for assistance with curriculum planning and the training of teachers. The provinces are to continue to provide education in English and Tok Pisin in the higher grades of primary school and in English in high school and university.

The Languages of New Ireland

The focus of this work is Tok Pisin, the pidgin/creole language which I claim is patterned on the Austronesian substrate languages found in New Ireland and East New Britain; and the Tigak language, a typical Austronesian language which I am using to exemplify the Austronesian characteristics of Tok Pisin. To provide a more specific context for the study, I will give a brief description of the languages of New Ireland in this section, and I will discuss the placement of Tigak within the Austronesian family in the following section.

New Ireland Province of Papua New Guinea is located several hundred miles off the eastern coast of the main island of Papua New Guinea. It includes the island of New Ireland itself, plus islands lying off its coast in all directions, including the St. Matthias Islands to the northwest, New Hanover and the Tigak Islands to the west, Djaul Island south of the northern tip, the Tabar, Lihir, and Tanga groups to the east, and Lambon Island (Siar) off the southernmost tip.

Most accounts of the languages in New Ireland Province list twenty languages. However, there are discrepancies in the numbers and the classifications. Lithgow and Claasen divided the twenty languages into three families (1968:3). These included eighteen Austronesian languages (earlier called Melanesian or Malayo-Polynesian), the Madak group of non-Melanesian languages, and Kuot (or Panaras) as a single Papuan isolate. Later researchers corrected the Madak classification to include the Madak family as an Austronesian language, resulting in only two language families represented in New Ireland (Capell 1969). Beaumont

(1972:15) placed Tigak in the Northern New Ireland subgroup that also included Tungag (Tungak), Tiang, Kara, Nalik, Notsi, and Tabar. Ross (1988) regroups Tungag (Lavongai), Tigak, Tiang, Kara, and Nalik together in the Lavongai-Nalik chain (see map 1.3). This grouping seems justified by the grammatical similarities of these five languages, as well as by the high cognate counts in the vocabularies (see Beaumont 1976:388). However, there are still gaps in our knowledge of the languages of New Ireland. It is thought that languages so far unclassified may be spoken in the mountains of southern New Ireland. I do know from personal contact that another language (probably Austronesian) was spoken on Djaul Island. As of 1996 the last five speakers were living in Sumuna village and gave me a small word list of this unrecorded language. None of the researchers on New Guinea languages I consulted listed the language of Sumuna (Beaumont 1972, 1976, Capell 1969, Lithgow and Claasen 1968, or Wurm 1975). I will discuss this dying language later in this chapter.

Map 1.3. Location of the Meso-Melanesian cluster and its subgroups (Ross 1988:259, map 12)

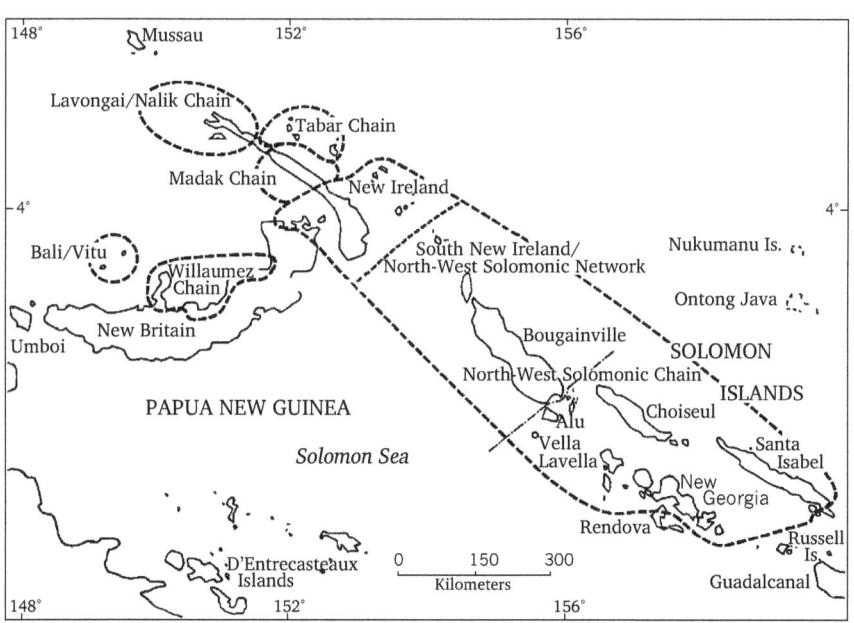

Tigak and the Austronesian Language Family

The Austronesian languages are a widespread and diverse group that extends from Madagascar to Easter Island and from New Zealand to Hawaii (Wurm 1975). Up to 10 percent of the world's languages may belong to this family (Dyen 1971:5). Capell (1969, 1971) divides the Austronesian languages in New Guinea into two subgroups, AN_1 and AN_2. Unfortunately, he reverses the labels of the two subgroups in his 1969 and 1971 works. Therefore, to avoid confusion I will relabel the subgroups as AN_M (for mainland) and AN_I (for island). The AN_M subgroup is confined primarily to the mainland of New Guinea and exhibits structural differences from the AN_I subgroup. These structural differences were probably acquired by close contact with the surrounding Papuan languages. The most striking differences between the two groups are the SOV word order and postpositions of the AN_M subgroup (like their Papuan neighbors) as opposed to the SVO word order and prepositions of the AN_I subgroup. Capell says that languages in the AN_M group have "basically NAN [non-Austronesian] structure" and "seem to be at root NAN languages with a veneer of Austronesian lexicon and less grammar" (1971:334). (A study of this convergence is beyond the scope of the present work, but I will discuss later in the chapter the opposite situation on New Ireland in which a non-Austronesian language is succumbing to the surrounding Austronesian languages.)

The AN_I group includes most of the languages of the coastal areas and the islands off the coast of the large island of New Guinea itself (including New Ireland and New Britain). Tigak and the other New Ireland Austronesian languages belong to the AN_I group, and I will use Austronesian without a subscript to refer to this group for the remainder of the study. This group (AN_I) shares many features in common with the rest of the Austronesian family throughout the Pacific and Indian Ocean area, including the SVO word order, many other structural features, and much basic vocabulary (see appendix 1 for comparisons of vocabulary items). This situation is expected for genetically related languages that probably diverged recently from a common Oceanic ancestor. The divergences exhibited by the modern languages are also normal when groups of speakers become isolated and when various groups come into contact with other languages. Because of my familiarity with Island Tigak, I will use it as the illustrative example of a typical Austronesian language.

Tigak is spoken on the northwestern tip of New Ireland and the many small offshore islands in that region (see map 1.4). With a little over 10,000 speakers, it is second in population in New Ireland only to Tungag (with approximately 14,000 speakers). According to Ross (1988) Tigak is a member of the Lavongai-Nalik chain of the New Ireland network of the Meso-Melanesian cluster of the Western Oceanic languages of the Austronesian family. In contrast, Wurm (1975) lists the New Guinea Austronesian languages as belonging to the Eastern Oceanic group. Capell (1969) reports the widely held opinion that the area including New Ireland and the eastern tip of New Britain was the original immigration area for speakers of Austronesian languages in the New Guinea region and that the languages spread from that area to the rest of New Guinea. The Austronesian speakers probably came from the west about 5,000 years ago. This hypothesis fits the folklore of northern New Ireland. For example, the Tigak people believe that they (and perhaps the Tungags) were the first to arrive in New Ireland.[5] They claim their language and people spread from the northern tip southeastward and into New Britain. The similarities in languages and culture corroborate this claim. The people of northern New Ireland to this day have closer ties to the Gazelle peninsula (the area of the Tolai/Kuanua[6] speakers) than to the middle and southern sections of New Ireland (see map 1.3 showing the proximity of New Ireland and New Britain).

Map 1.4. Lavongai-Nalik chain of New Ireland
(Lithgow and Claassen 1968)

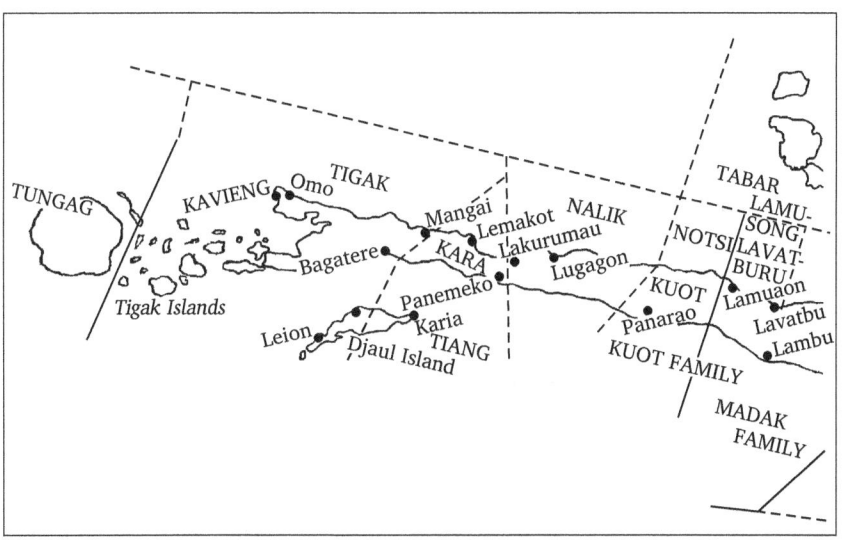

---

[5]There were actually already inhabitants on New Ireland. The Kuot (Panaras) people (and perhaps others of whom there is no record) were undoubtedly there before the Austronesian speakers arrived. The language attrition situation with the Kuot speakers will be discussed later.

[6]Tolai and Kuanua are alternate names for the same language.

Language Contact Phenomena in New Ireland

The northern tip of New Ireland within a fifty-mile radius around the provincial capital of Kavieng provides a study in miniature of the overall linguistic situation in Papua New Guinea. Within this small area there are eight indigenous New Ireland languages, plus English, Tok Pisin, and Kuanua (or Tolai from East New Britain). The interaction among these languages illustrates many language contact phenomena. In this section I will give an overview of the types of language maintenance and shift that are currently observable in northwestern New Ireland. These phenomena range from language maintenance due to isolation and ethnolinguistic pride through the bilingual use of different codes (including diglossia, borrowing, codeswitching, convergence, and language shift), attrition, and death. The contact phenomenon of pidgin/creole development will be discussed in chapter 6 for Tok Pisin, and the convergence of Tigak toward Tok Pisin and English and of Tok Pisin toward English is the topic of chapter 7. The languages involved within this region that are of concern to this study[7] include four different language families—Austronesian, Papuan, Indo-European (English), and Tok Pisin.[8] I will be referring to the languages shown on map 1.5 from (and including) the Tungag language to the west of Kavieng through the Kuot language to the east.

---

[7]There are other languages spoken in the area because of migration from other parts of Papua New Guinea and elsewhere. The Chinese (and to some extent Korean) speaking business people in Kavieng do not affect the local language situation in terms of structural influences. These speakers usually restrict their use of Chinese (or other L1) to within their ethnic community. For communications with others they use Tok Pisin and/or English. Few of them learn any of the local languages.

[8]Although I am stating that Tok Pisin is not in the same language family as the other languages involved in the contact situation, I do not completely agree with Thomason and Kaufman's (1988) assertion that pidgins/creoles do not belong genetically to any of the languages involved in their formation. I would claim that a pidgin/creole is, in fact, more closely related to the language family supplying the morphosyntactic frame (i.e., the composite matrix language). Since the composite matrix language might not be a single language, I do agree with them that genetic relationships are more difficult to pin down than in cases of languages undergoing normal, gradual transmission from one generaton of speakers to the next. To continue applying the "family" relationship metaphor to pidgins/creoles, perhaps a reversal of the model is needed. Instead of a single "parent" language producing multiple branches ("descendents"), a pidgin/creole may be viewed as a single descendent of multiple "parent" languages.

Language Contact Phenomena in New Ireland

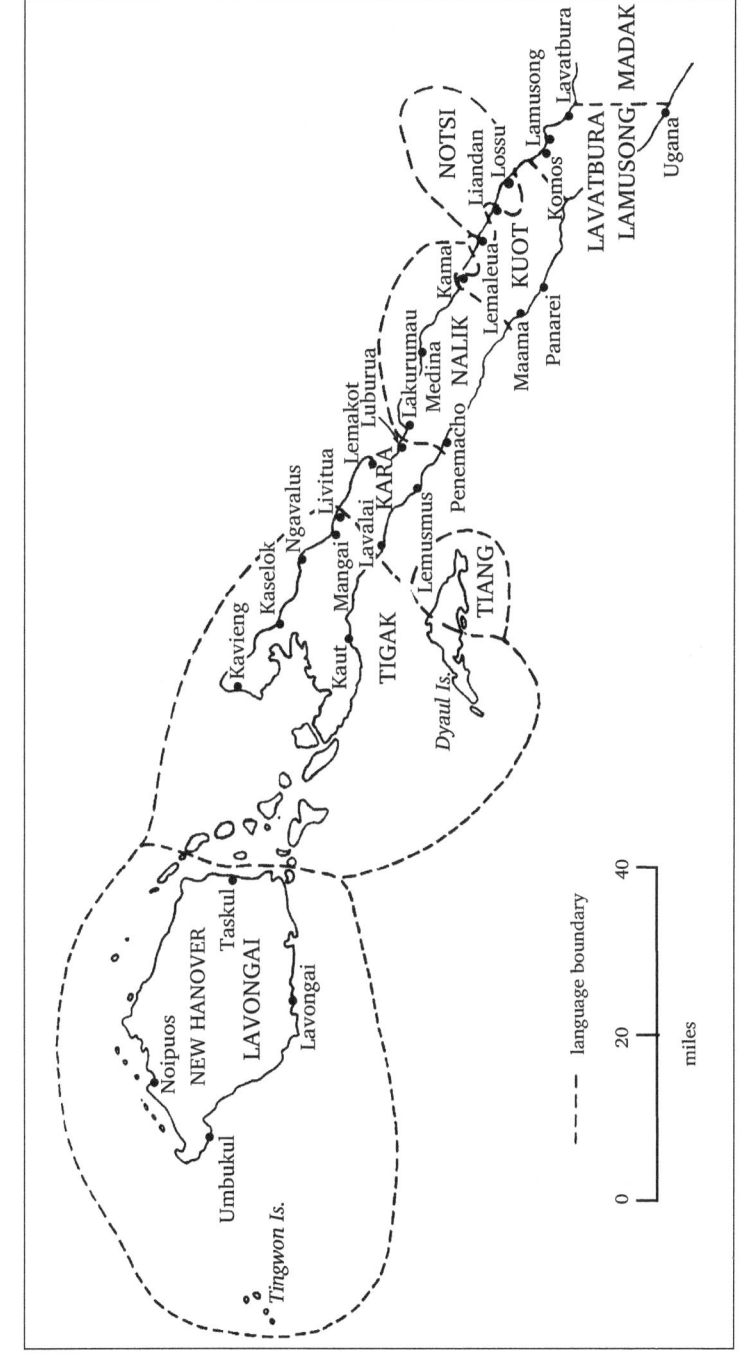

Map 1.5. Northern New Ireland languages (Beaumont 1972:16)

Contact produces change through exposure. Harris and Campbell (1995:122) define LANGUAGE CONTACT as

> a situation in which the speakers of one language are familiar in some way with another. That is, contact is a situation...but the contact itself is not change. Contact is often a catalyst for changes through reanalysis or extension.

The languages of New Ireland exhibit changes, some of which are internally motivated and some of which are due to contact with neighboring languages. This work is devoted to the contact-induced changes.

Social, historical, and geographic factors, in addition to linguistic ones, affect the types of language change and the rates of such changes. The historical progression of the Austronesian languages in New Ireland was mentioned earlier. Kapanga points out that various social factors such as age, educational level, and gender have differing degrees of importance in different contexts, such as the community, the workplace, or church. These factors may cause people "to alter their linguistic behavior in order to be accepted by members of social groups other than their own" (1998:284). Examples of social factors influencing language behavior and the resulting language changes are discussed especially with regards to diglossia in New Ireland, to codeswitching and to language shift, attrition, and death in the next sections. (Also see Blom and Gumperz 1972, Bright 1997, Di Pietro 1978, McClure 1981, Scotton 1986, and Myers-Scotton 1993b concerning social factors which influence language behavior.)

The geographic influence on language change is seen in the more rapid changes evident on the mainland of New Ireland as opposed to New Hanover and the Tigak Islands. For example, Tigak speakers live on a number of small islands off the northwestern tip of New Ireland and in more than a dozen villages on the island of New Ireland itself. The island dwellers are more isolated from speakers of other languages and tend to be more conservative in their language usage. Speakers from the mainland who live near the provincial capital of Kavieng have frequent contact with speakers of many other languages: related Austronesian languages as well as English and Tok Pisin. Those mainland Tigak speakers who live to the southeast of Kavieng in the area bordering the Kara language area have more frequent contact with Kara speakers. Speakers from each of these areas show differing patterns of language change due to contact (or lack of it).

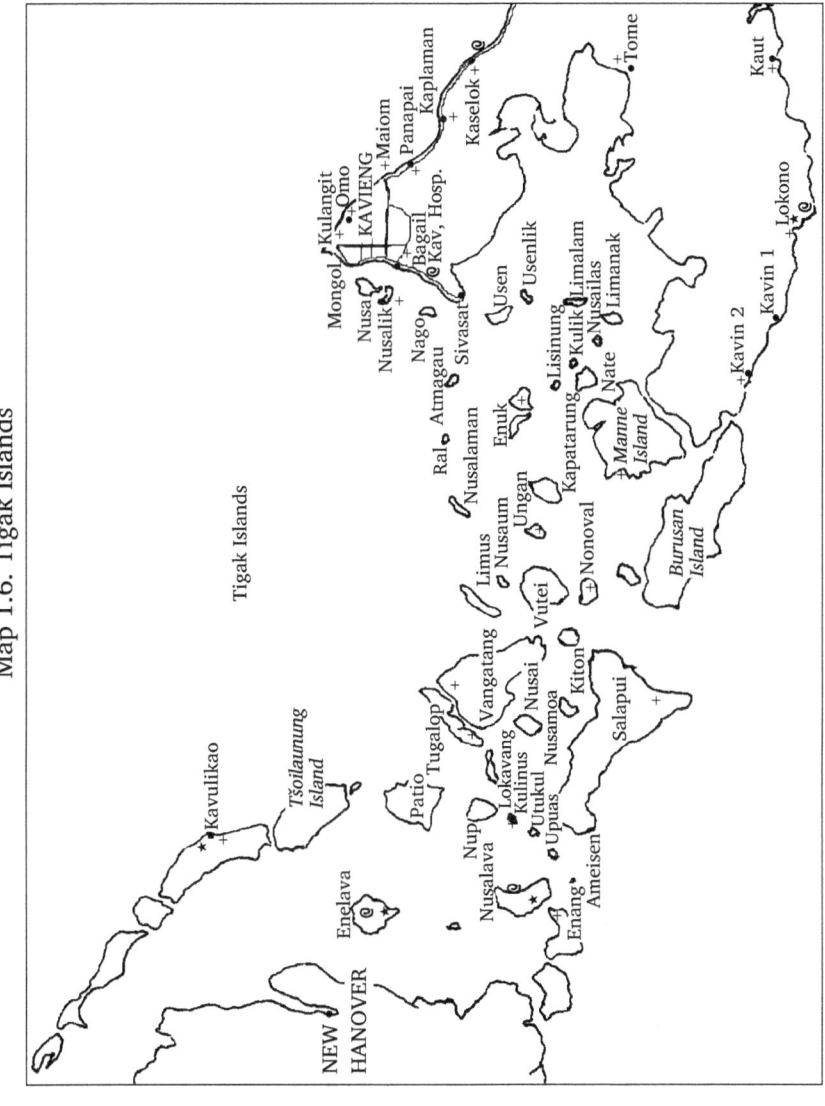

Map 1.6. Tigak Islands

The oldest available documents for the Tigak language are less than one hundred years old (Unknown 1911, 1921). These documents are not especially useful in determining change due to contact because they are translated materials done by Europeans translating from a European language (either English or German). The oldest useful material is the one hundred year old grammar of Duke of York, a closely related Austronesian language (Codrington 1974). Since long historical records of the Tigak language and most other languages of Papua New Guinea do not exist, the number and degree of contact-induced changes that can be discussed are not as numerous as for languages with a longer written history. I will rely on synchronic evidence including comparisons with other related languages and alternations in current usage.

Bilingualism

Lithgow and Claassen, referring to the people of New Ireland, assert that "most indigenous people have some knowledge of the adjoining languages" (1968:16).

Although it could be applied to the whole of Papua New Guinea, it is particularly true of New Ireland because of the relatively small population of each language group and the small physical territories and close proximity in which they live. Definitions for bilingualism have run the gamut from Weinreich's (1953) general description of using two languages alternately to Haugen's (1953) requirement that the utterances in each language be both grammatically complete and meaningful. In defining MULTILINGUALISM as "the use of more than one language," Clyne (1997:301) goes on to say, "the use of two or more languages in the long term depends on the need for those two languages" (p. 308). Myers-Scotton is more specific in defining BILINGUAL SPEECH "as showing either morphemes or lexical structure, or both, from two or more languages" (1998a:289). Papua New Guineans use more than one language because they need to, and the languages they currently use demonstrate how lexical structure is adopted from one language to another.

Some of the older Tigaks living on the more remote Tigak Islands speak only Tigak, but when spoken to in Tok Pisin or Tungag (the two most commonly known second languages for Island Tigak speakers) they will respond in Tigak, indicating at least understanding of the other language (passive bilingualism). It is not uncommon in New Ireland to hear a conversation in two languages, each interlocutor speaking his own L1 to the other. This pattern of passive bilingualism (called dual-lingualism by Lincoln 1979) is often the case in exogamous marriages. On the mainland of New Ireland, most people know at least some of the one or two nearest neighboring languages. For the mainland Tigaks, this other language is most often Kara. Kara speakers may also speak Tigak or Nalik, depending on where their village is located. Nalik speakers (Volker 1993:111) and Kuot speakers (Chung and Chung 1998) all speak some language other than Nalik and Kuot, respectively. Tungag and Tiang speakers are the least likely to speak a neighboring language because of their geographic isolation on outlying islands.

The single most commonly spoken language on New Ireland is Tok Pisin because almost everyone speaks it in some context to someone. In fact, Tok Pisin has almost taken over in all domains among the young Kuot population. Tok Pisin is still a second language to most New Irelanders, although it is the first language for a growing number of young people born into families of exogamous marriages who live in an urban center instead of a village.

English is the second most widely spoken language in the province, but the level of fluency varies greatly. As stated previously, for many years English was the official language of education in all of Papua New Guinea. Thus, in New Ireland, as elsewhere in the country, all students attending school were (supposedly) taught in English. Universal education is available to all through grade 6 (if the students can get to a school). Since grade 6 is the highest level of education for most Papua New Guineans, and since many never again use English after leaving school, a few English words are all that some know. For those who continue through the next level (grade 10), most can understand and speak some English. If graduates from the tenth grade or higher work in a town instead of returning to their village, they probably continue to use English, at least with expatriate business people. Those who have continued using English are usually very fluent. However, even fluent English-speaking New Irelanders still prefer Tok Pisin in social contexts involving speakers of other languages. English is also used as a means of "elite closure" in New Ireland, "limit[ing] access of nonelite groups to political position and socioeconomic advancement" (Myers-Scotton 1993c:149). I will discuss the diglossic use of these languages in the next section.

Another widely used second language in New Ireland is Kuanua (Tolai). Kuanua is the vernacular language from the Gazelle Peninsula of East New Britain around Rabaul. This area was the center for the German administration in New Guinea and was the center from which most missionary activity in the islands spread. Early Methodist missionaries quickly translated the New Testament of the Bible and the Methodist hymnal into the Kuanua language. They also trained local pastors and encouraged them to be responsible for their own churches. The Rabaul area became the training center for the Methodist (now called the United) Church in Papua New Guinea. Thus, Kuanua became the church language and is still used in United Churches all over Papua New Guinea. Since the missions were the first to provide education to the indigenes, Kuanua was also used as a school language until the Australian policy of educating only in English went into practice. Since most Tigaks are members of the United Church, most of those over the age of fifty were taught Kuanua in school. Tigaks younger than fifty years rarely know Kuanua. The situation is similar in the rest of New Ireland.

Diglossia

The situation I will describe of multiple language use among the Tigaks is also true among many of the language groups in the province. Because of the extensive bilingualism it is not surprising to find DIGLOSSIA. Ferguson introduced the term, and he characterizes a diglossic speech situation as one in which "two or more varieties of the same language are used by some speakers under different conditions" (1959:325). The languages are described as having a high (H) variety and a low (L) variety. He more completely defines diglossia as

> a relatively stable language situation in which, in addition to the primary dialects of the language (which may include a standard or regional standards), there is a very divergent, highly codified (often grammatically more complex) superposed variety, the vehicle of a large and respected body of written literature, either of an earlier period or in another speech community, which is learned largely by formal education and is used for most written and formal spoken purposes but is not used by any sector of the community for ordinary conversation. (1959:336)

Fishman (1967) extends the use of the term diglossia to include entirely different languages used in different domains. Papua New Guineans use languages in diglossic relationships in both Ferguson's original sense and in Fishman's extended sense. Mackey's (1986) "polyglossic spectrum" is an even better description of the situation on New Ireland. Among the Tigaks there are four languages (or codes) used in diglossic patterns. The use of vernacular (or everyday) Tigak and a code known as *maimai* speech fits Ferguson's (1959) original condition of the use of two varieties of the same language in mutually exclusive domains. A Tigak *maimai* is a spokesman for a feast or special occasion or ceremony. A *maimai* is required for any marriage exchange ceremony, place dedication, peace settlement, or funeral. He is usually one of the "big men" in the culture and becomes a *maimai* because of that position and his oratorical skill. *Maimai* speech is a Tigak variety, possibly an older form of the language that has been passed down from one generation to the next. Only another *maimai* can understand all the words spoken, but all Tigaks know the context and understand what is transpiring. The *maimai* will make his speech for the specific occasion in this special code, but will give directions or address individuals in vernacular Tigak. In this context, the *maimai* speech is the high (H) variety of Tigak and is restricted to use by the spokesman for a particular occasion. Vernacular Tigak is the low (L) variety, and all Tigak speakers use it for everyday, nonceremonial purposes.

The Tigak area also demonstrates Fishman's (1967) extension of the term diglossia to include entirely different languages used in different domains. Kuanua serves as a church language in the Tigak region. In the church it is used for reading from the New Testament and for singing hymns, but announcements, preaching, and praying are done in Tigak (or in Tok Pisin, depending on the speaker and the congregation). Tigaks do not use Kuanua as a second language in any other context.

Among educated Tigaks the most common situation of different language use in different domains involves Tigak, Tok Pisin, and English in a TRIGLOSSIC relationship. Tigak is spoken among relatives and in most situations in the village areas (except as discussed above). When meeting a Papua New Guinean from another village, especially if that meeting is in town, Tok Pisin is the language of choice (even if both speakers know the vernacular of the other). Should the conversation turn to business or education, the interlocutors may switch to English. If the other person is from Port Moresby or is an expatriate, the choice of language is English instead, at least to begin the conversation. If the conversation is entirely social and it becomes apparent that the interlocutors all know Tok Pisin, a switch to that language is usually made. When a Tigak enters a government office or a place of business and encounters someone he does not know, he opens the exchange in English. Even two Tigaks speaking to each other in the workplace on official business will normally employ English for that part of their verbal exchange. In this situation, Tigak is the low (L) variety used for the more intimate situations of home and family. Tok Pisin is a high (H) variety with respect to Tigak and is used in exchanges involving outsiders or an urban locale or for more formal social exchanges. With respect to English, however, Tok Pisin is the L variety and English is the H. English is used only for the most formal functions and mostly with real outsiders present. It is also used to demonstrate one's educated status. Tok Pisin is the social language and is the one used for friendly exchanges. Schiffman maintains that "diglossic situations tend to be unstable" and "often lead to language shift" (1993:115) unless each language has clearly distinct domains of use. I do not see a major language shift occurring among the Tigaks in the near future because the multiple linguistic varieties used by them are still used in distinct domains. However, some language shift is occurring among younger speakers raised away from the Tigak villages (including in Kavieng). This type of shift involves language loss and will be discussed below.

Dialect gradation, codeswitching, and borrowings

The Austronesian languages of New Ireland are so closely related that lexical similarities are common (see appendix 1 for vocabulary comparisons). The close geographic proximity of speakers of related languages has contributed to bilingualism, borrowing, and the convergence of linguistic forms (structural, lexical, and phonological) between neighboring languages. On the other hand, the lack of convenient modes of transportation and the physical barriers of mountains and ocean have contributed to the isolation of groups, which has produced and maintained the distinctions of small groups of speakers. These conditions have resulted in a gradual change in the languages of New Ireland from the northwestern tip to the southeastern.

From the degree of multilingualism and diglossia in New Ireland one might also expect codeswitching and borrowing to be very common, and they are. Myers-Scotton and Jake define "classic" CODESWITCHING as "the use of morphemes from two or more linguistic varieties in the same intrasentential clause (CP), with the grammatical frame derived from only one of the participating varieties" (2000b:manuscript). A switch is intrasentential if both varieties occur in the same sentence. Intersentential codeswitching is simply the use of more than one variety between sentences. Both types of codeswitching are common in New Ireland.

Alternation between languages at the word level has been the subject of much debate concerning the status of such alternations as borrowings versus codeswitches. Samar and Meechan (1998) and Poplack and Meechan (1998) claim that borrowings and codeswitches must be distinguished, but that this distinction cannot be made on single lexical items. They claim that most lone occurrences are borrowings. Poplack earlier had said that the difference could be determined "according to the degree of adaptation to the other language" and that codeswitches show "complete lack of adaptation" (1981:170). Borrowings, on the other hand, "will tend to be nativized phonologically, inflected with native morphological materials, and incorporated fully in the systems for word formation and sentence construction of the target language" (Hill and Hill 1986:346). Di Sciullo, Muysken, and Singh (1986) emphasize the conceptual differences between borrowings and codeswitches. Myers-Scotton (1993b, 1997a) and Myers-Scotton and Jake

(1995) claim that single items can be switches, but that the classification is difficult because the difference between switches and borrowings is cognitively based (i.e., the difference depends on how the lexeme is entered into the mental lexicon(s) of the speaker). A borrowed lexeme is entered into the speaker's mental lexicon of the recipient language (which may be the only language of the speaker), and it also remains a part of the lexicon of the donor language. For a bilingual speaker of both the recipient and the donor languages, that borrowed lexeme is entered into the mental lexicon of each of the two languages. In contrast, a codeswitched lexeme is entered only into the embedded language lexicon of the speaker. Halmari agrees that there are difficulties in pinning down specifications for a determination of the status of single-item switches. In her Finnish-English data she resorts to "phonological unassimilation as the determining factor which makes a lexical item a codeswitch rather than a loanword" (1997:17). I will not enter the debate here, but I will give some examples of different degrees of adaptation below. Some of those examples will illustrate why the criteria given above are not always decisive in classifying single lexical items as codeswitches or borrowings.

Because of the extensively shared vocabulary among Austronesian languages, it is difficult to determine what has been borrowed among those languages in New Ireland. As mentioned above, borrowings and single codeswitched items are sometimes impossible to distinguish, because the underlying difference is cognitive (see Myers-Scotton 1992a, 1992b, 1997a for full discussions). Borrowed items can occur in monolingual speech because they are part of the language into which they have been incorporated. For this reason monolinguals in the borrowing language can use borrowed items, whereas only bilinguals can engage in codeswitching. The performance-based difference most often used to distinguish loans from switches is the degree of adaptation. Borrowed items are more often adapted phonologically to fit the recipient language. For example, the name *Junior* from English has been adapted as *Dinia* in Tigak in accordance with the Tigak phoneme inventory and syllable patterns (see chapter 5 for Tigak phonology and syllable structure and below for the story of *Dinia*).

Not only is there a difference in who uses borrowed versus codeswitching forms, but there is also a distinction in the classification of borrowed forms. Cultural lexemes are forms that are missing from a given language because they are new to the speaker's culture. To fill these lexical gaps, forms are often borrowed from the source language. Cultural borrowings are the most common in all languages because they are not replacing lexemes in the recipient language but are adding referential power to that language. For example, Tigaks have borrowed the lexemes *ensin* 'engine' and *bensin* 'gasoline' from Tok Pisin to fill the lexical gaps for an outboard motor and the fuel to operate those engines, both items unknown in the culture until recent years. These lexemes "enter their ML [matrix language] lexicon *abruptly*" (Myers-Scotton 1992b:29, emphasis in original) and become established loans. Cultural borrowed forms are not directly related to codeswitching because they do not represent an alternative to the speaker.

Core vocabulary items are lexemes that already exist in the borrowing language. For this reason core borrowings are less common than cultural borrowings. A core item which is borrowed "typically starts out as a CS [codeswitched] form" (Myers-Scotton 1992a:34). When core borrowing does occur, the original forms are often forgotten in favor of the borrowed core items that now fill those semantic slots. For example, Tigak has borrowed lexemes for large numerals such as *handet* 'hundred' from Tok Pisin and English. Older speakers may still be able to name the Tigak form *sangsangaulung* 'one hundred', but they rarely use it, and younger speakers rarely know it. In borrowing, a cultural borrowed item from language B becomes a part of language A, filling a lexical gap in language A. In this case, the same form is an entry in both mental lexicons, that of the source language from which it originates and that of the recipient language into which it is borrowed. In codeswitching, however, one form does not replace another. Rather, each of the two languages retains its own form and separate entry in the mental lexicon for each language, respectively. Only core lexical items can start as codeswitches because those lexemes are the only ones that occur as different items in each language. Core borrowed items, therefore, enter a language in a gradual process (as opposed to the abrupt cultural borrowing process) in which codeswitching alternations precede the establishment of the borrowed core item.

Dialect gradation

According to Beaumont (1979) there are four dialects of Tigak: Island, Central, Western, and Southern (see map 1.7). I have no doubt that many changes occurred in the generation before I entered the Tigak region. The increased mobility and level of education of the population have initiated many of the changes. I can accept Beaumont's description of the Tigak linguistic patterns in 1969–70 when he was working in New Ireland, but I found fewer distinct boundaries between Tigak dialect areas by 1996 (Jenkins and Jenkins 1996b). Many of the regional characteristics he described have been leveled by intermarriages, greater mobility between villages, and more regular and long-term mixing in Kavieng. The Island dialect is definitely the most conservative dialect being the least likely to encounter innovations because of their more limited contact with nonislanders. However, the introduction and now common use of outboard motors has reduced their isolation greatly. Many Tigak Islanders regularly go by boat into Kavieng, some now even commuting to and from Kavieng daily. Improved road conditions on the mainland and the presence of public transportation vehicles traveling the length of the major road along the north coast of New Ireland between Kavieng and Namatanai provide the means for many New Irelanders from as far away as the Kuot and Notsi areas (see map 1.5) to go to Kavieng once or twice a week to buy and sell at the market or attend to business.

Map 1.7. Tigak dialects (Beaumont 1979:108)

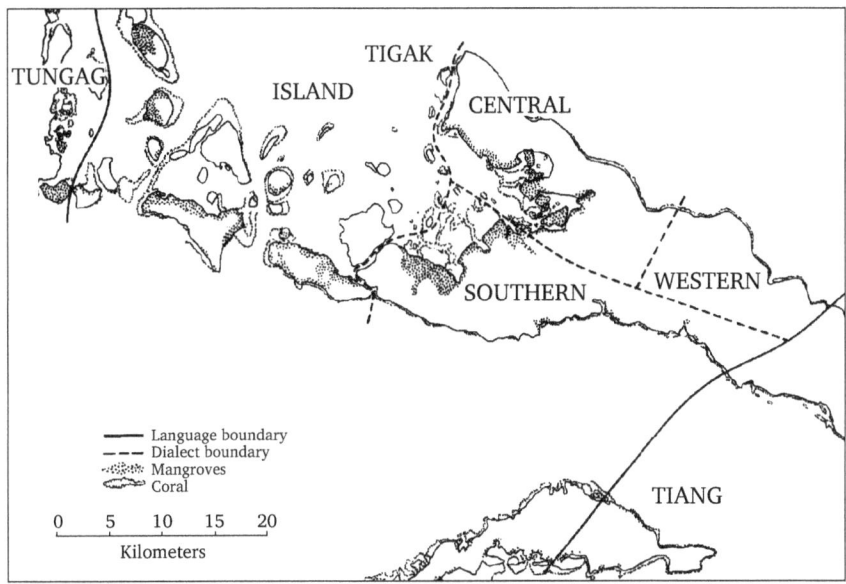

These changes in mobility have leveled many vocabulary differences within the Tigak language area. For example, Beaumont (1979) lists three words that he says are unique to the Island dialect and linked to Lavongai (Tungag). He claims that *bata* is used on the islands for 'rain/dark cloud' and *kuku/kungkung* for 'white cloud'. The latter form he states is used in the Central dialect for 'sky/heaven'. Presently, *bate* is used on the islands for 'white cloud', not 'rain cloud', and *kuku* is used for 'cloud covering /sky/ heaven'. In addition, he gives *ngarik* as the Island word for 'axe' and *gamui* as the form used in Central Tigak. On the contrary, today *gamui* is the usual form for 'axe' in the Island dialect, and the islanders claim that *anik* is a form used only on the mainland of New Ireland.[9] It is true, however, that many morphemes are shared between Island Tigak and Tungag. Beaumont notes that many of the Southern dialect forms are cognates with Kara. This is still true. There is, in fact, a gradient of changes as one travels southeast from Kavieng toward the Kara area. Much of the vocabulary in Manggai is also shared with neighboring Kara. However, all Tigak speakers know most of the vocabulary items used by other Tigaks even if they do not use those items in their daily speech, and many speakers now alternate between forms.

Most of the difference now is in phonology more than in vocabulary or syntax. Island Tigak has phonemically long and short vowels. This difference becomes harder to detect as one approaches the Kara area. The intervocalic voicing of /k/ is dropped near the Kara area, with much variation even in the same speaker. For example, in Manggai on the Kara border, the same speaker says *makago* and *makako* for the color 'blue/green'. There is definitely phonological convergence and some lexical borrowing between Island Tigak and Tungag and between Southern Tigak and Kara, but many of the vocabulary differences of the past are disappearing.

Codeswitching among New Irelanders

Codeswitching between New Irelander's first language (L1) and any other language in their linguistic repertoire is so common that many speakers do not realize when they switch. The switches occur most often in the town setting (Kavieng) because this is the place one is most likely to encounter speakers of other languages or persons from different areas of one's own language group. Switches also occur more commonly in informal, conversational discourses than in more formally structured interviews or narratives (cf. McClure 1981, Poplack 1981). Many Island Tigaks attended primary school on New Hanover and learned some Tungag while living on that island. Should one such Tigak meet a Tungag, the Tigak most likely switches between the two languages, using whatever Tungag he remembers. The switches that occur may involve single lexical items or entire phrases in Tungag. The Tungag probably understands Tigak but is less likely to use it in speech. As the numerically largest group

---

[9]The variation between these two forms, *nganik* and *anik*, reflects a possible internally motivated change occurring in Tigak. A discussion of this change is beyond the scope of this work, but it stems from the phonological conditioning of the form of the article (or noun marker) in Tigak, which varies according to the initial phoneme of the noun (for example, *ta lui* 'house' versus *tang ur* 'banana'). Some speakers trying to isolate the noun will disagree as to whether 'banana' is *ur* or *ngur*.

in New Ireland, Tungags are more likely to consider themselves more important than the neighboring Tigaks, and are therefore less likely to accommodate by using the Tigak language. Instead, a Tungag may respond in Tok Pisin. Only the more fluent bilingual Tigaks will speak entirely in Tungag. A similar pattern is followed when New Irelanders meet anyone from a neighboring language area. Both speakers are likely to alternate between the two languages, using the lexemes and expressions they know from the other language. Many New Irelanders are passive bilinguals in a neighboring language, and it is not uncommon to hear a conversation in which each is speaking his/her own language because each one understands the language of the other when he/she hears it.

Map 1.8. Tungag and Tigak

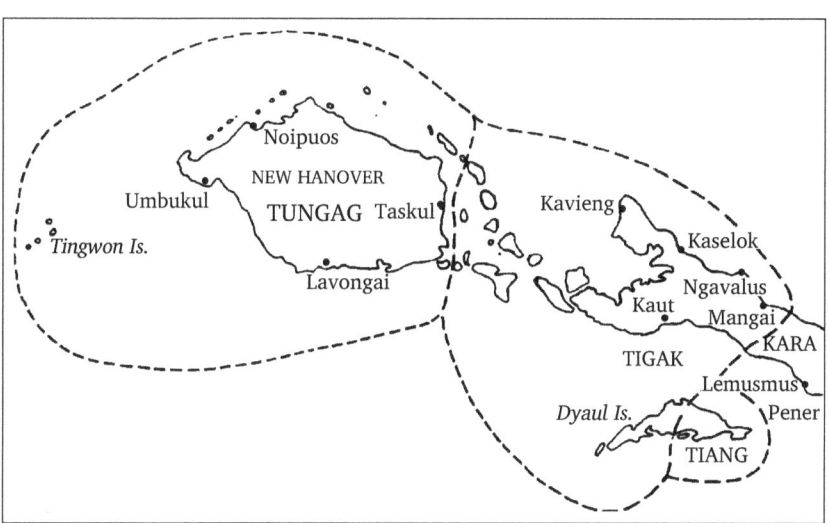

An even more common pattern of codeswitching represents Myers-Scotton's "unmarked choice" (1993b, 1993c, 1997a), which is the normal, or expected, pattern of speech within a given group. This pattern occurs among Tigaks only (or any other single ethnic group in New Ireland) and consists of alternating between Tigak and Tok Pisin. It is especially common among Tigaks in an urban setting. Tigaks communicating with other Tigaks use the vernacular to establish their ethnic identity and Tok Pisin to establish their urbanity. In interethnic groups in which Tok Pisin is the normal language of communication, switches also occur between Tok Pisin and English. These mixed groups of Papua New Guineans use Tok Pisin as their common language for friendly communication which marks them as **wantoks**,[10] but they use English to mark their membership in a more sophisticated, more highly educated group. In both cases, the codeswitching is a means of establishing identity in two groups simultaneously. It is "emblematic of dual membership" (Myers-Scotton 1997a:235).

Codeswitching can serve the function of exclusion as well as that of inclusion. Tok Pisin (in the case of a single ethnic group) and English (in the case of a mixed ethnic group) distinguish the speaker from a **bus kanaka**, 'village person'. But Tigak and English also serve the purpose of exclusion. In the first case, speaking Tigak excludes anyone who does not know Tigak, including some urban Tigaks. In the second case, speaking English excludes all except the educated Papua New Guineans (cf. Tabouret-Keller 1997 for the two aspects of the identification role of language, in-group versus out-group identification).

The very fact that most New Irelanders do engage in codeswitching indicates their remarkable multilingual proficiency. The level of proficiency (and therefore the degree of codeswitching) correlates with age and education level. The primary school children engage in codeswitching between their L1 and Tok Pisin, especially in schools in or near Kavieng. These schools have a greater mixture of languages represented in the student body, so Tok Pisin is more likely to be used on the playground and in the classroom. Young adults who have attended regional high schools (grades 7 through 10) or beyond know English and readily engage in codeswitching between English, Tok Pisin, and their L1. Among older adults codeswitching involving English is less common.

Factors other than age and education also influence switching patterns. According to Clyne (1987) switches may be triggered. A Tigak telling a story in Tok Pisin did not know the Tok Pisin word for a particular fish so he used the Tigak name. This Tigak name for the fish may have triggered the switch to Tigak for the rest of the sentence. (In the following examples Tigak is rendered in italics and Tok Pisin in bold.)

(1) **em i pulim huk na kisim...kisim**...*tang atulpot*
    3SG PM pull hook and get   get   ART mangrove.jack

---

[10]*Wantok* 'one talk' in the narrowest sense refers to another person who speaks the same vernacular, i.e., someone within the same ethnic group. In a broader sense it refers to anyone with whom you have a relationship within a given context—a good friend from school, a coworker, a fellow New Irelander, or even a fellow Papua New Guinean (if you happen to be in Australia or elsewhere).

	e	ga	ngan-i	∅
	and	3SG.S.AGR.PST	eat-TZ	3SG.OB.AGR

'He was fishing and got...got...a mangrove jack, and he ate it.'

A switch might also be triggered in the opposite direction by the use of a borrowed term. For example, during a discussion in Tigak about fishing, it was mentioned that a man, Ekonia, had bought an *ensin* 'outboard engine (TP)', and a switch was made to Tok Pisin when the speaker reported the result of Ekonia's having this engine (or what this engine made possible).

(2) na Ekonia ga togani tang **ensin** e tang vuul tana
ART Ekonia 3SG.S.AGR got ART engine an ART canoe his

em i go siksti nau
3SG PM go sixty now

'Ekonia got an engine, and now his canoe goes very fast.'

However, the use of a word from another language or of a borrowed word does not always produce a continued switch (1) or a later switch (2) into the other language, so the actual conditions that might produce triggering are unclear.

Switching patterns are also dependent on topic and other participants. In the absence of non-Tigak speakers, most conversation in the village concerning traditional matters is conducted in Tigak. However, when a topic changes, often the language switches as well. Even in villages on the more remote Tigak Islands, codeswitching occurs in the presence of residents of the islands who are not native Tigaks, but who have married a Tigak and have lived among them for some time. They are expected to at least understand Tigak, but concessions are made for their benefit, and they are included in the community through codeswitching with Tok Pisin. Switches to Tok Pisin are very common in the presence of an expatriate. Sometimes the speaker is unaware that he/she has switched. As I was walking along a trail between villages with several Tigaks, we were discussing what languages they use in different contexts. One middle-aged man spoke up,

(3) *O-o* **mipela olgeta taim** *mem etok lo etok siva!*
O-o 1PL all time 1PL.EXC.S.AGR talk LOC talk place

'O-o, we always speak in vernacular!'

McClure (1981) also points out the importance of the topic in addition to the setting, the participants, and the social identity projected in the codeswitching. The example above illustrates this to some extent, but it is even more apparent when discussions turn from traditional or everyday matters to religion or the church. Because many pastors assigned to churches in Papua New Guinea are not from the language group served by the church, many church services are conducted in Tok Pisin. On the Tigak Islands, the local people use Tigak for announcements and prayers, Kuanua (Tolai) for Bible readings and hymns, and the pastor often preaches in Tok Pisin. In the urban centers, the entire church service is in Tok Pisin (or sometimes English). Thus, a conversation carried on in Tigak will almost always include switches to Tok Pisin when religious matters are raised because Tok Pisin is the most widely used language in area churches. Education is another topic that brings about codeswitching, but in this case the switch usually involves English.

Another topic that often brought about a switch in conversations with my husband or me was a request for something. Greetings and social conversation would be carried on in Tigak with some exclamations (such as **ola man!**) in Tok Pisin inserted. After what was considered a polite interval, the Tigak would switch to Tok Pisin to express a need and then to English to make a request.

(4) ...*amoua   vo   mem   a   isa   e   Kavieng* **nau   mi**
    ...tomorrow   IRR   1PL.S.AGR.EXC   MA   go.up   LOC   Kavieng   now   1SG

   laik askim wanpela samting long yu   mi   gat   nid   long
   like ask   one   thing   of   you   1SG   have   need   for

   skul   fi   long pikinini bilong mi you got twenty kina?
   school fees   for   child   belong 1SG
   '...tomorrow we will go to Kavieng. Now I want to ask you something. I need school fees for my child. Do you have twenty kina?'

Cultural restraints can also exert pressure to switch codes. The Tigaks probably had no traditional greeting formulae. Greetings in Tigak today, using Tigak lexemes, are patterned after Tok Pisin. Using Tigak words for the greeting is a concession itself on the part of a Tigak. When a Tigak greeted us in Tigak, he/she immediately would switch to Tok Pisin or English to continue the greeting ritual, as in (5).

(5) Me: *lo moua ro*   'Good morning'
     Tigak: *lo moua ro*
              yu stap gut?   'How are you?'

The Tigak equivalent to the **yu stap gut** is *mug minang ro,* but I never heard a Tigak say this in Tigak. The reason was not clear until one day when we met a Tigak friend at the market in Kavieng. We had not seen Henri for several weeks. He greeted us first, and we continued the greeting in Tigak, not intending to switch to Tok Pisin or English.

(6)   Henri: *lo moua ro*   'Good morning'
      Me: *lo moua ro*
              mug minang ro?   'Are you well?'

At this point, Henri looked at us strangely and switched, not to Tok Pisin, which would have been the usual and friendlier switch, but to English. He asked, "Why?" After recognizing our innocent ignorance of what we had said, he explained that to him the only reason for someone to ask about his health when he had not been sick would be because that person expected him to have been sick because he/she knew of sorcery having been worked against him. No Tigak would ask such a thing of another Tigak. And no Tigak could bring himself to ask us, except by switching to Tok Pisin.

Codeswitches of single items also occur.[11] As widely noted, single item switches occur most frequently with nouns (Poplack 1980, 1981, Myers-Scotton 1992a, 1993a, Halmari 1997) and NPs (Treffers-Daller 1993). Among Tigaks such switches may occur in the same conversation with equivalent native Tigak words, as in (7). With verbs, the switched item may be unaffixed if it is intransitive (8), but will show Tigak morphology if it is transitive (9). A verb sometimes shows double morphology with a full Tok Pisin transitive form being suffixed with the Tigak transitive marker as well, as in (10).

(7)   *lisan-au ta* **kaikai** *ka-nig lisan-i ta pook ka-na*
      give-1SG ART food GEN-1SG give-TZ ART food GEN-3SG
      'Give me my food, give him his food.'

(8)   *vo nag* **go** *lo lana tang balus*
      IRR 1SG.S.AGR go LOC inside ART airplane
      'I will go in the airplane'

---

[11]Single-item codeswitching is not common in all language pairs. Kulick and Stroud (1987) report that most Gapun codeswitching with Tok Pisin is interclausal. The wide typological differences between Tok Pisin and this Papuan language may explain this fact.

(9) ri   kasinga-g   rig¹²   vuk   **was**-*i*   tang vakup pana
     ART   spouse-1SG   3PL.S.AGR   want wash-TZ   ART clothes with

   ta   **masin**
   ART   machine
   'My wife wants to wash the clothes with the machine.'

(10) **larim**-*i* 'leave-it'   < Tok Pisin **lar-im**   < English 'let-him'
     leave-TZ   leave-TZ

The Tok Pisin root verb **lar-** plus the transitive marker **-im** is reanalyzed by the Tigak speaker as the single morpheme verb root **larim** to which they add the usual Tigak transitive suffix *-i*. Example (10) illustrates the difficulty of separating single codeswitched items from borrowed items. As stated earlier, Myers-Scotton 1992a claims that most borrowed items start out as codeswitches. I know that for some Tigaks **larim-***i* is a codeswitch for the corresponding Tigak verb *talung-i*. However, for some (especially young Tigaks) *larim-i* is the only entry in their mental lexicon for the concept 'leave it'. It has, for those Tigaks, become a part of the Tigak language, and many of them do not even realize that it is borrowed. (One Tigak young man told me that Tok Pisin had borrowed the word from Tigak.)

Borrowings in Tigak

Despite the difficulties in separating borrowings from codeswitching of single lexical items, there are obvious established loans in Tigak that come from Tok Pisin, English, and other languages. Most of these established loanwords are borrowed from Tok Pisin, since this is the second language to which most Tigaks have the greatest access. The vocabulary of Tok Pisin came, in turn, from other languages, primarily English. In (11) is a short list of established loans in Tigak. In the list, the original source for Tok Pisin is given in parentheses. It is obvious from this list that most of the borrowed items are filling lexical gaps, but a few have simply replaced original Tigak forms. For example, the original Tigak *sangsangaulung* 'hundred' (lit., 'Rdp-ten' = 'ten tens') has been replaced by *maar* from Kuanua. This form is in turn now being replaced by the Tok Pisin form **handet** 'hundred'. Most number forms now used by Tigak speakers are from Tok Pisin, and only the numerals from 'one' to 'ten' are commonly heard in Tigak. Tigak *vuul* is equivalent to Tok Pisin **mun,** and the two are currently used interchangeably by Tigak speakers.

---

[12]The Tigak plural pronominal form is used in all contexts to refer to any woman who has had a child.

(11) Tigak item   Source
    maar   'hundred'   Kuanua
    Kalou   'God'   Kuanua
    talatala 'minister'   Tok Pisin/(Fijian)
    lotu   'worship'   Tok Pisin/(Fijian)
    abus   'meat'   Tok Pisin
    mun   'canoe'   Tok Pisin
    bensin   'fuel'   Tok Pisin/(English)
    buk   'book'   Tok Pisin/(English)
    dokta   'doctor'   Tok Pisin/(English)
    mani   'money'   Tok Pisin/(English)
    pepa   'paper'   Tok Pisin/(English)
    kaati   'small boat' English 'cutter'

The forms in (11) are all nouns, as are most borrowings cross-linguistically (Poplack, Sankoff, and Miller (1988), Treffers-Daller (1993:94) quoting Muysken's borrowability hierarchy). Because Tigak nouns are rarely affixed, they do not change form in either Tigak or Tok Pisin. With verbs it is easier to see adaptation into Tigak because of required affixation. Tigak does not have a generic term for 'to cook', but many different forms describing the traditional ways of cooking (such as *tuntun* 'to put into the fire', *sulai* 'to cook over a fire', *niningai* 'to boil', *taunani* 'to bake in hot stones', *nakas* 'to mumu'). Young adults who have lived outside the Tigak area and return now use *kuk/kukim* and *boil-i* from Tok Pisin/English. The Tok Pisin transitive form for 'boil' is **boil-im,** but Tigaks affix the Tigak transitive suffix *-i* to the Tok Pisin stem **boil** instead of the Tok Pisin transitive suffix **-im**. However, the transitive marker *-i* is not used by Tigaks with *kuk*, even though the Tok Pisin transitizer **-im** is suffixed in Tok Pisin. Rather, the Tok Pisin forms **kuk/kuk-im** have been borrowed into Tigak as complete intransitive and transitive verbs, *kuk/kukim*, respectively.

(12) ri   naa-g   **kuk**   [Tigak]
     ART   mother-1SG   cook
     'My mother cooks/is cooking.'

(13) a. vo   nag   **boil-i** tang dais   [Tigak]
        IRR   1SG.S.AGR   boil-TZ   ART   rice
        'I'll boil (the) rice.'

but

    b. *vo nag* **kukim** *tang dais*
       IRR 1SG.S.AGR cook ART rice
       'I'll boil (the) rice.'

(14) **bai** mi *boil-im* dais or **bai** mi *kuk-im* dais   [TP]
     FUT SG boil-TZ rice   FUT 1SG cook-TZ rice
     'I'll boil (the) rice.'   'I'll cook (the) rice.'

The use of the verbs above (and others) has become so widespread that even young children and monolingual Tigaks use them. They are established loans used by all Tigaks.

Some phonological borrowing from English into Tigak has also occurred. Several phonemes have been added to the Tigak inventory, mostly through the adoption of common English names, such as *Jems* and *Frank*, and some English tools such as *hamma* and *dril*. Although *dril* does not introduce any new phonemes into Tigak, it does illustrate the introduction of a new syllable pattern with consonant clusters (also seen in *Frank*). Mostly younger speakers who have some English fluency use these newer forms. Older speakers still adapt names and other borrowings to fit the native Tigak patterns. For example, one young adult Tigak friend was called *Dinia* by his parents and fellow Tigaks. Because it was not a traditional Tigak name, we asked about its origin. *Dinia* informed us that his parents had meant to name him *Junior* because they had heard expatriates called by that name. *Dinia* was the closest they (and other Tigaks with no English training) could come to pronouncing the English equivalent.

Another type of borrowing found in Tigak is borrowing at the conceptual or semantic level. As stated above, Tigaks traditionally did not have greetings. Culturally, conversation with or notice taken of another person depended on one's relationship with that person. For example, a Tigak must avoid speaking to or passing in front of an in-law or a cousin of the opposite sex. Tok Pisin greetings are adopted from English. Since Tok Pisin was previously used to communicate with speakers of other languages, greetings were no problem. As Tok Pisin speakers have returned to village areas, some patterns from that language have entered the vernaculars, including greetings. Tigaks have copied the concept from Tok Pisin and English and calqued Tigak words that match semantically. The translated words or phrases are put into a Tigak frame using the locative form *lo*.

(15) English: good morning
    Tok Pisin: **moning**
    Tigak: lo moua   (ro)
                 LOC morning (good)

In some cases the semantic borrowing involves an extension in meaning based on a Tigak lexeme. Example (16) provides such an example.

(16) vo   nag   **go** lo   lana   tang **balus**
     IRR 1SG.S.AGR go   LOC inside ART   airplane
     'I will go in the airplane.'

The word *balus* in Tigak is the name of a particular species of bird. It is a common Austronesian lexical item with this meaning. The form was borrowed into Tok Pisin with the same meaning, but in Tok Pisin was also extended to mean 'airplane'. Tigak (and most other languages of Papua New Guinea as well) has in turn borrowed back this extended meaning of the word to fill that lexical gap.

Language shift, attrition, and death

Northwestern New Ireland is a small area in which many languages are spoken. Most of the inhabitants speak an indigenous language as a native language, but not all do. In the previous sections I have given examples of several common contact-induced phenomena. Paulston says that "ethnic groups within a nation, given opportunity and incentive, typically shift to the language of the dominant group" (1994:77), and that the motivation for the shift is usually "economic advantage and social prestige" (p. 84) (see also Sasse 1992a, Gal 1988). The urban Tigaks, the Naliks, the Kuots, and the residents of Sumuna are in various stages of language shift, choosing to use different languages from that of their ancestors because of the opportunities those new languages provide. "Assimilation by choice will be the main cause of the worldwide decline of minority languages in the future" (Brenzinger 1997:282). Such is the present case in New Ireland and elsewhere in Papua New Guinea.

Various social and historical factors can influence a speaker's language choices. The languages discussed below will demonstrate some of the social and historical factors that have influenced the language choices of New Irelanders. These language choices have, in turn, produced language change. Young Nalik speakers are choosing a more technological lifestyle to which they have been exposed through education. This choice means more association with and use of Tok Pisin and English. Their Nalik is now converging toward these languages of wider communication. Kuot speakers are choosing to identify with their Austronesian neighbors and are giving up their language. Speakers of the Sumuna language were probably not culturally (or ethnically) different from the Tigaks and Tiangs located on either side of them, but they have already abandoned their own language in favor of the closely related neighboring Tigak language, probably because they were so much alike ethnically, culturally, and linguistically.

The historical accident of geographic location also influences language. As noted above, isolation increases the likelihood of vernacular maintenance (Lieberson, Dalto, and Johnson 1975). Below I will compare the more isolated Island Tigaks and Tungags who are conservative in their respective language use with Tigaks and other language groups on the mainland of New Ireland and on Djaul Island who are not isolated from other languages. Extended contact with numerically larger neighboring languages (in the cases of Kuot and Sumuna) and with prestigious introduced languages (such as Tok Pisin and English, in the cases of Tigak and Nalik) is affecting the vernaculars of New Ireland. New Irelanders are losing and/or changing their own languages under that influence. Details of the effects of Tok Pisin and English on the structure of Tigak are discussed in chapter 7.

Attitudes and beliefs about one's language also affect the degree of language maintenance (cf. Giles, Bourhis, and Taylor 1977). Some New Ireland groups are very proud of their linguistic and cultural heritage and actively work to see that the home language is used and taught to their children. Recent government support for the use of the indigenous languages in the early school years has prompted grass-roots support for and establishment of **tok ples pri skul** 'talk place preschool' (preschools taught in the vernacular). Vernacular education is being supported through grade 3 in many communities. However, the scale of linguistic vitality in New Ireland ranges from very strong language use and identity through shift to a language of wider communication, such as Tok Pisin and English, through language convergence and attrition in progress, all the way to the end of the scale with a dying (or already dead) language.

Lieberson, Dalto, and Johnson (1975) classify linguistic communities into four types. All four types are found in New Ireland. The Tungag language group on New Hanover is their indigenous superordinate type, an indigenous language group with power and prestige. As the largest (approximately 14,000 speakers) and one of the most independent and influential groups in New Ireland, the Tungags show strong ethno-linguistic vitality and language maintenance. As the authors would predict, little language shift is evident among the Tungags. The other types Lieberson, Dalto, and Johnson propose are the migrant superordinate (powerful outside groups who come into an area), the indigenous subordinate (native, but non-influential groups), and the migrant subordinate (migrant groups lacking prestige or influence). They predict little language shift in either of the superordinate types because these types have the power and influence to force their language on others or, at least, to maintain the language of their choice. The migrant superordinate groups of Papua New Guinea (and New Ireland) are the small but influential groups of expatriates who are the political advisors and businessmen of the country. Most of these groups are English speakers who have no intention or reason to give up the English language.

Within New Ireland, the Kuots would be the indigenous subordinate type of Lieberson, Dalto, and Johnson, being very few in numbers and lacking prestige among other New Ireland groups. This is the type of group in which the authors predict any shift to be slow because the speakers are in their own territory and in familiar surroundings. This gives them an advantage in maintaining their culture and language. Although the Kuots are shifting to Tok Pisin very rapidly now, this shift is the culmination of long and intimate contact with other groups. Every urban area of Papua New Guinea also has its own migrant subordinate enclaves. These are groups of speakers of a common vernacular who leave their villages and congregate in settlements in the towns. Members of this last type are the ones most likely to shift their language because they are in an environment using a different language and one in which they have little control. They must use the dominant language in order to survive. The dominant languages of the towns are Tok Pisin and English.

In the next sections I will describe examples of language shift, language decay, and language death found in New Ireland. Sasse distinguishes between *"normal language contact* situations and the pathological situation of *language decay"* (1992b:59, italics in the original). He continues, "theoretically, contact-induced loss...is motivated by the absence of the respective categories in the contact language, while decay involves loss of categories not motivated in this way" (p. 74). Contact-induced loss will be seen in loss of the alienable/inalienable distinction in Nalik due to the influence of Tok Pisin and English, both of which lack this distinction. Language decay will be seen in the case of Kuot through the neglect of the older generation to teach the language to the younger generations and encourage its use in daily life. Language death is defined as "the cessation of regular communication in the language" (Sasse 1992a:18). According to this definition Sumuna is a dead language, and Kuot is in the process of dying.

The following cases illustrate the more extreme end of the continuum of contact phenomena as compared to the cases of bilingualism, borrowing, and codeswitching discussed above. In each of the following cases some (or all) of the language is being lost due to the influence of contact with some other language(s). Such contact has been the case in New Ireland for centuries due to the close proximity of different languages (see the Kuot example below) and because the sea provides an avenue of travel between groups (see the Tigak example (2)). In the next section I will discuss the language shift of urban dwellers. Next I will describe a case of linguistic convergence in progress among the Naliks, followed by a discussion of the Kuot language shift. Finally, I will give a brief account of the dying language of Sumuna on Djaul Island.

Language shift among urban dwellers

Kavieng is the capital of New Ireland Province. Of the approximately 5,000 inhabitants within or near the town limits, probably one half are members of the Tigak language-ethnic group. The other half are mostly local residents who have government jobs centered in Kavieng or jobs in a local business. Thus, most residents of the town are New Irelanders. However, some residents are from elsewhere in Papua New Guinea, especially business employees, and there is a small number of expatriates (fewer than thirty in 1996) who work for a foreign business, the government, or one of the church/mission groups.

Most Tigaks are married to another Tigak from a different but appropriate clan. Among the Tigaks who live in the vicinity of Kavieng, however, exogamous marriages are more frequent.[13] The ratio of Tigaks married to non-Tigaks is probably higher than for any other language group in New Ireland simply because Kavieng is in the center of the Tigak-speaking area. Kavieng's location in the middle of Tigak territory means there are more Tigaks in the area. However, because it is the provincial capital and the center for provincial government activities and offices, there are also as many non-Tigaks in the town as Tigaks. This mixture provides opportunity for more interethnic marriages.

---

[13]There is a bilateral cause and effect relationship between urban dwelling and exogamous marriages. On the one hand, persons living in an urban area are more likely to meet others from different language groups. On the other hand, couples in an exogamous marriage are more likely to live in an urban center rather than in either of the two different indigenous areas.

Map 1.9. Kavieng, capital of New Ireland Province

Children of these exogamous marriages who live in Kavieng are often not taught the language of either parent. The very fact that the parents are in the town indicates that they probably have jobs in government or business. Only the more highly educated Papua New Guineans hold these positions, and they are less likely to want to return to the village areas. Thus, their children have fewer reasons to learn a village language. Those parents want their children to know Tok Pisin and English. The fact that they are educated in an urban school also means they are not taught a vernacular language in the school. All these children grow up using Tok Pisin as a street language and often as their primary school language. They are the traditionally defined creole speakers of Tok Pisin, in that Tok Pisin is their L1. These urban children who are educated beyond grade 6 also become the more fluent speakers of English, which is the official (and practical) language of education beyond the primary school level.

A similar situation holds for non-Tigak families living in Kavieng. Even among endogamous marriages in the town (including some Tigak couples), the L1 of the parents may not be taught to the children, simply because the children do not hear that language outside the home. Some of the reasons for this situation are cultural. A Papua New Guinean home is much more open than a typical Western home. The people really do live mostly outdoors, so usually a group of people gathers anywhere one person is seen outside. Papua New Guineans are also accustomed to accommodating others in terms of language. It is rare that everyone in such an urban gathering speaks the same L1, so Tok Pisin (and sometimes English) is the normal means of communication. Although the children growing up in this environment do not all speak the L1 of the parents, they often understand some of it because of relatives who appear from time to time who may not speak Tok Pisin to them.

This does not mean that no urban children speak an indigenous language. Many of the families do teach their traditional language to the children and do use it within the family and ethnic circle. However, the number of urban dwellers growing up without learning an indigenous L1 is increasing. There is no stigma attached to a young person's not speaking the language of his parents. In fact, in some ways a young Tigak who does not speak the Tigak language is looked upon as special. This lack is a mark of having been raised in a town and/or educated on the outside. It means that their parents were successful and important people who had the means to provide such a lifestyle. Nor is this lack detrimental for the non-Tigak speaker in terms of communicating with his clansmen and other **wantoks** because Tok Pisin and English provide that means of communication. Should there be a person who does not speak either of these languages with whom one needs to converse, there are always others in the group who can translate.

Tigaks (and most Papua New Guineans) do take pride in their ethnicity, and language is a major aspect of their identity. They express concern over language loss, but they want other members of the language group to maintain it. "Ethnic identity does not always coincid-e with the language used...[and] the language we associate ourselves with need not be the one we use in our day-to-day lives" (Eastman 1984:259) (see also Bentahila and Davies 1992). A Tigak speaking another language still considers himself to be a Tigak. He is a member of a Tigak clan regardless of the language he speaks, and clan membership is the most important aspect of a Papua New Guinean's identity. Although the shift is slow, there is a decrease in the number of speakers of the indigenous languages as opposed to Tok Pisin and/or English in urban centers. I do not foresee this shift reversing.

Nalik: A case of language convergence in progress

Nalik is spoken in the area between Kara and Kuot to the east of Kavieng (see map 1.10). It is the easternmost language in the Lavongai-Nalik chain of northern New Ireland. Published work on the language includes a grammatical description (Volker 1998) and a report on changes in the use and structure of the language (Volker 1993). As is common in New Ireland, all Naliks are bilingual, but among the younger generation Tok Pisin is taking over in more and more domains of use, even to the point that Nalik is no longer the primary language among young Naliks. Education is highly regarded, and all Nalik children attend primary school. A high school is located at Medina in the middle of the Nalik area, so a higher percentage of Naliks have had access to more education than have the people in many other parts of New Ireland. However, English is the language of the school system. Vernacular preschool education was just being introduced in the late 1990s. For this reason, most Naliks are fluent in English, and all are fluent in Tok Pisin. Although most Naliks a few generations ago knew at least one of the neighboring languages, today few speak even one fluently. Kara to the west and Tabar (from an island to the east) were the most commonly known languages because of trading interactions among those groups. Although intermarriage with the neighboring Kuot people is common, few Naliks have ever learned that non-Austronesian language.

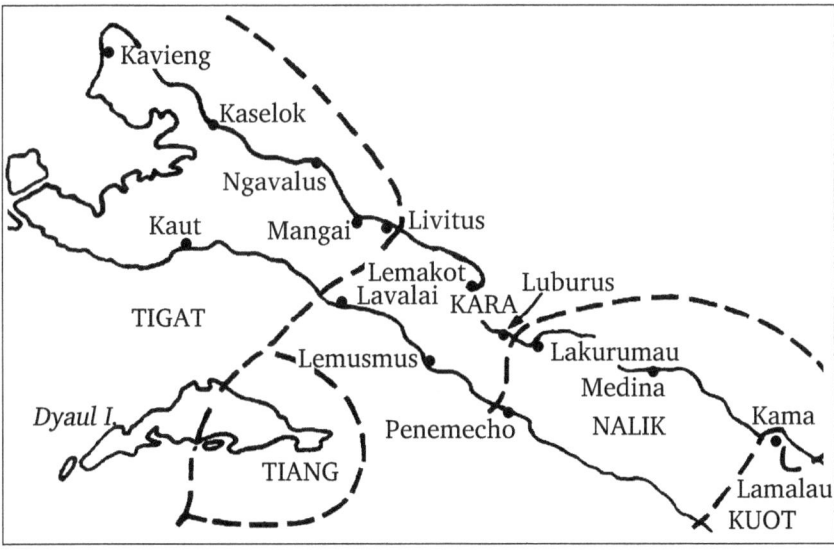

Map 1.10. Nalik language area

This shift in language use among the Naliks is producing changes in the language itself as it converges in style and structure toward Tok Pisin and English. Woolard (1989) pointed out that convergence often indicates a language shift in progress. Although Nalik is still a viable language, there is evidence that a shift has begun. In the lexicon, Tok Pisin lexemes are replacing even core vocabulary, such as *anti* 'aunt', *gaat* 'have', and numbers (Volker 1993). Although core vocabulary items are not usually the first lexical items to be lost, Smith (1983) has noted that lexical losses are usually an early sign of language attrition. Myers-Scotton and Jake (2000b) also give evidence for the early acquisition of content morphemes in language contact situations. Semantic changes under Tok Pisin influence are also occurring. Volker gives the example of the semantic convergence of the native Nalik forms *lagaf* 'hot' and *vulvulazai* 'hard' to Tok Pisin **hat** 'hot/hard', such that in Nalik *lagaf* now is used for both 'hot' and 'hard' to the exclusion of *vulvulazai*.

Language contact can also affect discourse styles and pragmatics. I will discuss substrate influences on Tok Pisin discourse style in chapter 6. Nalik, however, supplies an example of pragmatic convergence in the opposite direction. Nalik speakers are adopting pragmatic characteristics of the acquired languages (Tok Pisin and English) and moving away from those of the L1. Formerly, Naliks never made accusations directly, but vaguely hinted in the presence of an offender in order to shame the offender without direct confrontation. English is blamed for the more direct styles in use today, even among village leaders who openly accuse an offender in public meetings.

Campbell and Muntzel state that "the most obvious prediction one can make about dying languages is that their structure is very likely to undergo a certain amount of change" (1989:186), that these changes include loss of distinctions, variability introduced because rules become optional, and morphological reduction, and that these changes are due to the influence of a dominant language. Examples (17) and (18) illustrate these changes in Nalik. Grammatical convergence is seen in changes in the use of the alienable/inalienable possession markers. Older Nalik speakers distinguish inalienable possessions (such as body parts and blood relatives) in a common Austronesian pattern by suffixing the possessed noun with a pronominal form referring to the possessor. In (17a) and (18a) the first-person singular pronominal form (*-nagu*) is suffixed to the inalienably possessed noun. Alienable possessions are indicated with separate genitive forms, demonstrated in (17b) and (18b) by the free forms *saraga* 'my' and *sina* 'his/hers' (see Tigak examples under "Possession" in chapter 4). Within any mixed age group of Naliks one finds disagreement as to what forms require an inalienable suffix. Younger Naliks today do not make the distinction, following the pattern adopted from Tok Pisin and English.

(17) a. *a   mit-**nagu***
      ART hand-my
      'my hand'

   b. *a   mit   saraga*
      ART hand   my
      'my hand'

(18) a. *dama-**nagu***
      father-my
      'my father'

   b. *a   nalik   sina*
      ART boy   his/hers
      'his/her son'

Thus, the current forms used by young speakers are the (b) forms above, compared to the traditional inalienable forms in (a). These young Naliks form all possessives according to the alienable pattern. (The examples are adapted from Volker 1993:117–118.) This loss of distinction between the two patterns demonstrates Andersen's two strategies for dealing with gaps due to language attrition. He states these strategies as follows:

> Whenever possible use free morphemes...strung together linearly in the most transparent fashion to express your meaning...Whenever there are different devices to express the same basic meaning, use only one of these devices. (1982:100, 102)

Both strategies are followed by young Naliks in that they have chosen to use only one possessive construction, and the one they have chosen is the one formed by linear strings of free morphemes. The more frequently used words are also the first ones to lose the inalienable/alienable distinction, probably because these are the words most often borrowed from Tok Pisin and English, such as *papa* 'father' or *brata* 'brother'. These lexical items replace the vernacular terms (i.e., they are core borrowings).

Sociolinguistic factors such as age and gender can also be relevant to language behavior and language change (cf. Fischer 1958). Among the Naliks, younger male speakers are the first ones to lose the alienable/inalienable distinction. Not only do more older males and more female speakers maintain the distinction, but they maintain it for more lexical items. Volker (1993) mentions two other social factors that also influence the convergence (or lack of it) of Nalik toward Tok Pisin/English patterns. The first is, surprisingly, that young Naliks educated and living outside New Ireland tend to be more conservative in Nalik usage than their peers living in New Ireland, even those living in the Nalik area. I suggest that the reason lies in the fact that they remember the Nalik of their parents from earlier times in the home and that the innovations have not been reinforced because they have not heard them from other Nalik speakers in the village.

The second (and more expected) fact is that children of the more prestigious families from which the *maimai* (spokesman for a special occasion) come are also more conservative. It has been widely observed that discussion of traditional topics leads to more conservative vernacular language use. These young people would be exposed to the more traditional aspects of the culture and trained to revere those aspects. Proper language use would be among those traditional values.

Within the theoretical framework I am using, the convergence noted in Nalik could be interpreted as evidence of a composite matrix language. Myers-Scotton defines CONVERGENCE as "the use of morphemes from a single linguistic variety, but with parts of their lexical structure coming from another source" (1998:290). Using the alienable/inalienable possession example discussed above, all the morphemes indicating possession come from Nalik, as do the morpheme order and the structure of the possessive constructions, but the lexical-conceptual pattern comes from Tok Pisin, which lacks a distinction in possession types. Thus, the Nalik language variety spoken by the younger generation is a composite of Nalik morphemes and structural patterns based on the abstract lexical structure of Tok Pisin. Admittedly, the examples given here are few because Nalik data are not readily available. Thus, my argument in the case of Nalik convergence is very tentative. One could also argue that this loss in possessive distinctions is merely natural simplification. I cannot dispute that position on the basis of my limited data. However, viewed as a part of the total linguistic situation in New Ireland and as just one more example of the influence Tok Pisin is having on the indigenous languages there, the argument for convergence seems justified.

The variation among speakers in the usage of alienable versus inalienable forms also indicates that speakers are at different stages in a process of language attrition. Schmitt (2000b) suggests three stages in language loss, the first being the acquisition of content morphemes from the new language. Content morphemes, especially nouns and verbs, are the most psychologically salient of all morpheme types, thus easier to acquire (Myers-Scotton 1992a). As the speaker becomes more proficient in the new language he/she begins to use abstract lexical structure from that new language, even though some of the morphemes on the surface are still from his L1, especially late system morphemes. Naliks exhibit both of these stages. Some Naliks have replaced the native Nalik lexeme *dama-* for 'father' with the borrowed Tok Pisin lexeme *papa*. Those Naliks who are still at Schmitt's first stage of language loss use the appropriate Nalik inalienable construction given in (19a). The ones who have progressed to the second stage use the alienable construction for all possessive forms, as in (19b).

(19) a. *papa-nagu*
    father-my
    'my father'

   b. *papa   saraga*
    father my
    'my father'

The third stage is a complete matrix language turnover resulting in the new language becoming the speaker's matrix language. Nalik speakers as a group have not yet progressed to this third stage. The variation in alienable/inalienable constructions and the form these constructions now take, however, indicate that some Naliks are in the second stage of a language shift.

Although Labov (1966) popularized the idea of group linguistic variation as an aspect of socioeconomic stratification in healthy urban communities, King points out that "linguistic variation may also be maintained in dying languages in the absence of social differentiation, by fully fluent speakers of the language" (1989:140). Intraspeaker (and intragroup) variation in Nalik is an indication of change in progress. Interlanguage differences are affecting the vocabulary and the morphosyntactic structure of the language. Nalik is changing to become more like the languages which are replacing it as the primary vehicle of communication. However, it is not yet disappearing, only changing. Next, I will discuss a language that is disappearing in a very typical three-generational pattern.

Kuot: A case of language attrition in progress

When languages are in contact, speakers often have the choice of engaging in a conflict with the outside influence or of giving up some aspect of their identity by succumbing to that influence (Nelde 1986). The Kuot language (also called Panaras) is the only non-Austronesian language in New Ireland. The Kuot people have not resisted the influence of other languages surrounding them and may soon cease to exist as a separate Papuan people. The total population numbers about 2,500 speakers (Chung and Chung 1998). Kuot is bounded by the Nalik language to the west, the Madak language to the east, and is interspersed with Notsi speakers along the north coast (see map 1.11). Most Kuots are fluent in Tok Pisin, but many are not fluent in the Kuot language. Chung and Chung report that Kuot is often viewed and learned as a second language and that "it is not easy to find young people who are good at speaking their own language" (p. 5). Although the older and middle-aged speakers may use Kuot in most situations in the village, the younger Kuots use Tok Pisin exclusively, or Tok Pisin and English. Tok Pisin is, in fact, used in every domain by speakers of all ages. Kulick and Stroud (1987) report a similar situation in Gapun village on the mainland of New Guinea. In Gapun, Tok Pisin is becoming the single language everyone knows, replacing all local vernaculars, including their own vernacular Taiap. Many of the children under the age of ten know only Tok Pisin. This situation is universal among the Kuot villages.

Kuot is a dying language. In Campbell and Muntzel's (1989) classification system of types of language death situations, Kuot fits both the gradual death and the bottom-to-top death types. It represents a gradual shift from the use of Kuot to that of a dominant language, with Kuot being maintained only in ritual domains. It is also being lost from the bottom up because it is not used in the most intimate settings, the home and community. Only the current grandparent generation has a fluent knowledge of Kuot because, although that generation taught Kuot to the parent generation, they have not maintained the use of the language in all domains. Thus, the parent generation, by not using a large portion of the vocabulary and many of the syntactic constructions in Kuot, has gradually forgotten many of the semantic and morphosyntactic distinctions that only the elders can now use. This parent generation can communicate with the elders in a form of Kuot, but they have not taught the Kuot language to their children. Thus, the Kuot children today know little, if any, of the language of their elders.

The Kuot villages are divided into two groups, four on the east (or north) coast and five on the west (or south) coast of New Ireland. During rainy periods it is difficult to get to the villages on the west coast because of road conditions. There are high ridges with heavy jungle growth between the two coasts, and it is too far to go around New Ireland by boat from one coast to the other. Because of their greater isolation the west coast villages are more conservative in their language use; however, language maintenance is still not an important issue to them. Chung and Chung (1998) give evidence of this by the fact that Kuot is seldom used even in the family domain.

Map 1.11. Kuot language area

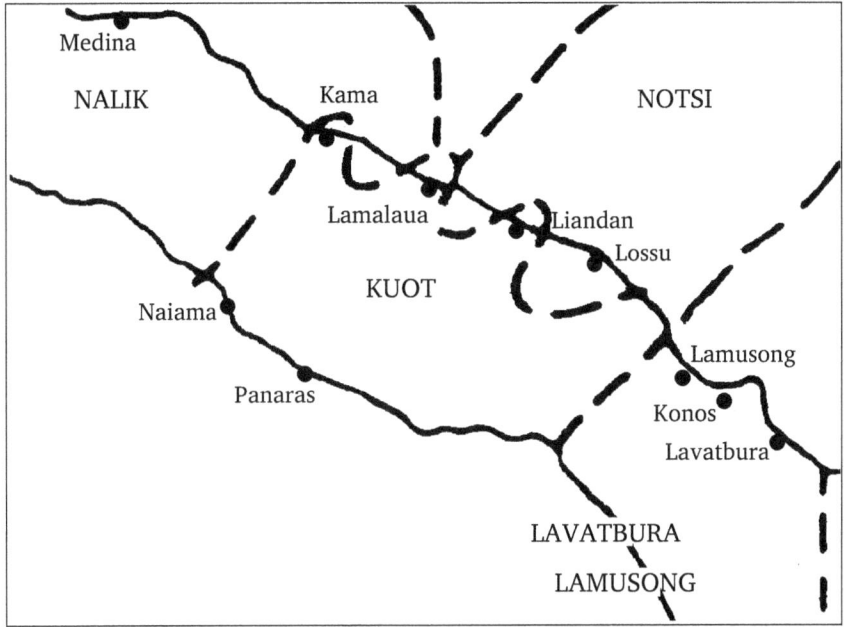

The geographic factor of being surrounded by Austronesian language speakers and the difficulty of Kuot (by comparison to Austronesian languages) are the primary reasons for the shift away from it. Other reasons for the shift to Tok Pisin include some different aspects in addition to those given by Kulick (1992:258) for the shift from Taiap to Tok Pisin. He attributes the change in Gapun village to a change in the worldview of the people; there is a degree of such change among the Kuots. Like the situation in Gapun, it is not primarily factors such as urbanization, industrialization, and migration patterns that have initiated the language shift among the Kuots (although increased mobilization through vehicular traffic has resulted in easier and more frequent contact with speakers of other languages). Extensive exogamous marriages have created kinship ties between the Kuot people and the neighboring Austronesian language speakers, thus weakening language and ethnic loyalty. Because it is the only Papuan language in New Ireland and is considered to be much more difficult than any of the neighboring Austronesian languages, no outsiders learn Kuot. Kuots themselves have traditionally been the ones to learn the languages of their neighbors, such as Nalik and Notsi, but speakers of those languages are now also using Tok Pisin. Kuanua, previously used in the United churches in Kuot villages, is even being replaced by Tok Pisin, the current language of choice for all functions in the religious observances among the Kuot people.

Language may be "a means of mediating between the past and the present" (Williams 1984:215), but "the new generations prefer speaking Tok Pisin to the difficult Kuot language, which will ultimately lead to the death of the Kuot language...the language decline seems to be inevitable and accelerating" (Chung and Chung 1998:6). Parents are not teaching Kuot to their children. Brenzinger warns that this tendency "might ultimately lead to the irreversible disappearance of the minority's original language" (1997:273) and that this displacement of the original language usually takes three generations (p. 282). The Kuots have already passed the three-generational pattern described by Li Wei (1994) and Milroy and Muysken (1995a) for immigrant groups, in which the oldest generation is monolingual in the ethnic language, the second generation is bilingual in the ethnic language and the new language, and the third generation is monolingual in the new language. Most elder Kuots (the grandparent generation) are not monolingual in the Kuot language, but they are the only Kuots who know the language well. The reason for the slower transition among the Kuots than among the Chinese immigrants to Britain described by Li Wei is that the Kuots are not displaced people but are the original inhabitants of their territory.

Linguistically, the evidence of language decay is abundant. Kuot has borrowed vocabulary from its Austronesian neighbors and from Tok Pisin and English and no longer considers them to be borrowed terms. Capell (1971:256) listed several Austronesian forms among the Kuot vocabulary items, such as *ula?* 'moon'. It is common for speakers to substitute entire phrases in Tok Pisin when they cannot recall the proper Kuot expression. Young people often make grammatical errors that shame them into switching to Tok Pisin. The older generation of men learned Tok Pisin away from the Kuot area, but the younger generations have learned it in their home villages and community schools, so it is a naturally acquired means of communication to them. Because every resident of each of the Kuot villages can now speak Tok Pisin, it is the natural universal form of speech in the villages.

English also affects the use of Kuot. As elsewhere in Papua New Guinea, English is the language of the educated, and it is a mark of high achievement and pride to a Kuot. Knowing English is a goal of many young people. It is not used extensively in the villages, however, because there are large numbers of Kuots who do not speak English. The youth do learn English in school, but although English is the official language of the schools, Tok Pisin is the unofficial and more often used language. Nearly all Kuot children complete primary school, but less than 50 percent complete the next level, grade 10.

The educational system shows no real support for maintaining Kuot. No community school in the language region has a single native Kuot teacher. In fact, only one village school has only Kuot students. The literacy rate is high (almost 95 percent) among adults for Tok Pisin, but drops to between 18 and 45 percent in Kuot and to 6 percent or less in English. The lowest literacy rates in all three languages are in the more linguistically conservative Kuot villages on the west coast. Kuot is not taught in any of the schools, and only in Panaras village on the west coast is Kuot even used among the children in the school. (This school also happens to be the only one in the Kuot region with an entirely Kuot student body.)

None of the above factors bode well for the survival of the Kuot language. Chung and Chung report that most Kuots feel that the language will die with the death of the current older generation (1998:6). Kuot illustrates "the actual process of abandoning a language [which] may be observed in a decrease in a) number of speakers, b) functional domains, and c) competence" (Brenzinger and Dimmendaal 1992:4).

Sumuna: A lost language

On Djaul Island to the south of Kavieng is an example of a language that is in reality dead. Previously three languages were indigenous to Djaul Island: Tigak, spoken in Leion village on the western end of the island; Tiang, spoken in three villages on the eastern tip of the island; and Sumuna, previously spoken in the north coast village of Sumuna (see map 1.12). I have found no written records of the existence of the Sumuna language. Rumors of an almost forgotten language in this village had reached us from our early days on the Tigak Islands in 1987. Until a survey trip to all Tigak villages in 1996 we had no confirmation of its existence or any other information about the language. The current inhabitants of Sumuna speak Island Tigak, but all were excited when we asked about *Sumuna Aino* 'Sumuna before/older' and were quick to verify that such a language was formerly spoken there, and in fact, some speakers (a total of five) were still alive. We asked permission to meet them and to ask them questions about the language. Three of the five speakers were present in Sumuna that day and were escorted to an open meeting area in the center of the village. All were quite elderly and each was accompanied by an offspring (child or grandchild). One was almost deaf and one was blind, but all three were happy to be asked for information only they could give.

These Sumuna speakers were probably already past the stage of Dorian's "semi-speakers" of Scottish Gaelic (1981), although they would fit her later definition as "the last, imperfect speakers of a dying language" (1983:158).

They no longer have other speakers to communicate with in the Sumuna language, since they are primarily isolated to their own homes. Sasse (1992b) distinguishes between semi-speakers and rusty speakers. A semi-speaker is one who never knew the language well because of imperfect transmission that prevented him from learning it well. A rusty speaker, on the other hand, once knew the language well but has forgotten it due to lack of use. It is impossible to know at this point if these Sumuna speakers were semi-speakers or rusty speakers. They were more like Hill and Hill's rememberers (1986) who could recall some words and formulaic expressions but could not really speak the language in everyday communication. The Sumuna language has already reached Knab's moribund state in that its "communicative networks are reduced and the language fails to fulfill its everyday communicative functions" (1980:232).

Map 1.12. Sumuna

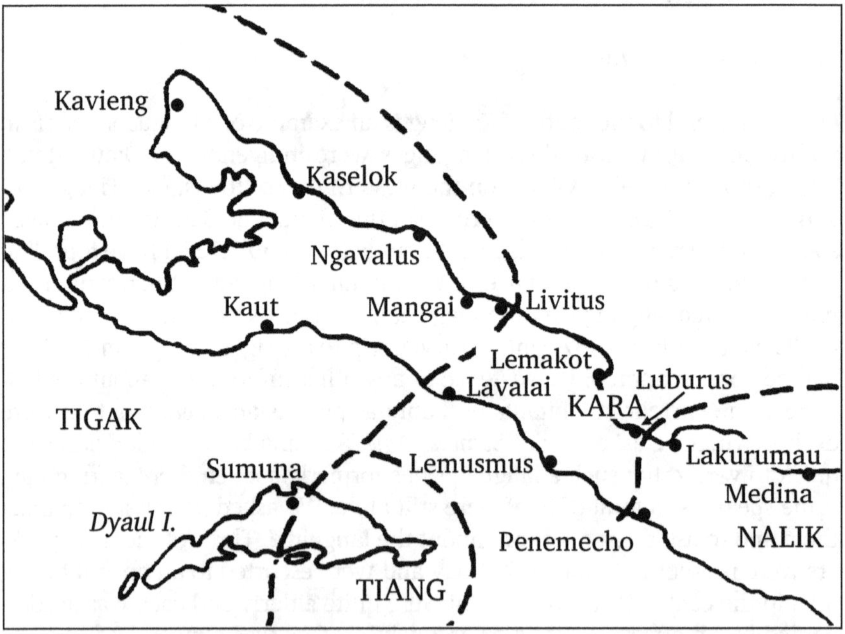

The history and earlier forms of Sumuna Aino (to use the name the residents of Sumuna use) are lost. This lack of information is one of the problems in studying dying languages (Dorian 1986). Other problems are the lack of choice of location and of speakers. The present residents of Sumuna could not tell us where the group came from or how they came to be mixed with Tigak speakers in Sumuna. It seems reasonable that they were on Djaul Island in the location of Sumuna before Tigaks came to live there. The residents of Sumuna did not express a negative attitude toward the language (as is the case among the Naliks and Kuots), but rather expressed regret that more people did not know the language better.

The reason for the loss of the Sumuna language is also a matter of speculation. Apparently, the loss was what Brenzinger and Dimmendaal (1992) call internal, coming from limited communication because of the restricted distribution of the language. The population of Sumuna is still small and could not have numbered more than 100 to 200 in the past. It is not likely in a linguistically tolerant society such as New Ireland that another language group moving into the area would deliberately pressure Sumuna residents to give up their own language. It is more probable that the original Sumuna residents were gradually outnumbered by Tigak speakers and shifted to the Tigak language. Because of the close relationship and highly cognate vocabulary, such a shift would not be difficult. Craig notes, "often death comes by a situation of languages in contact and shifting bilingualism" (1997:258). It is evident that previous generations of Sumuna speakers were bilingual in the Sumuna language and Tigak because the few remaining speakers of Sumuna now speak Tigak in daily communications. Another possible scenario is that the Sumuna language was a temporary, mixed language produced by Tiang and Tigak speakers who established a common village in the center of the island they share. Sumuna is located on the north shore nearest to the mainland of New Ireland and is on a small natural harbor making boat access easier than at either end of the island where reefs extend far into the sea.

The data I was able to gather in Sumuna reveal obvious similarities with both Tigak and Tiang, the other two languages spoken on Djaul Island. One cannot rely on these data for firm conclusions about the language, however, because of the obvious inconsistencies, undoubtedly due to the ages and possibly faulty memories of the subjects. For instance, in (20) the subject agreement pronoun used in the Sumuna Aino clause is the Tigak form *ga* '3SGSAGR', whereas in most other clauses (such as (21)) the equivalent form is *ik*. The form *ik* comes from neither Tigak nor Tiang, in which the equivalent form is *ka*.

(20) a. *tang anu ga visi a piu* [Sumuna Tigak]

    b. *a towar ga luk a piu* [Sumuna Aino]

    c. *nan ka luk a piu* [Tiang]
       'the/a man hit the/a dog'

(21) ***ik*** *mati* [Sumuna Aino]
    'he lies down'

This variation (*ga ~ ik*) could indicate the process of language loss. Schmitt (2000b) found that attrition affects content morphemes first, as content morphemes in the language being acquired are learned and replace those of the language being abandoned. System morphemes often are retained longer in situations of language attrition. Within the 4-M framework (Myers-Scotton and Jake 2000b) the subject agreement morphemes are late outsider system morphemes in Tigak, being structurally assigned and dependent on information outside the verb phrase in which they occur. Another system morpheme, the 3SG inalienable possession suffix, also shows alternation between Sunuma Aino *-nit* and the Tigak and Tiang equivalent *–na*. Example (22) illustrates this variation.

(22) a.   *isu-**na***   *mata-**na***   *goko-**na***   [Tigak]
    b.   *isu-**na***   *matai-**nit***   *goko-**na***   [Sumuna Aino]
    c.   *isu-**na***   *mata-**na***   *we:ya-**na***   [Tiang]
       nose-3SG   eye-3SG   neck-3SG
       'his/her nose'   'his/her eye'   'his/her neck'

The fact that even these late system morphemes are being replaced shows the degree of language attrition among these last speakers of the Sumuna language.

That Sumuna Aino was a distinct language is indicated by the extensive vocabulary that is unique to Sumuna Aino. It must also have been an Austronesian language like its neighbors, judging from the vocabulary that is shared and from the clause structure. Sumuna Aino may have originally been closer to Tiang than to Tigak. Discounting the vocabulary that is shared by all three languages, the number of lexemes shared with Tiang only is about twice the number shared with Tigak only. Those lexemes found in common among the three languages are also ones that are most commonly shared among Austronesian languages as a whole. It is also evident that Sumuna Aino influenced the Tigak spoken in Sumuna. There are several words from Sumuna Aino that have been borrowed by Sumuna Tigak (and which are not found in the vocabulary of Tigaks elsewhere), such as *tua(na)* '(his) skin' and *te:min* 'old woman'.

The clause structure and morpheme order is parallel in all three languages, as illustrated in (23).

(23) a. *tang anu ga   veak gi visi a piu*   [Sumuna Tigak]

b. *a   towar ga   iyaui   luk a piu*   [Sumuna Aino]

c.   *nan   ka   sak   luk a piu*   [Tiang]
ART man 3SG.S.AGR NEG hit ART dog
'the man did not hit the dog'

The apparently missing Tiang article in (23c) is not a missing article. The speaker actually used the independent subject pronoun *nan* instead of the noun phrase 'the man'. Literally, the Tiang would translate 'he he not hit the dog'. The construction would be identical in Sumuna Aino and in Tigak if the independent pronoun were used in each of those cases instead of the full NP.

The facts to be gleaned from my short list of elicited material are few. More questions are raised than are answered. This is only one of the problems involved in investigating a language that is already so moribund and out of use that even the data are questionable. What this situation does tell us is that languages sometimes do disappear. However, in the case of Sumuna Aino (as in all cases except that of sudden language death), the speakers have not disappeared; they have shifted to another language.

This section has provided an overview of language contact phenomena in progress among the Tigak people and surrounding language groups in New Ireland. The purpose has been to demonstrate the extent of the influences the languages of New Ireland have had on each other in the past and the extreme influences that new LWCs are currently having on the indigenous languages.

Predictions: Papua New Guinea's Linguistic Future

The policy and practice described in "National Language Policy" is a concession to the diverse linguistic situation in Papua New Guinea and the country's struggle to become a unified nation. Policy makers attempt to accommodate the local and international pressures for the preservation of vernacular languages of minority groups, as well as the opposing need for a national identity and the use of a language that will promote national unity. As Mushakoji stated, "language planning...is an exercise which cannot ignore the correlations of sociocultural trends and political power relationships" (1984:1). The linguistic conflict faced by Papua New Guinea is like that of many developing multilingual countries. This conflict has been seen by some as a struggle between the language of the soul and the language of national development (Alisjahbana 1984:47). Coulmas lists "eradicating illiteracy" and "protecting linguistic and cultural minorities" (1984c:5) as the two most serious problems facing underdeveloped nations. For governments, the conflict is often between providing education for its linguistic minorities (which includes everyone in Papua New Guinea) and providing other services, such as hospitals or utilities (Williams 1991).

UNESCO has been especially vocal concerning the responsibility of governments to protect and promote the vernacular languages of the people groups within its borders. Papua New Guinea has used this principle of language rights as the stated basis for support of vernacular education. The real reason for the push in vernacular education, however, is much more pragmatic than the protection of minorities. Papua New Guinea is becoming aware of the burdens of self-determination. The attempt at universal primary education in English has not been successful, so another approach is being tried. Papua New Guineans are a very pragmatic people. If something appears to work, they will try it. Positive results from beginning education in vernacular languages is well documented (Huddleston 1980), and international funding sources favor (or require) this approach. If vernacular education will improve the quality of education by providing a foundation on which to build higher levels of education, Papua New Guinea will try it. The goal is not, however, to continue education in the vernaculars, but to transfer the ability to read to the reading of a national language for the purpose of fostering national unity and expediting the goals of national and provincial governments. Alisjahbana affirms that

> We have to accept the fact and the necessity that many of these languages will decrease in importance through compulsory education in the modern national language, and through the increasing density of transportation and communication the world over (1984:54).

As Grenoble and Whaley point out, although some language planners argue "that literacy is essential to...language survival in the modern world...others argue that literacy actually facilitates language loss" (1998b:32). Mühlhäusler (1990) is one who maintains that vernacular literacy often leads to the loss of that vernacular language because the vernacular literacy is not continued but is only used as a bridge to education in a national language. This opinion fits the educational policy in Papua New Guinea regarding language. Although vernacular literacy is encouraged for preschool and early primary school, it is not officially continued beyond grade 3, when instruction in English is programmed to begin. The continuation of a vernacular literacy program is difficult in an endangered minority language for the very reason that it is an endangered minority language. Most such languages have no written tradition, therefore very little literature upon which to found a continued literacy program.

The reality of the language situation in Papua New Guinea is that many people are not maintaining their mother tongue or teaching it to their children. They are shifting to Tok Pisin and/or English, languages which they perceive will bring them socioeconomic upward mobility. Arasanyin quoted Bamgbose as saying that "language is like a currency, the more it can buy the greater the value it has" (1995:214). Bentahila and Davies attribute the Moroccan Berbers' attitude toward language as "rather like clothes,...to be maintained only as long as they are of use" (1992:204). This attitude is typical in Papua New Guinea where learning another language has never been unusual. The theory of the economic determination of language behavior is widespread among sociolinguists. Edwards calls it "of central importance" (1994:116). Grenoble and Whaley are even more emphatic, stating that "*economics*...may be the single strongest force influencing the fate of endangered languages" (1998b:52, italics in the original). The shift to a LWC is taking place in Papua New Guinea for these very reasons. The two languages to which most Papua New Guineans shift are Tok Pisin and English. The domains of use for each of these languages and the reasons behind the choices are very similar to the uses of Swahili and English in Africa reported by Scotton (1976). In Papua New Guinea English is the language of the educated elite, and Tok Pisin is a neutral locally developed pidgin.

Kulick maintains that the shift to Tok Pisin in Gapun of the East Sepik is not "pragmatic" or "socioeconomical," but "cosmological" (1992:249) because "the changes that have taken place there are not primarily material transformations...The changes that have occurred in Gapun are in many ways a result of the villagers' changing interpretation of their world" (p. 258). While it is true that the Papua New Guinean culture is changing, I do not believe the changing culture (and the accompanying language shift) is indicative of any great change in the Papua New Guinean worldview (although admittedly there is a connection between the two). The changes in marriage patterns, village allegiance, and residence patterns are a result of opportunities that were unavailable to previous generations. Papua New Guineans have always had a mythology about beings with secret knowledge who would bring prosperity to their followers (cargo cults). Traditionally, those beings were ancestors who would return with the cargo, and traditionally those ancestors, when they returned, would be white-skinned. Thus, the Papua New Guineans' association of English and Tok Pisin with Europeans' bringing prosperity and material goods is a natural outgrowth of traditional mythology. What is changing are the patterns of allegiance through which young Papua New Guineans are pursuing the dream of material gain they have always had. Where before the clan was the source of an individual's security, today education, a wage-paying job, and fewer family obligations provide that guarantee. The motivation behind the cultural changes and language shifts in Papua New Guinea is still primarily economic.

In terms of Kelman's (1972) dichotomy between instrumental and sentimental attachment, Papua New Guineans are instrumentally attached to some lingua franca (most often Tok Pisin or English) and sentimentally attached to their vernacular language. The instrumental attachment is proving to be by far the stronger one. One must use a lingua franca to engage in commerce with those from other language areas or to hold a wage-paying job in any town. Thus, outside the village context, use of a vernacular is restricted to the family and the (usually small) group of speakers of the same language who might be living in the same town. In the home, if the marriage is exogamous, a common language is more often spoken among the family members than is either of the parents' mother tongues. Regardless of the language used at home, children and adults will use a lingua franca in an urban environment because of the heterogeneous language situation. In such an environment neighbors and friends do not necessarily speak a common vernacular. Children learn a common language at school, and children and adults learn a common language in the neighborhood.

As stated above, the reasons behind the language policies of the past and the current policy in Papua New Guinea have been pragmatic (or instrumental), not sentimental. Although the current policy of beginning education in the vernaculars is stated in terms of the inherent value of all languages, the desired outcome of this strategy is the ultimate promotion of English as a national language. I believe the vernacular languages of Papua New Guinea will be maintained for the foreseeable future, but not because of vernacular education or strong sentimental attachments to these languages. They will be maintained until the development of Papua New Guinea reaches the point that transportation and communication are available and affordable to the majority of its peoples. In other words, geography and underdevelopment are the most important factors in Papua

New Guinea's current maintenance of its many vernacular languages. Lieberson, Dalto, and Johnston (1975) note that "spatial isolation of language groups and official educational policies" (p. 34) are highly correlated with language diversity. "[A] relatively high degree of isolation among lesser tongues tends to reinforce those languages" (p. 44). Too many Papua New Guineans are still isolated in their home areas by terrain and prohibitive airfares to hope for an improved standard of living through education or use of another language. Such citizens will continue to use the vernacular until education and mobility are available to them.

Kulick referred to language as an identity marker and suggested that Papua New Guineans have in the past "purposely fostered linguistic diversity" (1992:2) to enhance this identity. But for Papua New Guineans clan identity is more important than language group identity. As noted by Edwards, although "language…is a highly visible marker of group identity,…it has also been acknowledged that language is *not* always essential for continued identity" (1984a:283–284, italics in the original). In this context the vernacular does have a degree of instrumental value to those who remain in the villages and depend on traditional cultural practices in their daily lives. One's personal welfare in Papua New Guinea is provided through a system of clan obligations. The use and maintenance of the vernacular is one instrument through which clan identity is reinforced. However, this cultural pattern is beginning to change. As it grows weaker and the pattern of nuclear family independence becomes more common, this instrumental hold on the vernaculars will also decrease. The growing number of exogamous marriages among educated Papua New Guineans (who meet their mates at schools outside their home regions) also weakens the connection between language and clan membership.

Language shift is already a noticeable feature of Papua New Guinean culture. Nekitel (1985) reports that in Womsis village in the West Sepik Tok Pisin is replacing the Abu' vernacular, and Kulick and Stroud (1987) report a noticeable shift from the Taiap language to Tok Pisin in Gapun village in the East Sepik. I have given examples of language shift in New Ireland above. My report on the Kuot language showed a loss of that vernacular parallel to the losses of Abu' and Taiap. According to Dorian "language loyalty persists as long as economic and social circumstances are conducive to it, but if some other language proves to have greater value, a shift to the other language begins" (1982:47). The educational system in Papua New Guinea is not designed to maintain the hundreds of vernacular languages under its jurisdiction. Under the Australian administration (from the end of World War I until independence in 1975), all education was in English. Today vernacular education is encouraged only for the earliest levels of school and only at a cost to the local community.

Supposedly, all children have access to primary level education (through grade 6). However, school attendance is not compulsory, and many children attend only sporadically. For some children the nearest school may be three to four hours away along difficult trails. Many teachers are not from the same language group as the children attending the school, so communications are not necessarily in a language the children understand in the lower grades since the teacher does not speak the vernacular of the students. The rates of school attendance vary from one part of the country to another, largely dependent upon the length of contact with foreign cultures. In isolated parts of the mainland, some children may not attend school at all. In the island regions of New Britain, New Ireland, and Bougainville long-term contact with European cultures has instilled an appreciation of the opportunities education can provide, and primary education is almost universal. The economic conditions of each area also affect school attendance. In some areas there are few opportunities to earn cash for school fees, so fewer children in those regions attend school for all six years of primary school.

In order to continue beyond grade 6, a student must pass an examination that qualifies him/her for high school. High school consists of grades 7 through 10. Each of the nineteen provinces of Papua New Guinea has a provincial high school, and some have more than one. There are also some private mission-operated high schools. Costs for high school are greater than for primary school. One reason for the increased cost is that the high schools are usually boarding schools serving students from an entire province. The mixture of students from many language groups in the student body is a major factor in the use of Tok Pisin and English as the languages of instruction at this level. The higher the educational level, the more English is used in the classroom instruction and materials. After grade 10 a student may apply for two years at a national high school upon satisfactory completion of another qualifying examination. There are only a half dozen national high schools in Papua New Guinea. With an average student body numbering less than 300, this means that fewer than 1,000 students per year complete the twelfth year of school.

As education has been increasingly provided by the national government, students have been removed from their language areas (after grade 6) and placed in situations of daily contact with speakers of many other languages. Since many of these students have already learned some Tok Pisin (or Hiri Motu or English in their respective areas), this LWC becomes the informal, or social, lingua franca. These students also learn English as a school subject and a language of instruction. From this educated class come the professionals, government employees, and business managers. Romaine notes that the factors leading to pidginization (or language death) include "encroaching diglossia, failure of children to acquire the mother tongue, schooling in a second language, resettlement, dispersion, and intermarriage" (1989b:371). Educated Papua New Guineans who get jobs upon graduation do not usually return to their language areas to work. They locate in towns where their particular vernacular may be virtually unknown. For them Tok Pisin and English become the languages of daily use.

Other members of their clan may join them in the town where they are employed, and these relatives also learn a lingua franca. Since Tok Pisin is easier to learn than English, and since it is in more widespread general use than either English or Hiri Motu, it is normally the language learned outside the formal educational context. The members of the educated minority who do not get jobs may return to their villages. These more educated citizens take with them their knowledge of Tok Pisin and/or English. In the less technical, less academic village environment, English is not likely to be the language they use. More often Tok Pisin becomes a social language in the village because others there will also know it, and knowing another language is a mark of education. It is also at the schools or in the towns that contacts are made with members of other language groups, which may lead to exogamous marriages. Often the children of these marriages are taught the native language of neither parent. For them Tok Pisin (and in some cases English) becomes the first language.

Although most Papua New Guineans are bilingual they do not use each language equally well or in the same contexts; rather, they use their several languages in a diglossic pattern. Papua New Guinea is, in fact, very similar to Tanzania in having what Abdulaziz describes as TRIGLOSSIA, "three languages with both varying and overlapping roles" (quoted in Eastman 1983:41). In Papua New Guinea English is the most prestigious variety (therefore, always High) and is used for government, international business, and higher education. Tok Pisin is used for social purposes and as a lingua franca between speakers of different vernaculars. It is a Low variety compared to English, but a High variety compared to the vernaculars. The vernaculars are used in the home or village and are always the Low variety. (See "Diglossia" above for a fuller example of triglossic language use among the Tigaks of New Ireland.) The above description of the use of English, Tok Pisin, and a vernacular does not mean that all speakers use all three languages in these different contexts. Indeed, only 10 to 20 percent of the population currently know all three languages. English will continue as the language of the educated elite. It is firmly entrenched in the university system and is closely tied to economic development. The ties with Australia from the long colonial association will not soon be broken. For interactions with the international community, English is the language of choice. Because English has a history of use in Papua New Guinea and because of its international value as a LWC, it is not likely to be replaced in international contexts. English is also used symbolically by Papua New Guineans as a sign of education and sophistication, much as Gal (1989) reports for the use of German among Hungarian speakers, and as Haarmann describes the use of English in Japan (as reported by Cheshire and Moser 1994). However, I believe the percentage of English speakers will continue to decrease nationwide, especially if the push for Tok Pisin use in schools continues.

Hiri Motu will also continue to decrease in use as Tok Pisin replaces it in its stronghold, the National Capital District. With less than 9 percent of the population speaking it and with more and more Tok Pisin speakers moving into the capital area, the sheer fact of numbers is in favor of Tok Pisin as opposed to Hiri Motu.

Although Lynch expresses questions about Tok Pisin's future because of the negative attitudes he has encountered toward the language, he does concede that "Tok Pisin is not going to go away: it is here to stay" (1987:397). Wurm is much more positive about Tok Pisin as shown in the following assessment of the linguistic situation:

> In Papua New Guinea, the development of a pidgin language...has produced a linguistic tool in that area...that has been playing a very important role in the competition for language use in the course of the gradual decay of the local cultures...In Papua New Guinea, it is not so much the language of the dominant culture of the former colonial masters, i.e., English, which is constituting a threat to the continued use and existence of the many languages of the local cultures, but this pidgin language which...has become the means of expression of a newly developed Papua New Guinean contact culture which is neither western nor traditional, but...is something peculiarly Papua New Guinean. (1986:534)

The functional allocations of Tok Pisin are expanding as the number of speakers of Tok Pisin is increasing. Because of the fact that Tok Pisin is easier to learn than English and is often learned informally on the school grounds or in the market, more people speak Tok Pisin as a lingua franca than speak English. Tok Pisin is more flexible (or less standardized) than English, so those who are hesitant to use English readily use Tok Pisin. There is also a growing sentimental attachment to Tok Pisin as a language more closely associated with Papua New Guinea than English is. It is neither a foreign language nor one of the local vernacular languages. Tok Pisin is being promoted as an indigenous alternative to English, and efforts toward standardization and formal educational use of Tok Pisin are increasing. It is "the language of modernization" (Litteral 1987:375), best fitting the needs of a country struggling to balance preservation of traditional cultures with the need and desires of its populace to share in modern economic and technological advances. Regarding the social functions of language, Smith states that

> normal language fills, in addition to its communicative one, an integrative function by serving to tie people into the social system. Language is used by society to mark the social statuses of an individual, and is used by him to affirm (commonly unconsciously) his position in the society. (1972:48)

In Papua New Guinea, Tok Pisin is serving this integrative function by providing a means of communication within this multilingual nation. Grimshaw (1971) notes that among the social functions of pidgin/creole languages is the enabling of diverse and hostile groups to develop a sense of unity. Wolfers states specifically that Tok Pisin "provides a sense of unity among New Guineans, where none previously existed" (1971:417).

I have discussed above how Tok Pisin, English, and the vernaculars mark a person's social status and indicate his/her membership in multiple groups. Except for regions of Milne Bay where English is used as a lingua franca, Tok Pisin is neither denigrated nor denied as Ferguson reported in 1959 to be the case with Haitian Creole. For these reasons and the fact that it is the single language spoken by the largest number of people in the country, Tok Pisin will continue to be the most often-acquired replacement for the vernaculars. I also predict that the percentage of mother-tongue Tok Pisin speakers will continue to increase, accelerating the shift to Tok Pisin until it becomes the language spoken by the majority of Papua New Guineans.

2
A Review of Literature on Language Contact Phenomena

This chapter gives a summary of some of the relevant literature concerning language contact phenomena. Neither the references nor the topics are exhaustive for this area of linguistics. The discussion will be limited to those references which are most directly applicable to this study or which are representative of a particular topic or point of view. General works on language contact and language change will be presented in the first section including related topics such as social factors and principles of second language acquisition (SLA). In the second section literature concerning bilingualism and diglossia will be discussed. The third section will cover the topics of code-switching and borrowing, and the fourth will cover language shift, attrition, and death. In the fifth section relevant literature on pidgins and creoles will be discussed, including general works and a discussion of the theories of the origin and of the formation of pidgins/creoles. Specific references to the pidgins of the South Pacific, especially Tok Pisin, the pidgin/creole spoken in Papua New Guinea, are discussed in chapters 1 and 6. A review of psycholinguistic research in the field of language processing concludes the chapter. Discussions of the theoretical models based on the results of this psycholinguistic research and on which this study in turn is based are found in chapter 3.

Language Contact and Language Change: General

Thomason defines a CONTACT LANGUAGE as

> a language that arose by some historical process other than normal transmission. Or to put it another way, a contact language is comprised of grammatical and lexical systems that cannot all be traced back to a single parent language. (1997:74–75)

Although Thomason is referring to pidgins, creoles, and mixed languages in this definition, it can also be applied to other language contact phenomena to limited degrees. Each form of contact phenomena described in this study has some degree of mixture of conceptual, lexical, and grammatical systems. Nelde defines CONTACT LINGUISTICS as incorporating three aspects: "language, language user, and language sphere" (1997:287). Language contact generally produces language change (cf. Edwards 1992). Changes in the language occur only after changes have occurred in the language user and in the language sphere. Bright (1997) discusses theories of language change and the factors that initiate such change. Hill and Hill (1986) provide an exhaustive example of an extended language contact situation in Mexico, detailing both the linguistic and sociolinguistic stimuli and results. Two other works that provide good summaries and reviews of language contact phenomena, their relationships to each other, and the terminology common to those areas of study are Clyne (1986) and Appel and Muysken (1987). The latter provides especially useful examples and explanations of much of the terminology. Two other works useful for general background on language contact and the types of language change induced by contact are Comrie (1989) and Thomason and Kaufman (1988). Comrie approaches the topic from the standpoint of universals and typology, and Thomason and Kaufman focus directly on contact situations.

In language contact situations factors other than language may be more important than language itself in determining the outcome of the contact. Alleyne emphasizes that "language is part of culture" (1993:167), and many of the examples in this study will demonstrate that cultural changes affect language changes. Edwards (1992) provides a typological model for minority languages that distinguishes between the speaker, the language itself, and the setting as types of variables that interact and must be considered in determining the effects contact may have on a language. I gave examples of different outcomes in "Language Contact Phenomena in New Ireland" in chapter 1. Other examples of sociolinguistic processes producing unique results are described by Gumperz (1964) and by Gumperz and Wilson (1971). Each demonstrates convergence in multilingual settings.

Not only do outside sociopolitical pressures affect language behavior, but individual and group beliefs about themselves also affect the outcome when people have linguistic choices. Giles, Bourhis, and Taylor's (1977) definition of ethnolinguistic vitality is applied by Giles and Johnson (1987) and by Allard and Landry (1992) to look at both subjective and objective factors which affect a group's beliefs about themselves and their language. Those individuals and groups who feel positive about themselves, their language, and their culture are more likely to maintain the language than those who feel inferior to another group. The latter are more likely to shift to the language of the other group. Two aspects of ethnolinguistic identity are described by Tabouret-Keller (1997). One approach is based on Giles' accommodation theory whereby a speaker chooses to accommodate others (or not) as a way of expressing either approval or disapproval. The other is based on Le Page's (1977) projection theory whereby an individual attempts to project specific aspects of his/her own identity through the use of language. Examples of different reactions to language change are given in the description by Dodson (1986) of the Welsh's desire to maintain their own identity, which led to renewed interest in their dying language, and the description by Bentahila and Davies (1992) of the willingness of the Berber and Jewish communities to shift from their own languages to Moroccan Arabic because they did not see language as part of their identity, but as a tool to expand their opportunities. As Eastman states, "there is no one-to-one correspondence between language and ethnic identity" (1984:274).

Bilingualism and Diglossia

Bilingualism is a prerequisite for other language contact phenomena such as diglossia, codeswitching, and borrowing; it must precede individual diglossia and codeswitching. Blom and Gumperz (1972) discuss codeswitching as a form of diglossia, and Edwards (1994) discusses diglossia as a form of societal billingualism. For purposes of discussion, however, I will compare bilingualism with diglossia in this section and codeswitching with borrowing in the next section (see also chapter 1 for discussions of bilingualism and diglossia in New Ireland).

Weinreich, in his classic *Languages in contact* (1953), consolidates distinctions previously made by others concerning types of bilingualism. Although he uses the terms "coordinative," "compound," and "subordinative" (pp. 9–10) as labels for the relationships between the mental representations of different bilinguals, the terms coordinate, compound, and subordinate are now used to designate these bilingual types. Paradis (1978b) provides a thorough, but concise, discussion of Weinreich's types. Macnamara (1967) focuses on levels (or degrees) of bilingualism by examining how well each language is known and how dominant one language may be over the other. He uses the coordinate-compound distinction to relate the bilingual's semantic interpretation to the method or context of acquisition of the languages.

One of the controversies involving bilingualism that has spanned decades is that of the effect of bilingualism on the individual. The general opinion has shifted from the view that the bilingual is handicapped by the division of his mental capacity between two languages to the current view that the bilingual has a distinct advantage over the monolingual because he has greater power of expression. See Grosjean (1989) for an analysis of the bilingual's competencies and Edwards (1994) for a review of the changes in position concerning the bilingual and intelligence.

General works on bilingualism include Haugen (1973), Romaine (1989a), and Edwards (1994). Haugen provides a review of other language contact phenomena in addition to bilingualism. Many of his ideas are applicable to the development of a composite matrix language (CML) and to a matrix language (ML) turnover in the Papua New Guinea context. He states that "under conditions of language contact the experiences of bilinguals are rarely so distinct that it is possible for them to keep the codes wholly apart" (p. 521). This situation could well promote the formation of a composite matrix language. (Another possible result of not keeping the two codes separate is a mixed language such as described by Mous (1994) or by Muysken (1981c).) Haugen continues, "the result is a more or less gradual shift from two codes towards one, with various intermediate codes in which elements from both of the two are involved" (p. 521). This closely describes a matrix language turnover. The more recent work of Edwards (1994) gives a comprehensive review of the linguistic and the sociopolitical aspects of bilingualism/multilingualism. He distinguishes types of bilingualism according to different criteria, such as social versus individual (cf. Fishman 1972b), active versus passive (based on how the languages are used), additive versus substractive (based on the effect on the speaker's linguistic repertoire), primary versus secondary (based on the circumstances of acquisition), and simultaneous versus successive (based on the order of acquisition). He relates speakers' attitudes toward language to both their worldviews, which determine language attitudes, and to their language behavior, which results from their attitudes, and relates each of these factors to language maintenance or attrition.

Ferguson (1959) introduces the term diglossia to describe a speech situation in which more than one variety of a single language is used in complementary domains (see also Ferguson 1991 and the more complete discussion of diglossia in chapter 1). Fishman (1967) extends the meaning of diglossia to include the use of two different languages and gives examples of each of the four possible combinations of bilingualism and diglossia that can occur. Mackey (1986) extends the concept once more and coins the term "polyglossic" for situations involving more than two varieties. Schiffman maintains that "diglossic situations tend to be unstable…due to an *imbalance of power* between the two (or more) varieties of a language that constitute the diglossic complex," and these conditions "often lead to language *shift*" (1993:115, italics in the original). Schiffman (1997) focuses on diglossia as a sociolinguistic situation. Francescato (1986) compares bilingualism with diglossia and lists the contrasting characteristics of each. According to him, bilingualism may result from either spontaneous or guided learning, and the languages may be acquired simultaneously or successively. Bilingualism may be collective or isolated (individual), it may be dynamic or not, balanced or not. In contrast, he proposes that diglossia only results from spontaneous learning, the languages are acquired successively, it is a collective phenomenon, nondynamic, and nonbalanced.

Codeswitching and Borrowing

As stated above, many language contact phenomena are related to or dependent upon bilingualism. Codeswitching by definition requires bilingual speakers. Individual diglossia (in Fishman's extended sense) is also dependent upon the speaker's ability to use more than one language. The relationships among these phenomena were discussed in chapter 1 with examples of each as they are currently occurring in New Ireland. Many useful references are given in that section. I will describe other research on these phenomena here, trying not to be too repetitious. Scotton (1986) discusses this relationship between codeswitching and diglossia and the various types of codeswitching which occur in diglossic communities. She also relates codeswitching and borrowing (see "Dialect gradation, codeswitching, and borrowing" in chapter 1 for a full discussion). Types of contact-induced language changes that are dependent on codeswitching range from core content morpheme borrowing through relexification using content morphemes from the other language (the embedded language, or EL), a change in the matrix language for the codeswitching portions, language shift, all the way to language death (Myers-Scotton 1992a). Two types of lexical borrowing are distinguished (Myers-Scotton 1992b). Cultural borrowing fills lexical gaps in the recipient language because the lexemes refer to new items in the culture. Such borrowings "enter their matrix language lexicon *abruptly*" (p. 29, italics in the original), so these borrowings are not related to codeswitching. Core borrowings, however, start as codeswitching items. They are alternatives to expressions already present in the recipient language but which eventually replace the original language terms. Hock, following Thomason and Kaufman (1988), notes that although lexical borrowing may be the most common type, "anything can be borrowed" (1991:384) given the right circumstances. Linguistic differences between codeswitching and borrowing are detailed by Hill and Hill (1986). (You may also compare this with Nivens' (2001) discussion.)

Although a speaker must know some of two languages in order to engage in codeswitching, the actual motivations for doing so are social (Di Pietro 1978, Myers-Scotton 1993b). The language choices "depend on the social features which are salient to the exchange" and are, in fact, "a negotiation of rights and obligation sets" (Scotton 1986:404–405). McClure (1981) notes that setting is not the determining factor in language choice, but it does influence that choice. The most important factor, according to her, is the identities of the participants. She also finds the discourse topic to be important, especially when the topic is culturally related to one particular code. (For a fuller discussion, see "Codeswitching among New Irelanders" in chapter 1.)

Many theories have been put forth concerning the patterns of codeswitching and the mechanisms of switching. Backus (1996) reviews and compares many of these theories as he applies them to his study of Dutch-Turkish codeswitching. Most of the theories advanced are limited to descriptions of switching points and suggested restraints on where switches may occur. Many of the restraints are applicable only to particular pairs of languages with counterexamples from other pairs. Among the proposed restraints are the Free Morpheme Constraint and the Equivalence Constraint (Poplack 1981), The Subject-Predicate Constraint, the Noun-Complement Constraint, the Verb-Verb Complement Constraint, the Conjoined Phrases Constraint, the Constraint on psychological Verbs (Gumperz 1982), the Congruence Constraint (Lipski 1978, basically the same as Poplack's Equivalence Constraint, also see Sebba 1998), semantic constraints on conjunctions (Pfaff 1979), government constraints (DiSciullo, Muysken and Singh 1986), and conceptual constraints (Shaffer 1978). Samar and Meechan (1998) compare the Null Theory of codeswitching, which proposes no grammatical constraints on switches, to the Nonce Borrowing Hypothesis, which states that single forms are not switches, but borrowings. They support the Nonce Borrowing Hypothesis. Clyne reviews the constraints proposed at that time and acknowledges that "there are general constraints on code switches" (1987:742), but there is no agreement on what those constraints are.

The theories relating to codeswitching that I have adopted for application in this study are the extended Matrix Language Frame (MLF) model and the Abstract Level and 4-M models developed by Myers-Scotton and Myers-Scotton and Jake. The structural characteristics of codeswitching are described and explained in Myers-Scotton (1993a). A summary of the MLF model and the foundations for the Abstract Level model are presented in Myers-Scotton (1995). A comparison of codeswitching with other language contact phenomena and the application of the MLF to other phenomena are given in Myers-Scotton (1997a). The more detailed developments of the Abstract Level and 4-M models are presented in Myers-Scotton and Jake (2000a, 2000b). A fuller discussion of the theoretical base for this study is given in the next chapter and in the applications of these theories throughout the study.

Language Shift, Attrition, and Death

Language shift, language attrition, and language death are related in a one-way causal effect: language shift often leads to language attrition, and language attrition often leads to language death. However, the progression does not necessarily proceed from one stage to the other in the case of an individual speaker, and even less so in the case of a community of speakers. Examples of each case were presented in chapter 1. Brenzinger (1997) notes the increasing failure of minority group parents to teach their ethnic language to their children when a different language is used in the schools and community. This means that many languages are being displaced. In such situations "two opposing languages are typically involved, one which is replacing and one which is being replaced" (p. 274). The displacement process, according to Brenzinger, usually takes three generations. An example of this three-generational pattern of language shift is described by Li Wei (1994) for a Chinese immigrant community in Britain. Another example is given in "Kuot" in chapter 1 for an indigenous community in New Ireland.

More than a language is lost when a language dies. Often the culture of the speakers also dies with the language (Sasse 1992a). According to Sasse, nearly half of the world's languages have disappeared in the last 500 years (p. 7). He gives three sets of factors that are relevant to a study of language death. First, the "External Setting (ES)...the trigger for the entire process" (p. 9). The ES includes the social, cultural, and economic factors in the environment. These factors influence the second set, Speech Behavior, which is the variable use of language. This variable language use leads to the third set of features, the Structural Consequences, including changes in all areas of the grammar. Unlike other linguists (e.g., Dorian 1981, Romaine 1989b, Campbell and Muntzel 1989), Sasse makes distinctions between the *"normal language contact* situations and the pathological situation of *language decay"* (1992b:59, italics in the original) that leads to language death. The source of the differences is in the type of speakers involved in each case. For example, a bilingual speaker may engage in borrowing, a normal consequence of language contact; but it is the semi-speaker that is involved in a situation of language decay.

The classic documentary of a dying language is that of Dorian (1981) describing Scottish Gaelic. Dorian describes the process of language death as a "transition from monolingualism in one language to monolingualism in another language, via a period of bilingualism" (1983:158). She goes on to describe four structural patterns which appear as language attrition advances: (1) a "marked reduction in the number of allomorphs", (2) a "single favored structure" where there are choices, (3) a "single high frequency member" to represent an entire "system of morphological markers," and (4) the regularization of syntactic forms. To the structural changes listed by Dorian (1983) and Campbell and Muntzel (1989) add overgeneralization of rules for both marked and unmarked features, variability because rules become optional, interference from the dominant language, and "stylistic shrinkage" (1989:195). They maintain that the speakers of a dying language may fall anywhere on a continuum from "nearly fully competent" to "rememberers" (p. 181). They catalogue four types of situations that produce language death. In a sudden death situation all speakers suddenly disappear. Radical death is the result of a self defense mechanism whereby the speakers stop using their language because of political repression. Gradual death is the result of a gradual shift to a dominant language, and bottom-to-top death occurs when the language is maintained only in ritual domains, but not in the home or community. Brenzinger and Dimmendaal describe the context of language death as resulting from a "generally hostile environment" (1992:4). Rabin (1986) compares language death and language revival and concludes that similar changes occur in a language during either process. Unfortunately, language revival is much more rare than language death.

Pidgins and Creoles

General references

Since the focus of this study is language contact in New Ireland and Tok Pisin is the subject of an entire chapter in this context, I will not repeat the references made elsewhere in this study that specifically apply to Tok Pisin and pidgins and creoles of the South Pacific unless they are applicable as general references. Among the more basic general works are the volume by Hall with his emphasis on the "sharply reduced" (1966:25) structure of pidgins and those by Todd (1974, 1984). More comprehensive works include Hymes (1971a), DeCamp (1971, 1977), DeCamp and Hancock (1974), and Romaine (1988). Hymes says of pidginization that it is "neither arbitrary simplification nor mechanical mixing" (1971b:66). DeCamp (1971) includes characteristics and definitions of pidgin and creole languages, theories of their origin, and relevant historical and sociolinguistic factors; and DeCamp (1977) summarizes the history of the field of pidgins/creole studies. Hancock (1977a) describes the problem of lack of information about early pidgins/creoles because of the lack of documentation on them. Hancock (1977b) provides maps and lists of pidgin/creoles around the world, categorized by lexifier language. This information also appears in Hymes (1971a). The two-volume set by Holm (1988a, b) is one of the most comprehensive for both theory and reference. The first volume discusses the theories of pidgin/creole origins, the major modern theories of their development (including the universalist and the substratist theories), and descriptions of the phonological and grammatical characteristics of pidgins/creoles. The second volume is the *Reference Survey*. Goodman (1993) provides the history and the current definitions of terms such as "substratum," "superstratum," and "adstratum" and how these terms are applied to modern pidgin/creole studies. Disputes over terminology are not limited to those terms. Samarin (1971), Calvet (1986), and Mufwene (1997) suggest various definitions, applications, and alternate terms for jargon, koiné, even pidgin and creole. A review and evaluation of major theories of pidgin/creole origins is found in DeGraff (1999b). He sorts the theories into three groups: universalist, substratist, and superstratist and discusses some of the questions associated with each group.

Meijer and Muysken (1977) provide a more historical perspective with a review of some of the major nineteenth and twentieth century linguists involved in pidgin/creole studies, including Adam, Coelho, Schuchardt, and Hesseling. The study of these linguists reveals how old the disputes over pidgin/creole formation are. Coelho was a universalist who claimed there was no substrate influence. Schuchardt was a substratist (and the originator of the pidgin/creole life cycle of pidginization, creolization, and decreolization). Hesseling was not a substratist, and he did not consider pidginization and creolization to be two different processes. Whinnom (1977a, 1977b) provides brief histories of the lingua franca (Sabir) that fostered the monogenesis theories of pidgin/creole origins.

Pidgin and creole languages are not developed in a vacuum. Alleyne (1971) provides a summary of the social factors involved in pidgin/creole formation. The sociohistorical background for Tok Pisin is given in detail in chapter 6. Mintz (1971) provides a comparable background for the Caribbean area. Stoller (1979) and Singler (1993) also maintain the importance of social factors.

Theories of pidgin/creole formation

There are many different theories concerning the processes involved in pidgin/creole formation, the most common being the division into superstratist, substratist, and universalist camps, although some theories do not fit neatly into any single category. More and more linguists are recognizing that some proposals from each camp have validity in explaining the development of pidgins/creoles (Slobin 1983, Mufwene 1986, 1990, 1996, Myers-Scotton 2001) and that other factors, such as language acquisition constraints (Schumann 1976, 1978, Andersen 1979, 1983b, Meisel 1983, Seuren and Wekker 1986) and general cognitive constraints (Slobin 1983, Meisel 1983) or other combinations (Whinnom 1971, Winford 1997) may also contribute to the process. These three major classes of theories are discussed below.

The SUPERSTRATE position as the primary source for pidgin formation is the least popular one of the three major groups. According to this view, the superstrate (or lexifier) language is the principal source from which a pidgin develops. It is primarily Chaudenson (1977) that espouses this view. He bases his position on fallacies he sees in the monogenesis theory of pidgin/creole origin and his view that the socioeconomic powers in early contact situations were the most influential linguistically as well. Although others do not claim to be superstratists, some approach pidginization as if the superstrate language is the target of the language acquisition process. I would place those linguists who espouse simplification as a primary factor in pidginization into this category (Ferguson 1971, Ferguson and DeBose 1977, Le Page 1977, Hatch 1983, Naro 1983) because their assumption is that it is the superstrate language that is being simplified. Others either explicitly or implicitly refer to the superstrate as the model for the developing pidgin (Voorhoeve 1971, Koefoed 1979).

The SUBSTRATE position, which has many adherents, maintains that the substrate languages are the primary contributors to a pidgin/creole because these languages determine the semantic and grammatical structure of the pidgin. Many of these substratists are discussed more fully in chapter 6. Representatives of the substratist position include Silverstein (1972), Thomason (1980), Mosel (1980), Mühlhäusler (1982), Alleyne (1986), Keesing (1988, 1991), Goulden (1990), McWhorter (1992), Rickford and McWhorter (1997), and Siegel (1999). A particular group of substratists may be called relexificationists. The primary proponents of this position are Lefebvre (1986, 1993, 1997) and Lumsden (1994, 1999). Lefebvre defines relexification as

> a process that builds a new lexical entry by copying the lexical entry of a lexicon that is already established (a substratum lexicon), and by copying (or relabeling) the phonological representations in this copied lexical entry with a phonological representation taken from the phonetic string of a different language. (1997:182)

Thomason (1993) does not favor Lefebvre's relexification hypothesis because it does not take into account all the languages involved in the contact situation and how their grammatical structures relate to each other. In addition, Lefebvre's relexification hypothesis neither states which superstrate morphemes are selected for copying, nor does it explain the conditions necessary for that selection.

The universalist position (based on the theory that UNIVERSAL principles govern language structure and the speaker's acquisition of language) has been most adamantly espoused by Bickerton (1977, 1981, 1983, 1992, 1999 inter alia), although he does not call himself a universalist. His claim is that language universals only apply to the creolization process (1977:50), in contrast to Kay and Sankoff (1974), who claim universal principles apply to pidginization as well. However, Bickerton's position rests on his Language Bioprogram Hypothesis (LBH) (1981), which claims that an innate (therefore, universal) language program governs how and what we acquire as a language. Much of Bickerton's writing is rebuttal to the critics of his LBH (e.g., Bickerton 1983, 1992). Bickerton is criticized primarily by substratists (whom he has vehemently attacked), such as Valdman (1983), Holm (1986), Singler (1992), Hancock (1993), Bakker and Mous (1994), and Siegel (1997, 1998). Other universalists include Muysken (1981b), Muysken and Smith (1986), Roberts (1999), and Rizzi (1999). Mufwene (1999) recognizes that each of these three major positions has valid points to make concerning pidgins/creoles. He supports Bickerton's LBH in L1 acquisition by young children. However, he disagrees with Bickerton's contention that children create language if there is insufficient input to acquire it naturally. Baker (1997), who also espouses language creation in the pidginization process, disagrees with Bickerton's claim that pidgin/creoles are the result of failed language learning. Givón (1979b), however, defends Bickerton's LBH. Other universalists are also criticized indirectly; for example, Romaine (1981) argues against Lightfoot's transparency principle that some creolists use to support universals in pidgin/creole formation. The debate between universalists and substratists is not new. Gilbert (1986) provides a brief history of this debate, going back over one hundred years to the debates between Schuchardt and Hesseling. He notes that similar arguments are made in support of each side. DeGraff (1999c) closes with a comparison of the arguments stated in that same volume (1999a) that is especially good at analyzing the consequences of each theory and posing questions relating to the problems involved in each position.

All of the above-mentioned creolists focus on the origins of particular pidgin/creoles, either as language creation using innate universal principles or as derivations from one common ancestor pidgin (both of which account for the similarities in such languages), or as combinations of groups of languages formed under particular sociopolitical conditions (which accounts for the differences among them). Myers-Scotton (2001) takes a different approach by focusing on the cognitive processes of language production that determine the particular role of each language involved in pidgin/creole formation and on the language production mechanisms that produce the distinctive structures that are characteristic of pidgin/creole languages. Using the extended Matrix Language Frame (MLF), the Abstract Level, and the 4-M models, she predicts the sources of morphemes and morphosyntactic structure for a developing pidgin/creole.

Psycholinguistic Research on Language Processing

Models of language processing

There are many models for language processing, some of which are overlapping or complementary and some of which are in opposition to each other. Some research has not resulted in well-developed models but has provided insights into the problems involved in conceptual research, the directions of inquiry needed, and areas that may not be productive. Johnson-Laird (1975) researched network and category list models of the mental lexicon and memory retrieval and found such models not to be productive lines of research.

Other research has produced results that are interpreted differently by different researchers. Dell proposes a spreading activation model (1986:283) based on speech-error data that confirmed categorical divisions in the mental lexicon and indicated that language processing occurs at different levels simultaneously. On the other hand, Levelt (1981) proposes that language processing is organized according to a natural order, either chronological or systemically arranged. He listed three principles of recall: maximal connectivity, return by first-in-last-out route, and minimization of memory load. In linguistics simplicity and generality are often held out as desirable goals (e.g., see Lass 1984 and Radford 1988) and the innateness of linguistic ability and constraints as axioms (Chomsky 1973, 1986). However, Fodor and Crain (1987), while accepting the fact of constraints in grammar, reject the assumption that such constraints are innate. They also dispute the idea that children form the most general and simplest rules during the process of language learning.

The models on which the theoretical structure of this study is based are of a class called COMPUTATIONAL models; that is, they are models based on "working memory, a processor, and a set of nongrammatical scheduling principles" (Ford, Bresnan, and Kaplan 1982:787). Bates and MacWhinney maintain that a model of language processing must be a performance model, as opposed to a parameter-setting model. They state two problems in the study of language acquisition to be "what is universal…and…what is variable" (1987:157). The only way to distinguish between the two is by studying actual performance. Fodor, Bever, and Garrett state that speech production is a rational act because the speaker must make choices between alternatives in order to achieve his/her intentions. They propose that there is an innate computational language that is "part of the common human endowment" (1974:388). They assume that in language production the speaker goes from semantic representation (the message) to deep structure to surface structure (a prelude to Chomsky's (1995) *Minimalist Program*). Fodor elaborates on the "theories of choice" (1975:27) saying that in any situation certain options of behavior are available, each with consequences in a preferential order, and that a person acts (or speaks) on that basis (cf. Myers-Scotton 1993b). According to Fodor natural languages are not the "medium of thought" (p. 55) because the language of thought is innate. He claims that there is a "consensus in the recent literature that there is a 'semantic' level of grammatical representation—a level at which the meaning of sentences is formally specified" (p. 125) and adds that there is no reason for the well-formedness of this internal language to be equal to that of any natural language. Fodor develops his characteristics of language processing as a system of modules that are "domain specific, innately specified, computational, hardwired, autonomous, and not assembled" (1983:36–37). Marshall (1984) provides a good summary of the history and development of modularity as a model of language processing. Garfield reduces Fodor's criteria to four of his own: "domain specificity, manditoriness, information encapsulation, and speed" (1987b:2). Hornstein (1987) and Marslen-Wilson and Tyler (1987) provide opposing views on modularity.

Levels of language processing

Just as there is no agreement among psycholinguists as to the nature of the cognitive process in general, there is no consensus concerning the process of language production in particular. One generally held view, however, is that language production and processing occur in stages with different functions being fulfilled at each stage or level. What is not agreed upon is the number of levels involved, although many of the differences in the number of levels are simply a matter of how they are named and specified. Chafe states, "conceptual structure and surface structure are different things" (1970:74), but that there is a relationship between the lexical units and the semantic roles they represent. Fry (1973:158–159) had very early specified five stages of speech production: semantic encoding (conceptualization), lexical encoding (word selection), morpheme encoding (morpheme selection and placement), phoneme encoding, and actual articulation. Schlesinger specifies a prelinguistic stage which is the "semantic representation underlying the utterance" (1977:170) and a "lexification" stage in which "the substitution of appropriate words for protoverbal elements" (pp. 171–172) occurs. Kempen (1977) proposes three levels: conceptualizing, formulating, and speaking. Garrett (1980) agrees to at least two levels of sentence processing, the functional and positional, but also concedes that a conceptual level must be prior to the other two. Levelt (1989) gives the most complete description of the encoding process of a message from the conceptual stage to the utterance stage. His model is described in more detail in "The Abstract Level Model" in chapter 3. Bock and Levelt (1994) expand upon the relationships among concepts, lemmas, and lexemes and how access failures may occur.

Just as all researchers do not agree on the significance of the various levels in the speech production process, neither do all agree on the basic units of production. While Ford claims that "a deep clause is a major sentence planning unit….No evidence could be found at all that the surface clause per se is important" (1982:798), Rosenberg (1977b) and Fodor, Bever, and Garrett (1974) had previously used speech error evidence to claim that the surface structure clause is the basic speech planning unit.

The actual chronological order of the speech production process is more widely agreed upon. Fry (1973) describes the process as having each level on separate moving conveyor belts with a time lag between levels. Levelt and Kempen propose hierarchical chunking patterns (1975:208). Other researchers (Kempen 1977, Rosenberg 1977b, Kempen and Huijbers 1983, Kempen and Hoenkamp 1987) agree that the different levels are active concurrently, each using the processed information from the previous level. Much of the evidence for the various levels in the speech production process and the incremental, but parallel, processing of the levels comes from the study of speech errors (Fromkin 1971, Nooteboom 1973, Laver 1973, Garrett 1975, 1980).

The mental lexicon and morpheme types

The role and structure of the mental lexicon is important to many aspects of language contact theories (see fuller discussions in chapter 3). The mental lexicon is more than a repository of lexemes. The lemmas that activate access to specific morphemes determine more than meaning. They also determine morphological requirements, syntactic position, and pragmatic limitations. Pinker notes that a child acquires limits of uses and forms as part of the lexical entry for each form. Children do generalize, but they "generalize along semantic/thematic lines" (1982:711). MacWhinney (1987b) also assigns the mental lexicon a major role in language acquisition and production. Chafe gives evidence from the study of intonation units as to how the lemmas are activated and how units are combined in speech production. He states that

> our minds contain very large amounts of knowledge or information, and that only a very small amount of it can be focused on, or be 'active' at any one time...it is better not to think about a 'kind' of memory, but about a certain limited amount of information in our minds being temporarily 'lit up'. (1984:3)

According to Chafe, pauses between speech units relate to "changes in the activation states of information in the speaker's mind" (p. 7). Our intentions activate certain lemmas. The first lemmas to be activated may be those lemmas related to content morphemes. At least, according to Osgood and Bock (1977), content morphemes are the most salient, and the most salient information occurs earliest in sentence production. The lemmas underlying the content morphemes activate other lemmas needed to provide required morphemes to fulfill our conceptualizations.

3
Theory, Methodology, and Hypotheses

The Matrix Language Frame (MLF) model was developed primarily in the context of explaining structural characteristics of codeswitching (Myers-Scotton 1993a [1997], 1993b, 1995, 1997a, Jake and Myers-Scotton 1997a). More recently the model has been extended (Myers-Scotton and Jake 1995) and refined by the introduction of the 4-M model (Myers-Scotton and Jake 2000b) and the Abstract Level model (Myers-Scotton and Jake 1995, 2000a). These extensions and refinements to the model explain the variations in the occurrences of different types of morphemes in language contact situations and the structural characteristics of contact varieties. Recently the extended MLF model has been applied to various language contact phenomena (in addition to codeswitching). These phenomena include second-language acquisition (Bolonyai 1998, Myers-Scotton 1998, Jake 1998), convergence and attrition (Myers-Scotton 1998), and pidgin and creole formation (Jake and Myers-Scotton 1998, Myers-Scotton 1997b, 2001). The following is a minimal summary of the MLF model and its extensions necessary to the discussion in the remainder of this book.

Models

The Matrix Language Frame (MLF) model

Distinctions and constituency types elaborated by the MLF model

Two distinctions are foundational to the MLF model. The first distinction is between the MATRIX LANGUAGE (ML) and any EMBEDDED LANGUAGE (EL). The matrix language is the language that is the morphosyntactic controller of a language contact discourse. It dictates the morphosyntactic frame of constituents. An embedded language is any other language contributing to the discourse (within the restrictions given below). The second distinction is between CONTENT and SYSTEM morphemes. A content morpheme is one that has either the feature [+Thematic Role-Assigner] or [+Thematic Role-Receiver] (including discourse-level roles such as topic or contrast). Most commonly, content morphemes are nouns, verbs, prepositions, and some pronouns. A system morpheme is any morpheme that neither assigns nor receives a thematic role. System morphemes include quantifiers, specifiers, inflections (such as for tense, aspect, possession, etc.), and some pronominal forms.

Under the MLF model, there are three types of constituents that appear in codeswitching. These constituents are matrix language ISLANDS (in which all morphemes are from the matrix language), matrix language + embedded language CONSTITUENTS (in which morphemes come from both the matrix language and the embedded language), and embedded language islands (in which all the morphemes are from an embedded language). I hypothesize that these same types of constituents appear in pidgins and creoles, although the matrix language itself is not one particular language, but a composite of languages contributing to the structure of the pidgin during formation.

Characteristics of the matrix language

The basis of the MLF model is the Matrix Language Hypothesis and the two related principles, the Morpheme Order Principle and the System Morpheme Principle, given below.

> The Matrix Language Hypothesis: ...the matrix language sets the morphosyntactic frame for matrix language + embedded language constituents.
>
> The Morpheme Order Principle: In matrix language + embedded language constituents consisting of singly occurring embedded

language lexemes and any number of matrix language lexemes, surface morpheme order (reflecting surface syntactic relations) will be that of the matrix language.

The System Morpheme Principle: In matrix language + embedded language constituents, all system morphemes which have grammatical relations external to their head constituent (i.e., which participate in the sentence's thematic role grid) will come from the matrix language. (Myers-Scotton 1993a [1997]:82–83)

The MLF model is cognitively based because it is founded on "a set of abstract principles which seem to apply...across different communities" (Myers-Scotton 1995:234). It is also lexically based in the sense that it claims the language production processes that generate speech are lexically based (p. 235). (These principles will be elaborated below.) Some of the identifying characteristics of the matrix language in bilingual speech (pp. 237–238) are that it may be the most unmarked (i.e., the most expected) under the speech circumstances, speaker judgments identify one language as the matrix language, and more morphemes in the overall conversation come from the matrix language.

Although the direct application of the MLF model to pidgins and creoles is a recent development, there is support for the idea in earlier research. As early as 1956, Taylor stated that

most of the evidence...suggests...that only and/or all languages originating in a pidgin or jargon, while genetically 'orphans,' may be said the have two 'foster-parents:' one that provides the basic morphological and/or syntactic pattern, and another from which the fundamental vocabulary is taken. (1956:413)

In her analysis of the Delaware-based Trader's Jargon spoken in North America Thomason noted that "it agreed with other pidgins in the specific features *only*...where those features coincide with structural characteristics of the Indian languages in the area of its origin" (1980:180, italics in the original). Silverstein reports that "speakers of Chinook Jargon were using their distinct native grammatical systems in modified form to communicate in the Jargon speech community" (1972:623).

The Abstract Level Model

Language production models: Psycholinguistic and linguistic background

Levelt (1989) proposed and articulated a detailed model of speech production in which the speaker first conceives of his/her message and retrieves from a mental lexicon the particular lexical items needed to encode this message. The process of language production begins in the "Conceptualizer." Within the mental lexicon the information about each lexeme is stored in LEMMAS. The information stored in the lemmas determines the meaning of individual lexemes (their lexical-conceptual structure) and the syntactic frame required by the individual lexemes to produce the conceived message (the predicate-argument structure). This information also refers to any morphological markers required by each lexeme within that message (the morphological realization patterns). The "Formulator" performs the processes of assembling the parts into larger constituents. The "Articulator" then performs the grammatical and phonological encoding to produce the actual speech.

Levelt's work was based on much previous psycholinguistic research. Foundations for his model are found in Kemper and Huijbers' (1983) experiments to test models of lexical processing. They interpreted the results of the experiments as indicating a two-stage process of lexical retrieval with a monitoring stage to guarantee grammaticality before the actual articulation stage. Earlier Kemper (1977:259) proposed the three stages of conceptualizing (content selection), formulating (syntactic form selection), and speaking (the phonetic realization of the speaker's intent). He suggested, "a syntactic construction is a pair consisting of (a) a conceptual pattern and (b) a syntactic frame" (p. 262) and that the formulation of speech requires both. This interrelationship between the conceptual and the morphosyntactic structure will be demonstrated repeatedly in the language contact phenomena discussed in this study. Earlier yet, Nooteboom had interpreted evidence from speech errors as support for a structural pattern to speech because "phonemic speech errors...do not at all occur at random" (1973:147). Such errors also provide evidence of a planning stage before articulation because most speech errors are anticipatory. Laver had reported evidence for a monitoring function during speech production because "slips of the tongue are usually detected and corrected by the speaker" (1973:132).

Garrett (1975, 1980) presented speech error evidence for at least two levels of sentence processing: the functional level handling such aspects as syntactic organization and grammatical categories and the positional level handling such aspects as word forms and phonetics. Garrett also agreed that the message itself was generated at a conceptual level prior to the other two levels. Kemper and Hoenkamp call the three levels "three subprocesses of speaking: conceptualizing, formulating, and articulating" (1987:202). They propose that the processes are incremental rather than serial, meaning that the different stages may be running concurrently with each other in an overlapping pattern.

Makkai (1978) found evidence for different levels of language processing in the study of phonological errors in bilingual speech. Different types of errors led her to postulate that mismatches between two languages can occur at different levels. She proposed that the phonological level was autonomous from the semantic and syntactic levels. The fact that processing occurs at different levels implies that it is done in stages (cf. Fromkin 1971 and Chomsky 1995). Bock and Levelt specify that the phonological encoding is a separate process from the grammatical encoding yielding "four levels of processing, the message level, the functional level, the positional level, and the phonological level" (1994:946), with the grammatical encoding including both the functional and positional levels. Fry (1973) specified five different stages: semantic, lexical, morpheme, and phoneme encoding, followed by motor control, which is the actual articulation of speech.

The lexical base for a grammar is endorsed by Pinker as a part of a computational model for both speech production and comprehension. He notes that children acquiring a language do not show all the generalizations that would be expected of them according to a transformational grammar model. Instead, children acquire limits on the uses and forms of a language as part of the lexical entries for those forms. Children do generalize rules, but they "generalize along semantic/thematic lines" (1982:711). MacWhinney (1987a) also supports a lexical model and discusses the role of the mental lexicon in both acquisition and production of language.

General linguistic theory is also based on the psycholinguistic principles above and supports the development of a theory of multiple abstract levels in language production. The semantic theories of Talmy (1985), Jackendoff (1990), and Rappaport and Levin (1998) deal with the relationship between the mental lexicon and semantic structure. Chomsky 1981 and 1995 relate to the language production processes and sequences of activation of information during language production.

The levels of the language production process

Following the proposals of psycholinguistic researchers, Myers-Scotton (1995:237) specifies four levels of language production as shown in figure 3.1 (adapted from Myers-Scotton and Jake 2000a, figure 1).

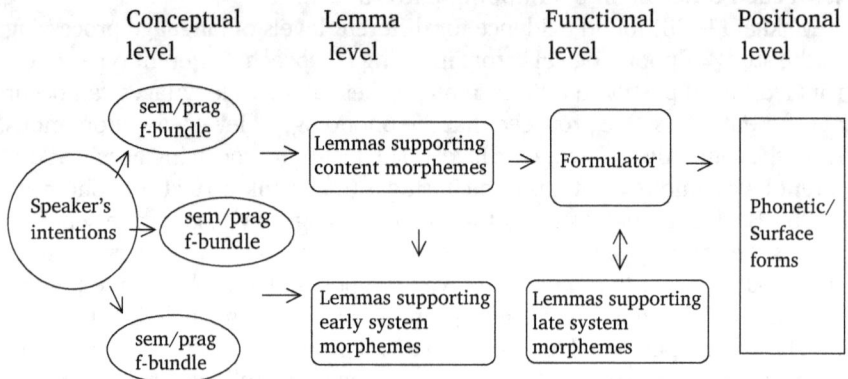

Figure 3.1. Abstract levels in language production.

At the conceptual level the speaker's intentions are generated. These intentions then select lemmas containing not only meaning (supporting content morphemes), but also syntactic requirements (supporting early system morphemes). These lemmas go to the formulator at the functional level and direct the formulator in setting up the morphosyntactic structure required (supporting late system morphemes). The importance of the conceptual level is reflected in Chafe's opinion that the "semantic structure [is] the crucial component of language" (1970:73). His description of lemmas states that they will have some universal common aspects (such as meaning), but that they will also have language-specific morphosyntactic requirements (such as word order). Sankoff applies the importance of the semantic level to pidgin/creoles in that the choice of expression in a pidgin/creole requires that "the item chosen must have appropriate semantic properties in order to be interpretable to interlocutors" (1983:243). At the positional level the actual phonological forms are selected and positioned.

However, these various levels of the sentence production process are not independent of each other since

> even though decisions made at the conceptual level refer to intentions, not utterance structures, the results of these decisions

determine the language or languages to be activated and set their structural roles. (Myers-Scotton and Jake 1995:991)

Grice (1968) notes that although an utterance may reflect the speaker's intentions, that intention, in turn, must be recognized by the hearer based on the structure of the utterance, so there must be a connection between intention and syntactic form. Lumsden (1994) gives an example of the connection between the psychological semantic range of the substrate possessives to the surface representations in Haitian Creole.

The mental lexicon of bilinguals is conceived by Myers-Scotton and Jake to be a single lexicon, but "with entries tagged for specific languages" (1995:986).[14] These entries are called lemmas, following Levelt. The "lemmas are characterized as containing abstract pragmatic information, in addition to semantic, syntactic, and morphological information" (p. 986). (Cruse (1986) does not use the term lemma, but he does provide insights into what kinds of information must be contained in a lemma.) These lemmas direct the selection and construction of lexemes and their placement within the syntactic structure of the utterance. They

> mediate between the conceptual level and the grammatical structures....Lemmas send directions to a 'formulator' that turns on the actual morphosyntactic procedures that will result in surface or positional level utterances. (Myers-Scotton and Jake 2000:4)

Since the matrix language sets the morphosyntactic frame for bilingual speech, the lemmas of bilingual speech must be congruent enough to fit into the matrix language frame activated. (If such congruence is lacking, embedded language islands may be produced.) In analyzing bilingual speech, the CP (Complementizer Phrase) is proposed as the appropriate unit of analysis. The problematic nature of using the sentence as a well-defined unit in speech analysis presented by O'Connell (1977) and the findings of Ford and Holmes that "sentence production does proceed basically by each deep clause being successively planned and uttered" (1978:44) support this choice.

According to the Abstract level model, although not completely autonomous, the abstract levels represented in each lemma may be split and activated for different languages at different stages during the production of bilingual speech. Since the types of information contained in the lemmas (the lexical-conceptual structure, predicate-argument structure, and morphological realization patterns) are accessed at different production levels in a contact situation, the resulting speech can reflect aspects of different languages, resulting in a composite matrix language. This characteristic of accessing different information at different levels of production explains many

---

[14]See Macnamara (1967) for arguments in favor of two separate linguistic systems in the bilingual.

aspects of bilingual speech, such as codeswitching restraints, adaptation of borrowed forms, convergence in second language acquisition, and the sources of pidgin/creole lexemes and constructions. This interrelationship of abstract levels and of the various languages involved in contact situations is acknowledged by Siegel with respect to pidgin/creole formation in that some superstrate free morphemes, if related in function or meaning to a substrate morpheme, may be "reanalyzed according to the substrate pattern" (1998:12). Hesseling implies the interaction between levels (and the importance of the conceptual level) in pidgin/creole formation very early (in 1933) when he describes the process as follows:

> they learn the surface structure of the European languages, although they make them suitable for their own manner of thinking...the slaves employ the foreign material in a way which is not in complete conflict with their inherited manner of expressing themselves. (1979:69)

Lumsden, as a substratist, emphasizes the control of the substrate semantic and syntactic levels in pidgin/creole formation.

> Where the superstrate and the substrate languages have lexical categories that contrast, the creole category should follow the superstrate pattern in phonological form, but the details of the syntax and the semantics of the creole category should systematically follow the substrate pattern. (1999:135)

However, Lumsden is not precise in his description. His "syntax" and "semantics" from the substrate would include all three levels of the Abstract Level model, allowing only the selection of the phonological form from the superstrate. In fact, there must be interaction (or congruence) between the substrate and superstrate at the conceptual level for any particular superstrate phonological form to be used. As will be shown in the following chapter, even those superstrate forms that do show sufficient semantic (lexical-conceptual) congruence to be selected are often reanalyzed to fit into the substrate predicate-argument structure or morphological realization pattern for that concept. This characteristic of the abstract levels being split and recombined in contact situations will be applied throughout this study.

The 4-M Model

Background to morpheme typing

The fact that different lexical categories behave differently under given conditions has long been acknowledged. Osgood and Bock (1977) report that salience is important in sentence production, with the most salient features occurring the earliest. They also note that content morphemes are the most salient. Bock and Levelt (1994) report a difference in speech errors dependent upon the type of morpheme involved, with most errors occurring with open class items. One of the distinctions on which Myers-Scotton (1993a) based her early formulation of the MLF model was the distinction between content and system morphemes. Jake (1994) discusses the discrepancy in the behavior of morphemes when classified by lexical category (noun, verb, preposition, etc.) or as open versus closed class (typified by nouns and verbs as open class morphemes and pronouns and prepositions as closed class ones). She demonstrates the weakness of each of these systems of classification by showing that the closed class lexical category of pronouns contains elements that do not behave the same way in bilingual speech production. In her study of embedded language pronouns occurring in codeswitching data, discourse thematic pronouns could always occur, but dummy pronouns from the embedded language never occurred. Indefinite pronouns sometimes behaved as content morphemes and sometimes as system morphemes, and personal pronouns varied according to the language. Thus, the only classification system that is consistent with the behavior of morphemes in bilingual speech is that of content versus system morpheme (see also the "Afterword" in the 1997 edition of Myers-Scotton 1993a).

Two principles from psycholinguistic research motivated the MLF model and the distinction it makes between content and system morphemes. These principles are that sentence production is (at least) a two-step process and that one language is always more active in bilingual speech than any other language(s) in the speaker's linguistic repertoire (Myers-Scotton 1995). If language production occurs in steps and one language can be more activated than others, then it is possible in bilingual speech for morphemes to be accessed at different stages in language production and from different languages at those different stages. The theory that the type of morpheme may depend on the stage at which it is activated was presented as a tentative 3-M model (Jake and Myers-Scotton 1998) and later refined to become the 4-M model.

The four morpheme types

The 4-M model of morpheme types as developed by Myers-Scotton and Jake (2000a, 2000b) is a refinement of the three-way distinction they had postulated in earlier works. The distinctions are based on the level of activation of the morpheme and the function it serves. As can be seen in figure 3.2 (from Myers-Scotton and Jake 2000b), conceptually activated morphemes are content morphemes and early system morphemes. Content morphemes are directly elected to fulfill the speaker's conceptual intentions and have the feature that they either assign or receive a thematic role. Nouns and verbs are prototypical content morphemes (such as English *house, work,* and *belong* from (24)).

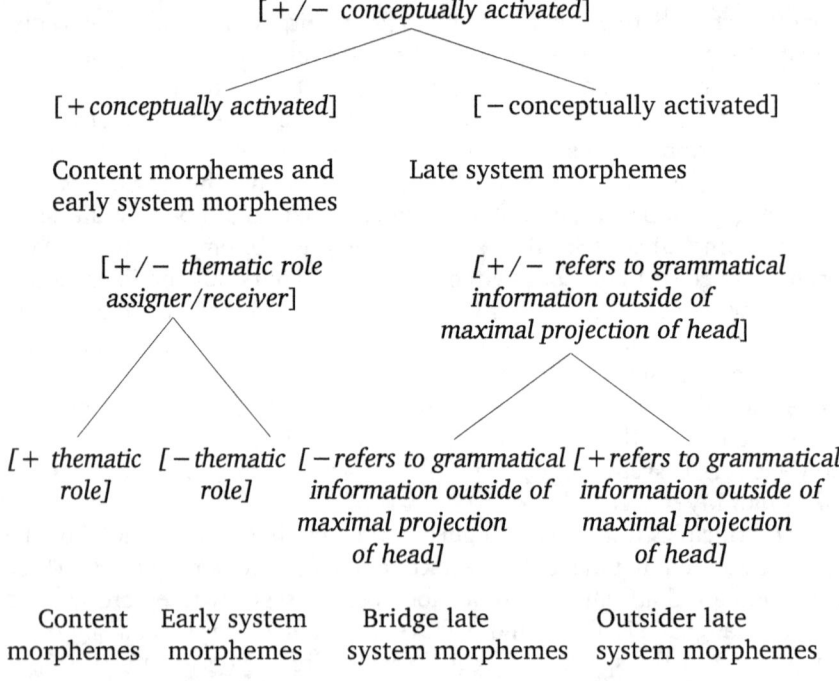

Figure 3.2. Feature-based classification of morphemes in the 4-M model.

Early system morphemes are indirectly elected by content morphemes, such as the preposition *at* in *look at*, or the articles *a* or *the* providing a definite/indefinite distinction to a noun. Although early system morphemes are conceptually activated (that is, they add some semantic content to the content morphemes with which they occur), they neither assign nor receive a thematic role. Both of these types are activated at the lemma level. Late system morphemes are not conceptually activated but are structurally assigned. The difference between the two types of late system morphemes depends on whether or not they must go outside the maximal projection of their head for grammatical information. The Tok Pisin possessive morpheme **bilong** in (24) is a late bridge morpheme, as is the Tigak *ina* in (24) and the English possessive *'s* in the glosses. Neither of these morphemes looks outside its maximal projection but relates the content morpheme **Sam**/*Sam* (the possessor) to the head of the NP (the possession: **haus**/*aisok,* 'house/work') of which it is a part. (Chapter 6 describes Tok Pisin as it relates to Tigak and other Austronesian languages.)

(24) a. **haus** *bilong* **Sam** [TP]
     house belong Sam
     'Sam*'s* house'

   b. *aisok* ***ina*** *Sam* [Tigak]
      work of Sam
      'Sam*'s* work'

Outsider late system morphemes do refer to information outside the maximal projection of their head. An example from English is the third-person singular subject agreement *-s* suffixed to the verb (e.g., *he run-s*). In Tigak, the subject agreement pronominals, *nag* and *rig* shown in (25), are late outsider morphemes because they refer to the subject of the clause, which is outside the verb phrase of which the subject agreement is a part.

(25) a. *naniu* **nag** *ngan-i tang ien*
     <u>1SG   1SG.S.AGR eat-TZ ART   fish</u>
     Subject VP
     'I am eating fish.'

   b. *tang ulina* ***rig****-a*   *poling-ani* *reg*
      <u>ART woman 3PL.S.AGR-PST listen.to-TZ 3DL.OB.AGR</u>
      Subject   VP
      'The woman listened to them(2).'

Table 3.1. Examples of the four morpheme types

Content	Early system	Late system bridge	Late system outsider
house	*at* in *look at*	*of* in *student of physics*	*-s* in *he runs*
Sam	*the* in *the book*	*'s* in *Ryan's car*	
work	*a* in *a man*		
belong	*-s* in *bicycles*		

The 4-M model relates the four types of morphemes to the speech production level at which each is accessed. Independent motivation for this four-way classification comes from the fact that the four types can be identified based on their syntactic behavior. Although both content and early system morphemes are activated at the conceptual level, only content morphemes assign or receive thematic roles. Late system morphemes are accessed later, and their form depends on grammatical or structural information. A bridge late system morpheme connects content morphemes to meet language-specific configurational requirements. An outsider late system morpheme is coindexed to a content morpheme outside of its maximal projection.

Evidence supporting the four-way classification of morphemes comes from codeswitching data, from studies of aphasia patients, and from second language acquisition data (Myers-Scotton and Jake 2000b). In codeswitching, embedded language late outsider system morphemes do not occur in mixed constituents because they are not accessed until the formulator level. Codeswitching data also reveal that only embedded language early system morphemes show double morphology because they are accessed at the conceptual level with the content morphemes requiring them to fulfill intentions, so they may be interpreted as a unit within the matrix language system and receive the matrix language system morpheme as well. Broca's aphasics find late system morphemes harder to produce and more often omit them than they do early system morphemes. In second language acquisition, some types of morphemes are also harder to acquire accurately. In second language acquisition data, content morphemes are acquired earlier than system morphemes, early system before late system, and bridge late system morphemes before the outsiders. Bolonyai (2000) found this same order of acquisition of morphemes in Hungarian children learning English as a second language. Schmitt (2000a) also found that the morpheme types are lost in the same relative order in which they are acquired. The difference in morpheme characteristics and behavior in pidgins/creoles has also been noted. Lumsden observed that not all morphemes are available for relexification, but that an overlap in semantics must exist first. "Since one of the defining properties of functional categories is their lack of denotational semantic content, it follows that functional categories should be immune to relexification in principle" (1999:140–141). However, Lumsden does not recognize the difference in behavior within his class of "functional categories." The functional category he describes above corresponds only to the late system morphemes of the 4-M model.

The matrix language determination of morpheme types

Since content morphemes may come from any language involved in a language contact situation (provided there is sufficient congruence), the same content morphemes are possible in a contact variety regardless of which language is the matrix language of a bilingual contact variety. However, the matrix language does exert control over which language can supply system morphemes. In her analysis of morpheme types within the lexical category of pronouns, Jake (1994) found that dummy pronouns do not occur as embedded language morphemes in codeswitching data because dummy pronouns are system morphemes. System morphemes only come from the matrix language. This restriction also holds for pidgin/creole formation because late system morphemes do not come from the superstrate (Hypothesis 3d). The absence of dummy pronouns in Tok Pisin will be discussed in chapter 6. Even though Tigak and English both use dummy pronouns as in (26a) and (26b) in which 'rain' is a verb, Tok Pisin (26c) reanalyzes 'rain' as a noun and does not use the dummy pronoun (26d).

(26) a. *ga   langit*   [Tigak]
       3SG.S.AGR rain

   b. *it's raining*   [English]

   c. **ren** **i**   *kam/pundaun/stap*   [TP]
      rain   PM   come/fall/stay (is)

   d. *em   ren
      3SG   rain

The Tigak *ga* corresponds to the English 'it' in (26) as a dummy pronoun. This Tigak *ga* is a late system bridge morpheme. In contrast to Tigak and English, Tok Pisin uses the content morpheme **ren** as the subject in (26c) instead of the third-person singular pronoun **em**. A late system morpheme is not expected to occur in a pidgin/creole if an alternate content morpheme construction is available. Tok Pisin/Tigak codeswitching data also confirm Jake's observation. In Tigak/Tok Pisin codeswitching the expression in (27a) is heard if Tigak is the matrix language of the bilingual clause (as is the case with fluent adult Tigak speakers), but not if Tok Pisin is the matrix language (as is the case with many young urban Tigaks who only know words and phrases from Tigak).

(27) a. *ga* **ren** [Tigak = matrix language]

   b. **ga* **ren** [TP = matrix language]

Additional evidence of the control of the matrix language over system morphemes is found in Tigak/Tok Pisin codeswitching data involving the doubling of pronouns. Tigak uses an obligatory subject agreement late system outsider morpheme in every clause to introduce the verb phrase. In addition, under certain discourse conditions (see chapter 5), Tigak may use an overt subject pronoun (a "discourse thematic pronoun" in Jake's terms), such as *naniu* in (28c), which is a content morpheme. Thus, if Tigak is the matrix language of the Tigak/Tok Pisin codeswitching, (28b)–(28e) may and may not occur as indicated. Example (28a) is the Tigak model. Tok Pisin is in bold type.

(28) a. *(naniu) nag-a puka*   [Tigak]
        1SG   1SG.S.AGR-PST fall   [*naniu* = Tigak (content)
        'I fell.'   pronoun, *nag* = Tigak
           (late system) pronoun]

    b. **mi** *nag-a puka*   [Tigak = matrix language]
        1SG   1SG.S.AGR-PST fall   [**mi** = Tok Pisin 1SG (content)
        'I fell.'   pronoun]

    c. *naniu* **mi pundaun**   [**pundaun** = Tok Pisin verb
        1SG   1SG fall   (content)]
        'I fell.'

    d. *nag-a* **pundaun**
        1SG.S.AGR-PST fall
        'I fell.'

e. *naniu Ø   **pundaun**
   1SG   1SG.S.AGR fall
   'I fell.'

As seen by the examples above, pronouns may be doubled in Tigak/Tok Pisin codeswitching if Tigak is the matrix language because Tigak has two slots in which pronouns may occur. The Tok Pisin pronoun may fill either of the two slots as in (28b) and (28c). A single subject pronoun may also occur if it is the Tigak late system subject agreement form, such as *nag* in (28d), because such a form most often occurs without the corresponding content pronoun in Tigak. However, a Tigak independent content pronoun, such as naniu in (28e), does not occur alone in codeswitching data because it never occurs without the corresponding subject agreement system morpheme in Tigak. If Tok Pisin is the matrix language, the possibilities are shown in (29).

(29) a. *naniu* **pundaun**   [TP = matrix language]
        1SG   fall
        'I fell down.'

   b. *nag-(a)*   **pundaun**
      1SG.S.AGR-(PST) fall
      'I fell down.'

   c. **naniu nag-a*   **pundaun**
      1SG   1SG.S.AGR-PST fall
      'I fell down.'

When Tok Pisin is the matrix language, only a single Tigak subject pronoun occurs, but it may be either of the two Tigak subject pronominal forms. The independent content pronoun naniu may be heard, as in (29a), but more often it is the subject agreement form nag, shown in (29b). Although this form is a late system morpheme in Tigak, and embedded language system morphemes are not expected in codeswitching, this subject agreement morpheme class is the one most often heard because it is obligatory in the clause, whereas the content pronoun is optional in most clauses. It also happens to occur in the same position in the clause as the Tok Pisin subject. The fact that the Tok Pisin speaker uses this system morpheme indicates that the speaker has reanalyzed the late system morpheme as a content morpheme. This morpheme is the more salient of the two choices because of its frequency. In fact, the non-Tigak speaker may never actually hear the independent content pronoun. The only exception to the pattern above is the pattern following the emphatic use of Tok Pisin pronouns, as in (30). Tok Pisin is the matrix language, and (30a) gives the Tok Pisin pattern.

(30) a. **mi, mi pundaun** [TP]
    1SG 1SG fall
    'me, I fell down'

   b. *nag,   nag-a   **pundaun**   [TP = matrix language]
      1SG.S.AGR 1SG.S.AGR-PST fall
      'me, I fell down'

   c. **naniu, nag-a   **pundaun**
      1SG   1SG.S.AGR-PST fall
      'me, I fell down'

Even though pronoun doubling does occur in Tok Pisin when the pronoun is used emphatically, I have never heard the use of both the Tigak independent pronoun and the subject agreement pronoun together by a non-native Tigak speaker, only the emphatic use of the subject agreement form, as in (30b). Again, this usage indicates a reanalysis of the Tigak late system morpheme as a content morpheme because this morpheme is the one most readily available to the non-Tigak. These data demonstrate that morpheme types do not always correspond cross-linguistically, but that reanalysis does occur to produce conformance to the structure of the matrix language.

Beyond Codeswitching: The Extension of the MLF and Related Models

As stated above, the MLF model was first applied to the bilingual phenomenon of codeswitching, but the principles on which it is based have proved to be explanatory for other language contact phenomena as well. The Abstract Level model's provision for the possibility of splitting the levels of information contained in lemmas and accessing one level from one language and other levels from a different language (or languages) during different stages of language production presents the possibility for a mixed morphosyntactic structure producing a composite matrix language. Even though "there is always a matrix language in bilingual constituents, and there is always only one matrix language at a time" (Myers-Scotton 1998:292), this matrix language may be a composite formed from different languages. Thus, the composite matrix language of Tok Pisin incorporates abstract grammatical features from more than one language, including English and multiple substrate languages. For example, in the Tok Pisin possessive construction **haus bilong Sam** 'Sam's house', the lexical-conceptual structure is from English, using the English content morphemes *house* and *belong*. However, these morphemes are used in a different way than in English. The grammatical structure comes from many Austronesian substrate languages, illustrated by the alienable possessive patterns shown in examples (13)–(16) of appendix 2. The English content morpheme *belong* is reanalyzed in Tok Pisin as a late system bridge morpheme to fill the morphosyntactic slot of the genitive marker in Austronesian languages (see the discussion in chapter 6). The more alike the languages involved are, the more the composite matrix language will resemble each of the languages and the more resistant that structure will be to less influential languages. Anderson's corollary to his "transfer to somewhere" principle for second language acquisition may also be applied to the development of a composite matrix language in pidgin/creole formation. "When any two or more forces promote a given interlanguage form that form is more likely to emerge and will resist restructuring longer than a form promoted by only one force" (1983c:182).

However, a composite matrix language is not necessarily static. Since in any bilingual speech "one [language] is more activated than the other(s)" (Myers-Scotton 1995:239), the particular level of activation determines the characteristics of the composite matrix language. By progressively accessing one language more than the original matrix language, a matrix language turnover can occur in which the language controlling the morphosyntactic structure of speech goes from one language through a series of CMLs to a different language. Di Pietro describes a matrix language turnover in his study of Italian-American codeswitching in which

> codeswitching behavior progressed from an initial stage in which stylized English expressions were buried within an Italian matrix...to reach a final stage in which English provides the matrix and switching into Italian is conventionalized and frozen. (1978:276)

Mühlhäusler's description of creolization also fits that of a matrix language turnover. He says that creolization is not so much expansion as it is "the replacement of one linguistic system by another one of comparable power" (1980:22). The convergence discussed in chapters 4 and 6 is also evidence of matrix language turnovers in progress.

Jake (1998) describes the development of a composite matrix language in SLA. Evidence of a matrix language turnover is that system morphemes from the second language appear in the bilingual speech (Myers-Scotton 1998:314). Bolonyai (1998) also describes the stages of development of a composite matrix language and the turnover that results in her study of Hungarian-English bilingual children.[15] Bolonyai (2000) and Schmitt (2000a) apply the 4-M model of morpheme classification to SLA and language attrition. Both of these studies found that the pattern of acquisition and loss of morphemes depends on the type of morpheme, which in turn depends on the level at which the morpheme is activated in speech production. More recently the matrix language frame and related models have been applied to pidgin/creole formation. The process is elaborated by Myers-Scotton (1997b, 2001) and by Jake and Myers-Scotton (1998). Gross (2000) applies the theory to the development of the composite matrix language in Berbice Dutch. The process of reanalysis described by Woolford (1979b) for the variation in complementizer use in Tok Pisin is a case of a matrix language turnover in progress. She reports the variation to be dependent on the age of the speaker and urban environment. Both of these factors are related to the degree of exposure to English, with younger Papua New Guineans more likely to be educated in English and urban dwellers more exposed to English in daily activities. The primary focus of this study is the application of the theories described above to the formation of Tok Pisin, and secondarily to the current language contact situations in New Ireland in Papua New Guinea. The former demonstrates the Austronesian influence on the morphosyntactic frame of Tok Pisin, and the latter reveals that the direction of influence has reversed, with Tok Pisin and English now affecting the indigenous languages.

Methodology

Data were collected from our first days of living on the Tigak Islands where I learned the language from local speakers in natural situations of daily living. We recorded daily conversations, remarks, and stories as the Tigaks themselves went about their normal activities. We later transcribed the tape-recorded speech for purposes of analysis and language learning. A Tigak co-worker also recorded conversations, meetings, church services, and stories in our absences. He was able to accomplish this recording more unobtrusively than when we were present. The Tigak

---

[15]Backus (1996) reports some opposing views on a composite matrix language and a matrix language turnover.

people knew that we were trying to learn their language and wanted to collect natural samples, so they soon became accustomed to these recording practices.

In addition to linguistic data, we gathered information concerning language attitudes and use by observation and by a survey questionnaire. My husband, several Tigaks interested in developing Tigak vernacular literature, and I conducted the survey. We elicited lexical items, phrases, and clauses from residents in each Tigak village in New Ireland in order to make dialect comparisons. In most villages we conducted the survey with a group of village residents of all ages. In one village we could only interview one elderly man and in another village only members of one family. Many dialectal differences were also pointed out to us specifically during conversations in which Tigaks from different areas were present. Each village is proud of its own version of the Tigak language (although the differences are quite minor), and speakers are glad to demonstrate their ability to identify another person's place of origin by his speech.

Most of the Tok Pisin data were gathered coincidentally with our Tigak language research because of the high degree of bilingualism and codeswitching in New Ireland. Some of the Tok Pisin data were recorded at meetings in Ukarumpa, Lae, and Port Moresby, all towns outside the normal Tigak-speaking context.

Hypotheses

The hypotheses proposed here are based on the extended Matrix Language Frame (MLF), 4-M, and Abstract Level models. I will apply these models to the language situation of northwestern New Ireland and the language contact phenomena occurring there to test the hypotheses below. As discussed previously, the matrix language frame model is based on two oppositions—the opposition between the matrix language and other embedded languages in any bilingual speech and the opposition between content morphemes and system morphemes. The languages involved in contact situations perform different functions and supply different types of morphemes to fulfill those functions. The function of the languages and the distribution of the morpheme types are predictable under the extended matrix language frame and related models. Some of the hypotheses proposed below are testable and some are not. For example, Hypothesis (4c) is a prediction, the proof of which depends on future developments in Tok Pisin.

Hypotheses about the matrix language

A matrix language controls the morphosyntactic structure of all bilingual speech. For monolinguals there is only the one known language by which to structure speech. However, for multilinguals, or for those in contact situations, more than one language is available (to some degree). Even in multilingual situations with multiple languages available and in use, a single matrix language sets the grammatical structure of speech (although that matrix language may be a composite formed from more than one language). The following two hypotheses concern the matrix language of Tok Pisin (Hypothesis 1) and changes in that matrix language (Hypothesis 2). (See Hypothesis 1 of Myers-Scotton 2001.)

Hypothesis 1: The Austronesian substrate grammatical frame is the matrix language for Tok Pisin.

   a. This matrix language for Tok Pisin is a composite matrix language formed by splitting the abstract levels of language structure and recombining those levels to form a grammatical frame composed of aspects from different individual languages. Most of the conceptual structure, predicate-argument structure, and morphological patterns come from the Austronesian languages, but most of the phonological forms come from English, based on some degree of lexical-conceptual congruence between English and the Austronesian substrate.

   b. This composite matrix language is a result of compromises among the various Austronesian speakers, and the variations in Tok Pisin reveal the differences in the substrate languages producing the pidgin.

The almost identical structure of Austronesian languages and the large core of common vocabulary are widely attested features of these languages (Lynch, Ross, and Crowley 2000). The common structures are even more evident among geographically close groups of the languages, such as the Austronesian languages of New Ireland and East New Britain. The common characteristics of the Austronesian languages spoken in the region from which Tok Pisin spread in Papua New Guinea are exemplified by the Tigak language of New Ireland, described in chapter 4. The reflections of these structural features in Tok Pisin are described and illustrated in chapter 5. Examples of variations in Tok Pisin (such as the placement of the future marker bai) are explained by differences in the Austronesian substrate languages.

Hypothesis 2: The matrix language (especially a composite matrix language) need not remain unchanged in a language contact situation. Rather, the matrix language will change as the dominance of the languages in the contact situation changes.

    a. A matrix language turnover can occur with language shift from an L1 to Tok Pisin and/or English and can be seen in the changes in L1 and Tok Pisin usages and structures.

    b. As more Papua New Guineans become educated through the medium of the English language and as more urban dwellers establish employment ties with companies dominated by English speakers, the matrix language of Tok Pisin will converge to be more like English for those speakers.

Convergence is the first step in developing a composite matrix language leading to a matrix language turnover. Convergence is defined as a phenomenon in which abstract lexical structure comes from more than one variety, but all the surface forms come from a single variety. Changes in Tok Pisin structure reflecting convergence toward English are discussed in chapter 6. Evidence of convergence affecting the native languages of Tok Pisin speakers is described in chapter 1 for Nalik and Kuot and in chapter 6 for Tigak.

Hypotheses about morpheme types in Tok Pisin

The following hypotheses make claims concerning what types of morphemes from each contributing language will be found in Tok Pisin. These hypotheses parallel Hypotheses 2, 3, 4, and 5 of Myers-Scotton (2001).

Hypothesis 3: Content and early system morphemes can come from any language in the contact situation whether substrate or superstrate, but late system morphemes will only come from the substrate.

    a. Only content and early system morphemes from English occur in Tok Pisin.

    b. Some English content morphemes and early system morphemes are reanalyzed to serve as content or early or late system morphemes in Tok Pisin. Those reanalyzed English morphemes can thus fill Austronesian system morpheme slots.

c. There will be some congruence in lexical-conceptual structure for phonetically similar forms used.
   d. No late system morphemes from a superstrate will occur in Tok Pisin.
   e. Late system morphemes from the homogeneous Austronesian substrate will appear in Tok Pisin if congruent enough with a superstrate form.

In accordance with the hypothesis that content morphemes may come from any language in the contact situation, the sources of morphemes in Tok Pisin are discussed in chapter 5. Although English is the primary source of content morphemes, approximately 3 percent of the Tok Pisin lexicon in New Ireland and New Britain is from German (Laycock 1970). Germany was the political power with its seat of government in Rabaul from the late 1800s until WWI. German's contribution to and influence on Tok Pisin are discussed early in chapter 5.

Hypotheses about constituent types in Tok Pisin

The following hypotheses suggest ways in which constituent types are changing and will change in Tok Pisin as the language stabilizes and as the body of speakers changes.

Hypothesis 4: Constituent types will change during the pidgin/creole formation and stabilization processes.

   a. During pidgin/creole formation most embedded language islands from individual substrate languages are single lexemes or short phrases due to the extensive use of superstrate (or lexifier) content morphemes.
   b. As the pidgin develops and stabilizes, the morphemes from the superstrate actually become morphemes of the pidgin. They are completely incorporated into the pidgin itself so that speakers acquiring the pidgin do not need access to the superstrate to acquire those morphemes.
   c. As Tok Pisin becomes a creole and as it becomes more widely used as a national language, especially among educated Papua New Guineans who know English, there will be more codeswitching between Tok Pisin and English, resulting in more mixed (matrix language + embedded language) constituents and embedded language islands (with English as the embedded language).

The extensive lexification of Tok Pisin from English is well attested and obvious to anyone hearing the language. With estimates of 75 percent or more of Tok Pisin lexemes being from English (Laycock 1970, Mihalic 1971, and Ross 1992) there are few, if any, stretches of two or more lexemes from any given substrate language. The fact that the matrix language for Tok Pisin is a composite matrix language formed from many mutually unintelligible, though structurally similar, languages means that each individual substrate language is an embedded language. The fact that the number of different substrate languages is large also contributes to the smaller possibility of substrate embedded language islands of more than a single lexeme from any one language. Evidence for the claim that the superstrate morphemes of an established pidgin are actually part of the pidgin and no longer from an embedded language is found in the morphological adaptation of the lexemes, the frequency of their use, and the fact that bilingual speakers who know only Tok Pisin and an indigenous vernacular codeswitch between the two languages and incorporate Tok Pisin words into their vernacular. The changes in Tok Pisin discussed in chapter 6 describe a language that is expanding and changing as its body of speakers grows and changes. Among those speakers who are educated in English and those who work in businesses and government departments that require extensive use of English, more and more English words and phrases enter Tok Pisin.

4

Tigak, a Typical Austronesian Language

Since the primary purpose of this study is to demonstrate within a particular theoretical framework the connection between Tok Pisin and the Austronesian substratum, using Tigak as a typical Austronesian language, this chapter provides a brief grammatical sketch of Island Tigak. Before Beaumont's work (1976, 1979) in Central Tigak, there was little published material on the Tigak language. Material from the nineteenth century (Codrington 1974 [1885]) gives some vocabulary and basic grammatical outlines of several Melanesian languages, including the closely related Duke of York language of the South New Ireland/North-west Solomonic network (see map 1.3 in chapter 1).

The Austronesian languages of the islands of Papua New Guinea (the AN_I group described in chapter 1) have many features in common with each other and with Austronesian languages outside Papua New Guinea. Many of the following Austronesian characteristics are discussed in Lynch, Ross, and Crowley (2000) and are illustrated by my own data from Island Tigak (Jenkins 1996, 1998). That they are common to Austronesian languages can be seen by the similarities with Tolai as described by Capell. In fact, he lists as common characteristics of Austronesian languages "(i) [s]tructural features typologically identical or very similar from language to language, and (ii) morphemes or lexemes actually shared between the languages" (1969:47). A basic core of these features is described below as manifested in Island Tigak of New Ireland.

Tigak Phonology, Syllable Structure, and Stress

Phonological characteristics

The phonological systems and syllable types of Austronesian languages are not as complex as those of many language families. The number of phonemes is small compared to most languages of the world, often numbering in the teens and low twenties. Tigak is typical with the following phonemic and orthographic inventory (Jenkins 1998).

(31) /a b d e g i k l m n ŋ o p r s t u ß/
     <a b d e g i k l m n ng o p r s t u v>
     <A B D E G I K L M N Ng O P R S T U V >[16]

There are no affricates or consonant clusters in the Tigak phonological system. The most common phonemic complications of Austronesian languages involve the vowel system. In Tigak twenty-one diphthongs occur, including the five long vowels that contrast with the short vowel counterparts. Sequences of three or more vowels are common in Austronesian languages. Monomorphemic sequences of three vowels occur in Tigak.

(32) p*ouak*   'two'
     aius   'rest'
     papan*iau* 'Moorish idol fish'

Some four vowel sequences occur at morpheme boundaries (which are also syllable boundaries in those cases).

(33) **tui-ai**   'to bow/be bowed over'[17]

Syllable final obstruents are devoiced in Tigak, as is common in Austronesian languages. The devoicing becomes apparent with the pronunciation difference that occurs when a suffix is added or a form is reduplicated.

---

[16]The additional orthographic symbols < c h f h j w y > are also used for words borrowed from English, especially for proper names such as Charles, Frank, Hannah, and James, or for cultural loan words such as *hamma* 'hammer', *yist* 'yeast', and *wain* 'wine'. However, these symbols are not used in writing native forms.

[17]An epenthetical palatal glide (corresponding to the high vowel it follows) forms the onset of the second syllable of the vowel sequence. Since this glide is predictable, it is not phonemic. For example, /pouak/ → [pou.^{w}ak], /aius/ → [ai.^{j}us], /tuiai/ → [tui.^{j}ai].

(34) /rig/ [rik] → /rig-a/ [ri.ga]
      3PL.S.AGR   3PL.S.AGR-PST

(35) /togan/ [to.gan] → /tog-togan/ [tok.to.gan]
      'have' (VT)   'have/be' (VI)

Syllable structure

The canonical Tigak syllable shape is CV with no consonant clusters. Vowel sequences, however, complicate the interpretation of syllable structure. Tigak does not have phonemic tone, so the Tigak syllable is not a tone-bearing unit. Neither is the Tigak syllable a timed unit, since some syllables are of longer duration than others. The one obligatory element in a Tigak syllable is a vowel. Thus, the vowel nucleus is the basis for defining a Tigak syllable.[18] Beaumont (1979) interpreted a sequence of two vowels as a complex syllable nucleus. I agree with his interpretation. Applying Occam's razor, the sequence interpretation of diphthongs and long vowels is more economical. The alternative interpretation would force the postulation of an extremely large set of additional phonemes made up of long vowels and diphthongs. However, such an interpretation requires that a two-vowel sequence be accepted as a single syllable nucleus. Thus, a Tigak syllable nucleus (N) may consist of either one or two vowels, giving us the following four syllable types: N, NC, CN, CNC. All of the above are variants of the basic pattern (C)N(C) in which the syllable nucleus consists of either one or two vowels. Onsets and codas consist of at most one consonant.

(36) N   *a.lu*   'again'   *ai.mug* 'last'   *lu.ai*   'calm'
      NC   *ot*   'thing'   *aong*   'very'
      CN   *ga.ra.ma* 'men's house'   *ai.no* 'before' *piu*   'dog'
      CNC   *gaan*   'day/time'   *gaus*   'rope'   *ma.sut* 'bush'

---

[18]Determining that vowels form the nuclei of syllables does not settle the question of Tigak syllable structure. The large number of diphthongs (many of which are unambivalent sequences such as /eo/ and /ea/) and the contrast in long and short vowels (as in *gup* 'parrot fish' and *guup* 'night/dark') form many sequences of two or more vowels in Tigak. There are also many single syllables with a sequence of two vowels, such as *kais* 'left' and *vaum.lea* 'chief'.

Stress

As is common in Austronesian languages, Tigak word stress falls on the first syllable of the word.[19] Grammatical particles, such as subject agreement pronominals, mood and aspect markers, and articles (noun markers) are not stressed.

(37) *tang 'u.li.na 'la.pun ri.ga*[20] *me 'kau.li 'tau.ni ta 'ko.no*
ART woman old.one 3PL.S.AGR MA paddle toward ART beach
'The old woman paddled toward the beach.'

Tigak Word Order

The basic word order of Tigak follows the general AN_I pattern of SVO. However, the most typical clause will contain only the VP, according to the formula of (38).

(38) CP → (Comp) (SADV) (NP) (SADV) VP (SADV)

A subject agreement marker (and object agreement marker for transitive verbs) is required as part of the VP. An overt NP subject (or object) is required only under certain discourse conditions, such as the first mention of a participant, when there is a change of subject/object which is unclear from the context, or for emphasis.

(39) *(ta piu) ga   kagat-i-reg   (ta ve-lakek)*
      (ART dog) 3SG.S.AGR.PST bite-TZ-3DL.OB.AGR (ART 2-child)
      'The dog bit the two children.'/'It bit them(2).'

Most clauses do not contain an overt subject NP (or object NP). The information required for these elements is contained within the VP in the form of the obligatory subject agreement marker and the object agreement suffix (for transitive verbs). These agreement markers are pronominal forms related to the independent pronouns given in table 4.1. The subject agreement marker occurs in every clause and is the first element of the verb phrase. In chapter 5 I will relate this Austronesian subject

---

[19]There are exceptions to the first-syllable stress rule in Tigak: the second syllable is stressed if it is heavy, meaning that the nucleus is a long vowel or a diphthong.

[20]The plural subject agreement pronominal is used to refer to a woman who has born a child.

agreement marker to the Tok Pisin predicate marker **i**. Sentence level adverbs, such as *nago* 'yesterday' or *emug* 'later', may occur in any of the optional slots for SADV shown in (38). As is expected in an SVO language, modifiers follow the head (as in (40) and (41)), and there are prepositions (as in (42)).

(40) ta piu **ro**
 ART dog good
 '**good** dog'

(41) rig-a kas **papeis**
 3PL-PST swim fast
 'They swam **fast**.'

(42) ta pook **ke** Sam
 ART food GEN Sam
 'food **for** Sam'/'Sam's food'

Interrogatives and imperatives are not marked with different syntactic arrangements. Each is indicated with intonation as in English. Imperatives may omit the second-person subject agreement pronominal. Two imperative forms appear to be contractions of the third-person singular subject agreement pronominal with the verb. These two are given in (43).

(43) *gima!* 'come!' < *gi ima* 'he comes'
 ginang! 'go!' < *gi inang* 'he goes'

Questions in Tigak involve neither inversion nor movement. The appropriate question word is used in situ, as in (44) and (45).

(44) nug inang **eve?**
 2SG.S.AGR go where
 'Where are you going?'

(45) **nasi** gi ima?
 who 3SG.S.AGR come
 'Who is coming?'

Tigak Word Categories

The multi-categorial status of many words in Austronesian languages was noted by Codrington in 1885 when he wrote that "it has been already observed that in the Oceanic languages words may be, and commonly are, various parts of speech according to their use" (1974:131). In Tigak, as well, lexemes often fill multiple category slots. Nouns are often derived from verbs, either by conversion, reduplication, or suffixation, and some verbs are derived from nouns by affixing the causative prefix *la-* and the transitive suffix *-i*, as in (46).

(46) *aisog*   'work'   V, N   (conversion)
     kap-kapis 'plant'   N from V   *kapis* 'to plant'   (reduplication)
     ain-ino-ai 'leader'   N from ADV *aino* 'before'   (suffixation)
     la-isan-i 'to name' V from N   *isan* 'name'   (affixation)

In some cases one cannot make a determination of which category is the original basis of classification.

As will be noted in the next section, there are also questions on the status of other lexical items, such as adjectives and articles in Tigak (and other Austronesian languages). Some linguists question whether there are actually adjectives in some Austronesian languages (Bugenhagen 1995). There are only a few adjectives, at best, in Tigak. Most Tigak words that correspond semantically to English adjectives are more often stative verbs or nouns.[21] For example, the Tigak lexeme *ro* 'good' in (47) often occurs in the adjective slot of the NP formula given in (52).

(47) *tang ien* **ro**
     ART fish good
     'good fish'

That fact alone does not justify classifying *ro* as an adjective since other categories (such as nouns and verbs) may also occur in that position (cf. *ulina* in (62) and *ong* in (51)). Further evidence for its status as an adjective is the fact that it also occurs in the predicate slot of an equative clause as in (48). The fact that *ro* cannot be used with the article, or noun marker

---

[21]Since conversions between nouns and verbs are very common it can sometimes be difficult to assign a particular lexeme to one category or the other. Bugenhagen (1995) gives good tests for category membership and guidelines for deciding among the categories of verb, adjective, or noun. Also see Braine (1987) for arguments on both sides of the distributional versus semantic question of category membership.

(49a), disqualifies it as a noun. Instead, a noun (such as *ot* 'thing') is required with the article and *ro*, as in (49b).

(48) ga   ro
     3SG.S.AGR.PST good
     'It's good.'

(49) a. *tang ro
        ART   good
        'a/the good'

     b. tang ot   ro
        ART thing good
        'a/the good thing'

Many words used as noun modifiers are actually verbs. None of the evidence given above precludes classifying *ro* as a verb, meaning 'be good'. Unambiguous verbs can fill the same slots that *ro* fills above. In addition, the lexeme *ro* can occur with common verbal affixes in an adverbial slot.

(50) la-takil   a-*ro*-i   tang vakup
     CS-hang   CS-good-TZ   ART clothes
     'Hang the clothes properly.'

Prefixation with a causative morpheme is a common means of converting another part of speech to that of a verb or adverbial modifier. From the discussion above it becomes clear that classifying many Austronesian lexemes is not straightforward. Many lexemes can, in fact, have membership in multiple categories. Since *ro* can be affixed in the same way as other verbs but cannot serve as a noun, a classification as a verb seems appropriate. This classification does not prevent its use in the adjective slot of a NP. However, the one slot *ro* does not fill is that of a main verb. For this reason I have classified *ro* as a Tigak adjective since this classification does not preclude any of its observed functions.

Adjectives and adverbs can also be derived from verbs, nouns, or other adjectives as illustrated in (51).

(51) tang vivilai **ong**   '**evil** lifestyle'   Adj from V **ong** 'to wrong'
     latugi **ekising**   'put it **aside**'   Adv from N **kising** 'edge'
     latakil **aroi**   'hang s.t. **properly**'   Adv from Adj **ro** 'good'

The Tigak Noun Phrase (NP)

The noun phrase (NP) in Austronesian languages can be deceptive and can vary from one language to another, but there are general characteristics. Beaumont (1979) gives a basic NP string for Central Tigak as follows:

(52) NP → article (quantifier) N (adjective) (determiner) (possessive)

However, in Island Tigak the quantifier precedes the article, so that (52) becomes (53). A NP with every slot filled is given in (54a). Such a long NP is rare, however, and would more likely be stated as a clause as in (54b).

(53) NP → (quantifier) article N (adjective) (determiner) (possessive)

(54) a. *sakai na natu-na laklik ang i Lisum*
    one ART child-3SG little this of Lisum
    'this one little child of Lisum'

  b. *na natu-na laklik ang ga te Lisum*
    ART child-3SG little this 3SG.S.AGR GEN Lisum
    'This little child is Lisum's.'

The head noun of a Tigak NP is not marked for person, number, or gender with two exceptions. The article (or noun marker) of a proper name or kinship term distinguishes a woman who has borne children. Other females receive the same article designation as males. A few kinship nouns have prefixes to indicate dual or plural number, as in (55a) and (55b). All other plurals are specified (within discourse standards) by the plural quantifier *(ma)mana(n)* as in (56a) and (56b).

(55) a. **va**-*lapan*
    pair-spouse
    'married couple'

  b. **na**-*lakek*[22]
    PL-child
    'children'

---

[22]The plural prefix *na-* is not the same morpheme as the personal article *na*. It is perhaps a shortened form of the basic plural quantifier *mana*.

(56) a. ta **mamana** piu
    ART PL   dog
    'dogs'

b. ta **maman** ot
   ART PL thing
   'things'

Independent pronouns can also be the head of a NP. The pronominal system (discussed later) does distinguish for person, number, and motherhood.

Articles

Beaumont (1976:390) states, "articles are used in all the languages [i.e., Austronesian languages in New Ireland], though often with little semantic significance." In fact, the article in Island Tigak is basically a noun marker whose form is based on the noun category (personal or common) and which is phonologically conditioned for common nouns (Jenkins 1998).[23] For personal names and some kinship terms, the articles *na* and *ri* mark the noun. The form *ri* precedes a noun referring to a woman who has borne a child. The form *na* is used with all other personal names.

(57) **na** Ekonia   'Ekonia' (a man's name)
    ri Karak   'Karak' (a woman's name)
    na tigana   'his son'
    ri naag   'my mother'

Before common nouns (except for some kinship terms) the noun is marked with a form of /taN/ (where N is nasal). This article is always written as either *ta* or *tang*, but the specific form depends on the initial segment of the noun it precedes as illustrated in (58). The written forms are predictable with *ta* occurring before voiceless consonants and /l/, free variation before nasal consonants, and *tang* elsewhere.

(58) **ta** siva   **ta ~ tang** masut   **tang** gaan   **tang** ot
    'a/the place'   'a/the bush'   'a/the day/time'   'a/the thing'

---

[23]Beaumont (1979) actually claims that there is a definite/indefinite distinction in Central Tigak. I did not find such a distinction in my limited survey of the mainland Tigak villages. Island Tigak certainly lacks such a distinction.

Further phonetic variation results from bi-directional assimilation with nouns beginning with /ß/ *v* and /r/ *r*. This assimilation produces the phonetic forms:

(59) *tang vuul* → *[tam buul]* 'a/the canoe'
 tang rei → *[tan dei]* 'a/the wind'

The article always occurs with a Tigak noun except in some locative phrases in which it is optional.

(60) *lo lana (ta) lui* 'inside a/the house'
 lo (ta) laman 'to/on/at the water'

Tigak (and other Austronesian) articles are actually noun markers that are early system morphemes. The Tigak article is accessed at the conceptual level with the content noun that requires it, but the only semantic content is in identifying the type of noun (i.e., common noun, person, a mother). I will claim in chapter 5 that there is insufficient congruence between the Austronesian substrate articles and the English superstrate articles for articles to occur in Tok Pisin.

Complex noun phrases

As stated above adjectives follow the head noun in a Tigak NP (cf. *ro* above). This order is not the same as in Tok Pisin, so it would seem that Tok Pisin does not follow the Austronesian pattern in this point. However, other Austronesian patterns may have provided the model for Tok Pisin. Codrington notes such a construction in his comparison of Melanesian languages. He observes, "when two nouns are in juxtaposition, it may be that one qualifies the other and does the work of an Adjective without becoming one" (1974:143). There is a complex noun construction of this type in Island Tigak (much like a serial verb construction) in which a more specific noun follows a more generic one. Thus, instead of an adjective following the noun, (53) above would become (61), omitting other optional elements. This construction is illustrated in (62).

(61) NP → article N N

(62) *na lapun ulina* or *na ulina lapun*
 ART old.one woman ART woman old.one
 'old woman' 'old woman'

The choice of the noun order in (62) is determined by the focus. The noun in focus is the head noun, the first noun of the pair.

The Tigak Pronominal System

Austronesian pronominal systems commonly differentiate between singular, dual, and plural number, and sometimes include a trial or paucal distinction. They also differentiate between inclusive and exclusive first person but distinguish gender only for a woman who is a mother. Although four classes of pronouns used as independent (or emphatic) subject or object, possessor agreement, verb phrase subject agreement, and verb phrase object agreement are common, the forms are often related. Tigak independent pronouns are given in table 4.1. Except for the irregular singular forms, the bolded portions are the basic forms that also occur in the other classes. The independent pronouns can fill the noun slot of a NP. As seen in the table, the feature that distinguishes the independent pronouns from the forms used as agreement markers is the article (or noun marker) morpheme (*na-*) prefixed to the basic form, as in **na**-*mem* 'we (PL, EXC)', **na**-*nu* 'you (SG)', and **na**-*ri-tul* 'they (TR)'. Thus, the independent pronouns that can fill NP slots do contain both obligatory elements of a NP: the article and the nominal form.

Table 4.1. Tigak independent pronouns

	Singular	Dual	Trial	Plural
1 Inc		naka**rag**	naka**ratul**	**naka**ra
1 Exc	naniu	na**meg**	na**memtul**	na**mem**
2	na*nu*	na**mug**	na**mitul**	na**mi***
3	na*ne*	na**reg**	na**ritul**	na**ri***

(* -*g* is suffixed to form the subject agreement forms)

The four-way distinctions in number and the inclusive/exclusive distinction in the pronominal system make the Austronesian system exceptionally marked among the world's languages. For this reason, such distinctions are not expected in a pidgin/creole, though these same distinctions do occur in Tok Pisin, as we will see in the next chapter.

The Tigak Verb Phrase

The verb phrase and the equative clause

As shown in (38), the verb phrase (VP) is the only obligatory element of a Tigak clause. However, within the VP are obligatory constituents that supply the participant (or argument) information required by the verb. The VP may be defined by the general formula in (63) in which the constituents enclosed in parentheses are optional and those enclosed in square brackets are required for specified verb classes.

(63) VP → (IRR) SAGR (NEG) (PRE-V) $V_{t/\emptyset}$ (MOD) $[OBAGR]_t$ $([PCOMP]_\emptyset)$

The subject agreement pronominal is an obligatory element of the VP and is the first element of the predicate occurring in every clause. I will claim in chapter 5 that this pronominal element is the model for the Tok Pisin predicate marker *i*. In Tigak the subject agreement pronominal carries the only indication of tense beyond specific temporal adverbs. This pronominal is suffixed with *-a* for past tense. Present and future are not distinguished in the VP. (Marking future tense is one function of the irrealis marker *vo* which occurs VP initially.) The object agreement pronominal is obligatory for transitive verbs but does not occur with any other verb class.

An overt object NP is optional (in the predicate complement slot) under the same discourse constraints as those controlling an overt subject NP. If there is an overt object NP that is in focus, then that focused NP can be fronted to the beginning of the entire clause, as in (64).

(64) ***(ta lakek ang)*** *(ta piu)*   ga   kagat-i-Ø
      (ART child that)   (ART dog)   3SG.S.AGR   bite-TZ-3SG.OB.AGR
      '(That child), (the dog)/It bit him.'

The predicate complement constituent may also be another complete clause, as shown in (65) Clausal complements are common with psychological verbs.

(65) ga   nol-i   Ø   auneng   ***vo gi***
      3SG.S.AGR.PST think-TZ   3SG.OB.AGR   like.this   IRR   3SG.S.AGR

      vil-i-Ø   tang vuul
      make-TZ-3SG.OB.AGR   ART   canoe
      'He thought that he would make a canoe.'

The Tigak Verb Phrase 115

Other elements that may fill the predicate complement slot will be discussed below with the equative clause.

The pre-verb constituent may come from one of several categories (see also "Tense, mood, and aspect" below). This slot is usually reserved for particles indicating aspect (such as completive *po* in (66)), mood (such as deontic *ke* in (67)), or qualification (*sa,* in (68)). It may also be filled with the auxiliary verb *vuvuk* (69).

(66) rig-a   (veko) **po** sang
     3PL.S.AGR-PST (NEG) CMP   arrive
     'They (had) (not) arrived.'

(67) mug   **ke**   tug[24]
     2DL.S.AGR must   stop
     'You(2) must stop.'

(68) nane   ga   **sa**   marol
     3SG.PRN 3SG.S.AGR.PST   just   silent
     'He was just silent.'

(69) nag   **vuvuk** inang e   Kavieng
     1SG.S.AGR want   go   LOC Kavieng
     'I want to go to Kavieng.'

Tigak has a null copula in equative clauses, so an equative predicate has no overt verb. If the verb is considered to be ∅, formula (63) still describes the equative predicate with the PCOMP constituent being obligatory. The predicate complement may be a noun phrase, an adjective phrase, an adverb phrase, or a comparative phrase. Specifically, the equative phrase could be described as in (70) with examples in (71).

(70) EQP → SAGR (PRE-V) $V_\emptyset$ PCOMP

(71) Equative Clauses
     a. ga   ta   lita   [NP COMP]
        3SG.S.AGR ART woven.wall
        'It [is] a woven wall.'

---

[24]The negative *veko(n)* does not occur with *ke*. To negate (67) a negative obligatory form, *pata*, is used; the negative would be *mug pata tug* 'you(2) cannot stop'.

b. *tang iai   ga   vugvuga*   [ADJP COMP]
   ART tree   3SG.S.AGR   (very) tall
   'The tree [is] (very) tall.'

c. *tang vuul   ang   ga   losilik aong*   [ADVP COMP]
   ART canoe that 3SG.S.AGR   near   very
   'That canoe [is] very near.'

d. *gi   malan ta-na   tivu-na*   [COMPARATIVEP COMP]
   3SG.S.AGR like   to-3SG.OB   grandfather-3SG.OB
   'He [is] like his grandfather.'

Transitive and intransitive verbs

Tigak has several classes of verbs based on transitivity. Some verbs are semantically transitive but unmarked for transitivity even though requiring an object, as in (72), and others incorporate the object into the semantics of the verb, as in (73). These transitive verbs do not take either of the two transitive suffixes *-i* or *-ina*.

(72) *(nanu)   nug   me   **suka**   ta   pook*
     2SG.PRN   2SG.S.AGR   MT   get   ART   food
     '(You) come get the food.'

(73) *nag   **bak***
     1SG.S.AGR   catch.crabs
     'I am catching crabs.'

Two classes of marked transitive verbs are distinguished by the type of object taken and identified by the form of the transitive marker. Some transitive verbs belong to one class only and some belong to both. Transitive verbs taking objects which are semantically patients are identified with the transitive suffix *-i* plus the appropriate person/number object marker (the bold portions in table 4.1).

(74) *ne   ga   **kuus-i-mem**   pa-na   ta   pasak*
     3SG.PRN   3SG.S.AGR.PST   tell-TZ-1PL.EXC   with-3SG.OB   ART   news
     'He told us the news.'

Transitive verbs taking objects which are obliques are suffixed with the transitive marker *-ani* (~ *-ana*)25 and the appropriate object agreement form.

(75) tang ue   gi   ***polong-ana-reg***
     ART crocodile 3SG.S.AGR listen-TZ-3DL.OB.AGR
     'The crocodile is listening to them(2).'

Some transitive verbs may take either patient objects (76) or oblique objects (77). (The transitive marker *-i* is deleted before a vowel-initial object suffix, as in (76)).

(76) ga   ***pol-om***
     3SG.S.AGR.PST lie-2SG.OB
     'He lied to you.'

(77) reg-a   ***pol-ani-?-∅***   kula...
     3DL.S.AGR.PST lie-TZ-3SG.OB.AGR because...
     'They(2) lied about it because...'

Some verbs may be used transitively (77) or intransitively (78).

(78) ta popo gi   ***ngek***
     ART baby 3SG.S.AGR cry
     'The baby is crying.'

(79) gi   ***ngek-i-mug***
     3SG.S.AGR cry-TZ-2DL.OB.AGR
     'It is crying for you(2).'

Some transitive verbs are made intransitive by reduplication as in (80).

(80) a. ***ngeik-i***   (VT)   'to move something (an object)'

    b. ***nga-ngeik*** (VI)   'to move, change location (a person)'

25The *-an* is also used as a valence reduction marker to form stative verbs and to form a passive construction, as in *ga kagat-an ta piu* 'he/she/it was bitten by the dog' versus *ta piu ga kagat-i-∅* 'the dog bit him/her/it'. Another form, *ani*, is used as a preposition, as in *kuskuus ani tang ue* 'story about a crocodile'. Either form is a possible source for the transitive construction in (75). I favor the interpretation of *-ani* as a bimorphemic form composed of the valence reducer *-an* and the transitive suffix *-i*.

Other transitive verbs (81a) are made intransitive by a valence reduction suffix, *-ai*, as in (81b).

(81) a. *rig-a* **akaung-ani-∅** *ta lakek tigari*
    3PL.S.AGR-PST praise-TZ-3SG.OB.AGR ART child male
    'They praised the boy.'

 b. *kara* **akaung-ai**
    1PL.S.AGR praise-VR
    'We give praise.'

Some intransitive verbs (81a and 82a) are made transitive (81b and 82b) with a causative prefix, *la-* or *a-*.

(82) a. *rig* **sinug** *lo lana ta garama*
    3PL.S.AGR sit LOC inside ART men's.house
    'They are sitting inside the men's house.'

 b. *ga* **la-sinug-i-∅** *ta sula lo lana ta*
    3SG.S.AGR.PST CS-sit-TZ-3SG.OB.AGR ART spear LOC inside ART

  lui
    house
    'He put the spear inside the house.'

(83) a. *tang anu gi* **kos** *eno*
    ART man 3SG.S.AGR board(vehicle) in.front
    'The man gets in in front.'

 b. *gi* **a-kos-i-ri** *ka-na maman ot*
    3SG.S.AGR CS-board-TZ 3PL.OB.AGR GEN-3SG PL thing

  lo ka-ri kar
    LOC GEN-3PL car
    'He loaded his things into their car.'

One pair of ditransitive verbs illustrates subcategorization differences that affect morphosyntactic structure. The Tigak verb *tave-i* 'to give to someone' requires the verb's object to be the recipient (84). The item given (if specified) is introduced with the instrumental/accompaniment preposition *pa-*.

(84) tang anu ga   **tave-i-∅**   ta lakek pa-na
    ART man 3SG.S.AGR.PST give-TZ-3SG.OB.AGR ART child with-3SG.OB

   tang ien
   ART fish
   'The man gave a/the child fish.' lit., 'The man gifted the child with fish.'

The verb *lisan-i* 'to give something' requires that the object be the given item (85). The recipient is introduced with the personal locative *su*.

(85) tang anu ga   **lisan-i-∅**   ta piu su-na
    ART man 3SG.S.AGR.PST give-TZ-3SG.OB.AGR ART dog LOC-3SG.OB

   ta lakek
   ART child
   'The man gave a/the dog to a/the child.'

I will show in chapter 6 how convergence of Tigak toward Tok Pisin affects the use of these two verbs.

Serial and compound verbs

Serial verb constructions are common. Two or more verbs are used in a single verb phrase with one set of affixes for the series and one set of the free forms used to mark subject/object agreement and any tense-mood-aspect markers that are appropriate.[26] In (86) the series of two transitive verbs *(tivan-i* and *gavan-i)* are used with only one subject agreement pronominal *(nug)* and one aspect marker *(a)*, both preceding the verbs. A single transitive suffix *(-i)* and object agreement pronominal (∅) are suffixed to the last verb only.

(86) **nug   a   tivan gavan-i-∅**   ta laman i-na
    2SG.S.AGR MA pour throw-TZ-3SG.OB.AGR ART water GEN-3SG

   tang niik
   ART coconut
   '(You) go throw out the water of the coconut.'

---

[26]Crowley (1987) classifies serial constructions in Bislama as those constructions in which each verb has its own set of markers. Givón (1987) considers both types as serial constructions (i.e., constructions with more than one verb but only one set of markers and constructions in which each verb has its own markers).

A similar construction is seen in verb compounds that are formed by combining two verbs into one. Examples of their functions include emphasizing an action, as in (87) or expressing the manner of the action, as in (88).

(87) mem-a **tug-bat-i-∅** ta pas-pasal
1PL.EX.S.AGR-PST stop-block-TZ-3SG.OB.AGR ART RDP-walk
'We forbade/prevented the journey.'

(88) ritul **ru-pisin-i-∅** ta motange
3TR.S.AGR run-away-leave-TZ-3SG.OB.AGR ART snake
'The three of them run away from a/the snake.'

Tense, mood, and aspect

Tense, mood, and aspect are marked in different ways in Tigak. Tense is most often indicated with temporal adverbs, except for the past tense marked on the subject agreement pronominal forms with the suffix -a (see (87) and (90)). Example (84) uses ga '3SG.S.AGR.PST'; the non-past form is gi. Singular forms are often irregular. Irrealis mood is marked by vo in clause initial position of (89). The indication of future tense is only one use of the irrealis mood.

(89) **vo** nag inang e Kavieng (amoua)
IRR 1SG.S.AGR go LOC Kavieng (tomorrow)
'I will go to Kavieng (tomorrow).'

(90) nag-**a** inang e Kavieng (nago)
1SG.S.AGR-PST go LOC Kavieng (yesterday)
'I went to Kavieng (yesterday).'

Aspect markers (91) and the negative marker (92) occur between the subject agreement pronominal and the verb.

(91) rig-a **po** polong-ani ka-ri etok...
3PL.S.AGR-PST CMP listen.to-TZ GEN-3PL talk
'They listened to their talk...'

(92) nag **veko** kalapang
1SG.S.AGR NEG know
'I don't know.'

The verb *kalapang* 'to know' from (92) is also used with other verbs as the habitual aspect marker as in (93).

(93) gi **kalapang** saleng pa-na ka-na piu
 3SG.S.AGR HAB hunt with-3SG GEN-3SG dog
 'He always/usually hunts with his dog(s).'

Prepositions

Most Austronesian languages have prepositions, as is typical for SVO languages, but they usually form a very small class. In Tigak, for example, there are only seven common prepositions. Three of these forms, *lo, e,* and *su,* are semantically general locative forms used in mutually exclusive contexts determined by the nominal object.

(94) nag inang **lo** (ta) lui [before a common place name]
 1SG.S.AGR go LOC (ART) house
 'I'm going to the house.'

(95) rig inang **e** Rabaul [before a proper place name]
 3PL.S.AGR go LOC Rabaul
 'They are going to Rabaul.'

(96) a. ga lisan-i-Ø **su** Kipang [before an animate
 3SG.S.AG.PST give-TZ-3SG.OB.AGR LOC Kipang recipient]
 'He gave it to Kipang.'

 b. ga lisan-i-Ø **su**-na
 3SG.S.AGE.PST give-TZ-3SG.OB.AGR LOC-3SG.OB
 'He gave it to him/her/it.'

Three of the prepositions are genitive forms (also with mutually exclusive functions) (see the next section for examples of these possessive forms). The seventh preposition is *pe/pa-* 'with'. It is used to introduce an accompaniment or instrument. The form *pe* is used before a person's name or a kinship term. *pa-* is used elsewhere with the appropriate pronominal object suffix.

(97) mug inang kum **pe** na tama-mug
 2DL.S.AGR go together with ART father-2DL.OB
 'You(2) go with your(2) father.'

(98) ga   nak-i-∅   ta   mit-ig   **pa**-na   (tang iai)
     3SG.S.AGR.PST hit-TZ-3SG.OB.AGR ART hand-1SG with-3SG (ART stick)
     'He hit my hand with it/(a stick).'

Pana is also used to introduce speech clauses (see example (109)).

Possession

Possession is indicated in various ways in Austronesian languages, and Tigak is no exception. The most widespread distinction is that between alienable and inalienable possession. An alienably possessed noun is marked with a preposed genitive *ka-*, to which is suffixed the appropriate pronominal agreement (99a), or with a similarly formed postposed genitive phrase with *ta-* (99b).

(99) a. **ka**-na   lui
         GEN-3SG house
         'his house'

   or

   b. *lui*   **ta**-na
      house   GEN-3SG
      'his house'

To specify the possessor by name, a genitive phrase follows the noun, and the free prepositional forms *te* and *ke* are used, as in (100).

(100) a. ta   lui   **te**   Sam
         ART house GEN Sam
         'Sam's house'

   or

   b. ta   pook   **ke**   Sam
      ART food   GEN Sam
      'Sam's food'

There is a semantic difference between the postposed *ka-/ke* and the *ta-/te* forms. The former denotes 'benefactive' possession. Thus, the specific meaning of *ta pook ke Sam* is 'food for Sam'. With a pronominal construction indicating benefactive possession the *ka-* prepositional phrase is postposed, as in (101).

(101) ta   pook **ka-na**
     ART food GEN-3SG
     'his food' (lit., 'food for him')

Inalienably possessed nouns (usually body parts or kinship terms) are simply suffixed with the appropriate pronominal, as in (102).

(102) *ngur-i-g*[27]   and   *tiga-**mug***
     mouth-Ø-1SG   sibling.same.sex-2DL
     'my mouth'   'your(2) brother/sister'

Proper names of people and places (103) cannot be marked in either way.

(103) **ka-m   Punai* or **Kavieng-i-g*
     GEN-2SG Punai   Kavieng-GEN-1SG
     'your Punai'   'my Kavieng'

Subordinate Clauses

Subordinate clauses are structured no differently than main clauses in Tigak. Just as there are coordinating conjunctions *e/ve/ave* 'and', *kisang* 'but', *ne* 'then', and *vo* 'or', most types of subordinate clauses are introduced by a particular subordinating conjunction occurring in the Complementizer slot of the complement phrase. The following examples illustrate the most common types of subordinate clauses. The subordinate clauses are in square brackets, and the conjunctions are bolded.

(104) Conditional clause
     rig   *veko* *kaskaas* *akamusi* *tang* *aisog* [***vouneng*** *tang*
     3PL.S.AGR NEG be.able complete ART work if   ART

---

[27] The vowel insertion is a morphophonemic rule to separate the two consonants and satisfy syllable structure requirements in Tigak.

      vaap   rig   veko angasigiri]
      people 3PL.S.AGR NEG help.them
      'They cannot finish the work [**if** the people don't help them].'

(105) Reason clause
      *nag   inang e   Kavieng [**kula**   nag   veko pe   togoni*
      1SG.S.AGR go   LOC Kavieng because 1SG.S.AGR NEG still have

      ta   pook]
      ART food
      'I am going to Kavieng [**because** I have no more food].'

(106) Purpose clause
      *rig   a   ngaungaul [**ina**   ngan]*
      3PL.S.AGR MA fish   [in.order.to eat]
      'They fish [**in order to** eat].'

(107) Manner clause
      *gi   pasal [**malan te** tamana   (gi   pasal)]*
      3SG.S.AGR walk [like   of father.his (3SG.S.AGR walk)]
      'He walks [**like** his father (walks)]'

(108) Time clauses
    a. *vo rig   sinug etang [**tuk** vo rig   maat]*
       IRR 3PL.S.AGR sit   there [until IRR 3PL.S.AGR die]
      'They will sit there [**until** they die].'

    b. *nug   ke   maiak [**kula**   tang ulan gi   singan]*
       2SG.S.AGR must fish   [before ART moon 3SG.S.AGR shines]
      'You must fish [**before** the moon comes out].'

(109) Speech clauses
    a. *riga   kuusau **pana** ["laak lo   lui"]*
       3PL.S.AGR.PST tell.me with [go.up LOC house]
      'She said to me, [Ø "go into the house"].'

    b. *gi   kuusom   **auneng** [nug kos   enos]*
       3SG.S.AGR tell.you(SG) [like this 2SG.S.AGR board in.front]
      'He is telling you [**to** get in in front].'

Both direct and indirect quotes may be introduced with either of the speech conjunctions.

Relative clauses in Tigak have no introductory conjunction or relative pronoun. These clauses are usually marked by simple juxtaposition following the NP to which they relate (110), or sometimes by the use of a form that also serves some other function, such as a deictic (111).

(110) vo   rig   tave akuruli-Ø   ne   ang [ga
      IRR 3PL.S.AGR give plenty-3SG.OB.AGR 3SG.PRN that [3SG.S.AGR

  togtogon]
  have]
  'They will give plenty to the one [who has].'
  [lit., 'They will give plenty to that one [he(who) has].']

(111) a. **gare** ta   salan
         here ART path/trail
         '**Here** [is] the path.'

  b. ina   so   mig   vili tang ot   [(gare) ga   veko
     in.order what 2PL.S.AGR do   ART   thing here   3SG.S.AGR NEG

  nos]?
  straight
  'Why do you do the thing [**(that)** is not right]?'

The antecedent of the relative clause may be any noun in the clause, and this antecedent must be referred to within the relative clause by the appropriate agreement pronominal. In (111b) the antecedent is *tang ot*, the object of the main clause. The coreferent is the subject of the relative clause and is marked with the third-person singular subject agreement pronominal *ga*. Since the relative clause always follows the noun antecedent, it often occurs at the end of a sentence. The only grammatical clues to distinguish such a relative clause from a following independent clause are the intonation, which indicates it is part of a larger unit, and the fact that there is no coordinating conjunction joining the two clauses, which eliminates its status as a second independent clause.

When the relative clause is modifying the subject of a clause, it will not be at the end of a sentence but will immediately follow the subject.

(112) tang   atul   [naga   ngauli-Ø   nago]   ga
      ART   tuna   [1SG.S.AGR.PST hook-3SG.OB.AGR   yesterday]   3SG.S.AGR

      vugvuga   aong
      big   very
   'The tuna [I caught yesterday] was very big.'

In (112) the subject of the main clause *(tang atul)* is the antecedent for the object of the relative clause. The pronominal coreferent is the usual null third-person singular object agreement. Only a time antecedent (113) has no coreferent in the relative clause.

(113) lo   tang gaan   [gi   sang]   ta   nalakek   rig   me   elau
      LOC   ART   time   [3SG.S.AGR   arrive] ART   children   3PL.S.AGR MT   run
   'At the time/when [he arrives] the children come running.'

Discourse Characteristics

At the discourse level, tense and participant reference are similar. Once each is established there is little overt marking through the remainder of the discourse. For tense, once the time frame is given, the discourse is often delivered in the unmarked or non-past tense.[28] Similarly, once the subject and object are overtly named with an independent NP, only the pronominal agreement markers are used until there is a change of participant or until emphasis or clarification is deemed necessary. Plural marking for number is also treated as unnecessary once the fact is established. Since the pronominal agreement markers indicate number, quantitative expressions are rarely repeated.

Embedding is a relatively rare feature of Tigak discourse; however, many clauses are often strung together with coordinating conjunctions. Sequences of events are normally chronological. One prominent feature of Tigak narrative discourse is head-to-tail linkage, by which the previous clause is repeated at the beginning of the subsequent clause. The translation in (114) demonstrates this characteristic, which is common in many Papua New Guinea languages.

---

[28]The unmarked form is non-past because it serves for both present and future time frames. Only the past is overtly marked, and then only on the subject agreement pronominal.

(114) Pukuntap went fishing. He paddled to Nonoval. He reached Nonoval and turned toward Limus. When he arrived at Limus he floated on the water toward the reef. Over the reef he dropped his fishing line…

The characteristics of Austronesian languages described in this chapter are especially common among the languages of New Ireland and New Britain. In the next chapter, I will show that these features are also prominent in Tok Pisin and hypothesize that they are features of the composite matrix language frame of this pidgin.

5

Is Tok Pisin an Austronesian Language?

One often-cited characterization of pidgins and creoles is that they have the grammar of one language and the lexicon of another. The fact that the (so-called) lexifier language is almost universally termed the SUPERSTRATE has promoted the assumption that the lexifier language is also the most influential language in pidgin formation.[29] This assumption has contributed to the characterization of pidgins as simplified (or sub-standard) versions of the lexifier language. An opposing perspective of pidgin formation that surfaces repeatedly is that of the influence of the SUBSTRATE languages. Because most pidgins and creoles have developed in situations involving multiple substrate languages, it has been difficult to isolate a single substrate language from which all aspects of a particular pidgin/creole grammar come. For this reason the influence of substrate languages has often been denigrated. This fact is also true of Tok Pisin (TP).

The theories so far advanced concerning the origin of pidgins/creoles have not been able to explain adequately the combinations of features found in these languages or to classify their relationship to other languages. Indeed, Thomason and Kaufman (1988) claim that pidgins and creoles do not belong to a genetic family but result from abnormal transmission. The transmission is abnormal because the language is not learned from one generation by speakers in the next generation as a first language (or mother tongue). A

---

[29]I will use the term SUPERSTRATE to refer to the languages of the traditional political powers and SUBSTRATE to refer to all other languages involved in the pidgin/creole situation in accordance with the normal usage in the literature. No implication of social value is intended by either of these terms.

pidgin is acquired as a second language. In the formative period, the speakers acquiring the pidgin are speakers of many (or at least several) different native languages. Although the transmission of a pidgin may be abnormal compared to the way most people learn a language from their parents' generation and in turn teach it to their children's generation, the development of pidgin/creole structure and the source of their lexemes may be seen as a very normal process under the theoretical framework of this study. According to the matrix language frame theory one language controls the grammatical structure in codeswitching while both languages can supply morphemes. In the contact situation of pidgin formation, no single language is available to all speakers to supply the grammatical frame, so a composite morphosyntactic frame is established drawing on the structures of the different languages involved. The Abstract Level model explains how features from more than one language can be incorporated into a composite matrix language by splitting the abstract levels of language structure and combining different levels from different languages. The Tok Pisin pronominal system (presented later in this chapter) is an example of how the lexical-conceptual structure and morphological realization patterns of the Austronesian substrate are combined with the lexical-conceptual structure and phonological forms of English. The 4-M model characterizes four types of morphemes. Content morphemes (and early system morphemes), being conceptually activated, are more accessible to non-superstrate speakers than late system morphemes. For this reason superstrate content (and associated early system) morphemes are more likely to appear in a pidgin/creole than the late system morphemes, although some of them will be reconfigured in the pidgin to serve grammatical functions. For the same reason (accessibility to all speakers), content morphemes are the most likely type to be adopted from the substrate languages. I will demonstrate below with Tok Pisin how the structure and the vocabulary sources can be predicted by applying the principles of these models.

Tok Pisin does not fit neatly into the traditional descriptions of pidgin and creole languages. This fact has stimulated much debate concerning the theories of pidgin formation. The Abstract Level and 4-M models show promise as explanatory models for pidgin/creole formation, just as they have for other language contact phenomena. These models allow predictions of which aspects of grammar and vocabulary will come from specific languages. These theories incorporate many of the divergent characteristics of other theories that previously showed no connection, thus permitting a coherent model of pidgin/creole grammatical structure and vocabulary. I give a brief sociolinguistic and historical sketch of Tok Pisin followed by a discussion of the theoretical framework used in this study, applied to pidgin formation and, finally, by the application of the model to Tok Pisin.

Sociolinguistic and Historical Background of Tok Pisin

The success of Tok Pisin as a lingua franca in linguistically diverse Papua New Guinea is a natural consequence of its history. Mühlhäusler defines a PIDGIN as

> a contact language used among people who have no other language in common. It is a second language to those who use it, and its use is restricted to a limited number of situational contexts. (1982:442)

A pidgin is normally considered to be a much more simplified language than any of the languages involved in its formation. In contrast, the traditional notion of a CREOLE is as a pidgin (or jargon) that is the native language of its speakers (see for example, Holm 1988a, 1988b, Todd 1974, Mühlhäusler 1982). As a native language, a creole is used in all contexts and is, therefore, a more complete (or expanded) language than a pidgin.

These definitions have presented problems for the classification of Tok Pisin as a pidgin or a creole. The number of native speakers is very small compared to the number for whom Tok Pisin is a second language, so for most speakers it is still a pidgin based on that criterion. However, the Tok Pisin used by most of its speakers is neither simplified nor restricted. There are speakers of Tok Pisin for whom it has become the primary language. As such it may be used in all contexts, and the speaker may actually be more fluent in Tok Pisin than in his/her L1. From its inception Tok Pisin has been used primarily among native speakers of different indigenous languages communicating with each other, rather than as a means of communication with foreigners (Sankoff and Laberge 1974). In fact, it is this "high usage among speakers of mutually unintelligible substrate languages, rather than between superstrate and substrate speakers" (Rickford and McWhorter 1997:244) that has produced the remarkable expansion in the use and structure of Tok Pisin. (The fact that grammatical expansion occurred before there were native speakers of Tok Pisin has also been noted by Sankoff (1979) and Romaine (1988).) Even before independence in 1975, Papua New Guineans used Tok Pisin as a common means of communication to begin to build a sense of national unity. The domains of use have steadily expanded even among speakers of a common vernacular. Although Tok Pisin is a creole for the small group of speakers for whom it is the native language, for most speakers it is an EXTENDED PIDGIN:

> [a pidgin] which, although it may not become a mother tongue, proves vitally important in a multilingual area, and which, because of its usefulness, is extended and used beyond the original limited function which caused it to come into being. (Todd 1974:5)

For Papua New Guineans, Tok Pisin is not a substandard variety of English (an opinion many English-speaking expatriates hold). Rather, it is a prestigious lingua franca, necessary in many contexts and appropriate in even more.

At the time of the 1980 census (Romaine 1992:87), Tok Pisin was the most widely spoken language in Papua New Guinea with approximately 45 percent of the population over age ten speaking it and only 9 percent speaking Hiri Motu (Sankoff 1980b:20). Approximately 22 percent of the population spoke some English. These percentages are still probably representative of the linguistic situation in Papua New Guinea, except that the percentage of Tok Pisin speakers is growing, and the percentage of Hiri Motu speakers is dropping. For most speakers of Tok Pisin, it remains just one of a number of languages in their linguistic repertoires. It is currently the native language of only a small number of Papua New Guineans who grow up in towns and whose parents speak different first languages. Even though, under traditional definitions, this situation means that Tok Pisin is only recently becoming a creole (and for a relatively small number of speakers), I would agree with Wurm that in "actual use...[TP] corresponds to that of a real creole" (1980:237).

Wolfers notes that Tok Pisin's "vocabulary, its special expression, even its grammatical structure, vary quite widely from place to place..., very largely under the influence of the particular traditional local languages" (1971:413). There are varying dialects of Tok Pisin in different regions of Papua New Guinea. The dialects reflect the linguistic differences in the vernaculars of the people. The rural and urban dialects of Tok Pisin also differ, with the urban dialect being more anglicized. Mühlhäusler (1979) calls a variety used by Australian expatriates since early colonial periods Tok Masta. This label can still be applied to the variety learned by many expatriate short-term residents, but it is not true Tok Pisin and is not the version learned by the indigenous people of Papua New Guinea (Wurm 1980). (We will see below that differences in the varieties of Tok Pisin can be explained using principles of the Abstract Level and MLF models.) The particular dialect of Tok Pisin with which I am most familiar is that variety spoken in the islands region of New Ireland and New Britain. Except when specified to be otherwise, the variety of Tok Pisin under discussion throughout this work is the variety spoken in this islands region of Papua New Guinea.

Melanesian Pidgin English (MPE) is a cover term for the closely related (and mutually intelligible) pidgins/creoles used in Papua New Guinea (Tok Pisin), the Solomon Islands (Pijin), and Vanuatu (Bislama) (Holm 1988b). MPE is said to be descended from an early nineteenth century pidgin known as Beach-la-Mar (Churchill 1911; cf. Clark 1979). Thus, Tok Pisin is only one variety of a more widespread pidgin/creole spoken in the South Pacific. This variety is also known as Neo-Melanesian and New Guinea Pidgin. An accurate history of Tok Pisin is difficult to document because of the lack of written records and the scarcity of accurate descriptions of the multitude of languages spoken in the Pacific islands. This lack of documentation also makes it difficult to trace the sources of some Tok Pisin forms and structures. For example, Ross (1992:373) states that there are no prenasalized consonants, such as found in **umben** 'fish net' (Tok Pisin < Tolai *ubene*), in the languages spoken on New Ireland and New Britain. However, Tigak does have prenasalized obstruents, as was shown in examples in the section on noun phrases in chapter 4. The Madak language in the center of New Ireland also has prenasalized obstruents as evidenced by the pronunciation of the language name, *[mandak]*.

The various versions of Tok Pisin history fall into roughly three groups: Keesing (1988), who claims that Tok Pisin originated in the central Pacific from a nautical and trade jargon; Baker (1993, 1995, 1996), who claims Australian varieties of pidgin English (with Austronesian and Australian aboriginal input) as the source; and Mühlhäusler (1979, 1982, 1987a), who claims that Tok Pisin originated on the Samoan plantations and later developed independently of the Queensland variety or the other Pacific island varieties. Each of these scholars acknowledges a Queensland influence, but, except for Baker, they do not rank the Australian pidgins as the most important factor in the development of Tok Pisin. All agree that Tok Pisin changed after it arrived in the New Guinea islands, influenced by the indigenous languages.

Keesing suggests that the jargon of the Pacific whaling, sandalwood, and beach-la-mar trade was carried to the plantations of the Pacific (mostly in Samoa for Tok Pisin speakers) and from the plantations back to German New Guinea. Mühlhäusler proposes that New Guinean laborers were taken to Samoan plantations where they acquired an already established pidgin (possibly learned from other islanders who had acquired it in Queensland). Clark (1979) specifically credits the New Britain and New Ireland region of Papua New Guinea as the source of the MPE variety known as Tok Pisin. Baker is the most adamant that Tok Pisin (and its related dialects) originated in Australia and was carried to the Pacific islands from there. He stands alone in his claim that Eastern Australian Pidgin English "heavily influenced" (1995:4) Melanesian Pidgin English. Although his claim may have some merit for other varieties of Melanesian Pidgin English, it is not strong in the case of Tok Pisin. Both the historical record and his own data weaken his claim, as I will demonstrate below.

Goulden (1990) provides a short but detailed history of Tok Pisin with comparisons of the three major differences of opinion mentioned above. He divides the development of the language into three periods. During the first period, before 1865, the principle means of communication for Melanesians with Europeans were the nautical and trade jargons used with whaling ships' crews and overseers of the sandalwood and beach-la-mar trades. Keesing holds that a common nautical jargon was widespread in the Pacific by that time, but Mühlhäusler claims there were many varieties in different areas of the Pacific. Baker agrees that there were many varieties of pidgins in the Pacific but contends that New South Wales Pidgin English had a greater influence than any others.

During the second period, between 1865 and 1900, the plantation labor trade developed. Most of the early laborers were from Vanuatu and the Solomon Islands until Germany began establishing plantations in Samoa in 1869. The Queensland plantations had developed earlier, but most New Guinean workers were recruited for the German Samoan plantations during this time. Islanders from Vanuatu and the Solomon Islands probably carried the Melanesian Pidgin English variety of Queensland to Samoa. Thus,

> Tok Pisin evolved from a Samoan plantation pidgin that had its roots in Queensland Canefields English, accounting in part for the similarities among Tok Pisin, Pijin, and Bislama, as well as Australian forms of pidginized English. (Goulden 1990:17)

The Germans began establishing plantations on New Britain and New Ireland in the 1870s and 1880s. Some of the laborers on these plantations had worked in Samoa. Under the Germans most of the overt interclan hostilities were stopped. As a result there was more interaction between language groups and a greater need for a lingua franca.

The third period extended from the late 1800s until WWI. With German rule established in 1884, English was withdrawn as a possible target language for the New Guineas. This fact may explain why there are more English lexemes in other varieties of Melanesian Pidgin English than in Tok Pisin, which incorporated more German and indigenous vernacular lexemes.[30] The Germans did not encourage New Guineans to learn German.

---

[30]There are also more French lexemes in Bislama than any other Pacific variety because of the French involvement in Vanuatu.

For them the pidgin was an acceptable and useful neutral language. Mühlhäusler reports that for plantation laborers

> between 1887 and 1903 the seven most important recruiting areas were Northern New Ireland, Southern New Ireland, Gazelle Peninsula, Buka, Bougainville, and the islands east of New Ireland, and New Hanover, in that order. (1979:77)

Although there were New Guinean laborers on Samoan plantations until 1913, during those early years of the century most of the New Guinean laborers worked within New Guinea, but not necessarily within their own language areas.

Between the two world wars more regional differences developed in the pidgin of New Guinea. In the islands (the area in which this study is centered) the pidgin was used primarily as a means of communication among New Guineans from different language groups. They learned the pidgin from each other, not from expatriates of the lexifier language. In the highlands of the interior, on the other hand, the local people learned the pidgin from Australian patrol officers. This variety was "a heavily anglicised variety" (Mühlhäusler 1979:91). World War II continued the spread of Tok Pisin as young New Guinean males were recruited as carriers and laborers for the military. During that conflict Tok Pisin became the means of communication between the expatriate soldiers and the native New Guineans.

In support of his argument for an Australian origin for Tok Pisin (and other varieties of Melanesian Pidgin English) Baker (1993) lists 107 features and the year of the first record of each feature in several varieties of Pacific pidgins, including the variety of Tok Pisin of New Ireland and New Britain (his Dutch New Guinea). Of these features nine appear first in the islands region of Papua New Guinea, eleven do not appear at all in that region, fourteen do not occur in Queensland plantation pidgin, and five do not occur in either. Later he uses the argument that because most of the features are attested earlier in Australia than in Melanesia, the direction of transmission is obvious (1996:251).

I am not arguing for any particular historical origin for Tok Pisin. Rather, I am arguing that a particular model of language interaction in a contact situation best describes how and explains why the contact varieties develop as they do. Baker says that pidgins are created (1993:6), but they are created out of the linguistic repertoires of the speakers involved. Most of the so-called features discussed by Baker are actually content morphemes, which may come from any language in a contact situation according to the theories presented here. The lexical-conceptual and morphosyntactic structures of Tok Pisin as spoken in the New Guinea islands are Austronesian, the result of a composite matrix language formed by the speakers based on their own similar L1s. During my years in the area, I never heard even one of the structures Baker reports for Dutch New Guinea. He lists *man bush* as occurring in Dutch New Guinea before it occurs in Queensland. The form currently found in former Dutch New Guinea is **man bilong bus,** structured according to the Austronesian substrate languages. Anticipating one argument against his evidence for the direction of transmission, Baker writes,

> It might be argued that the data examined give an exaggerated impression of the importance of Australia simply because literate Anglophones with the time and inclination to record samples of pidginized speech were always more numerous in Australia than in other Pacific territories; had those who visited and worked in the islands left more substantial written records, it might have been possible to show that some of the MPE features attributed to Australian influence above had in fact originated in the islands. (1993:59)

As if responding to that argument, he continues that an equivalent amount of additional material gathered since he first compiled the data has revealed no change in the direction of influence, even though one would expect additional material to turn up more evidence if it were there. This justification does not follow from the facts. If there was an absence of written material because such material did not exist before the additional data were compiled, there is no reason to expect it to materialize as more data are gathered. In fact, Baker's own statements support the extended matrix language frame model as applied to pidgins and creoles. With reference to the person and number distinctions of Tok Pisin he says,

> There is no doubt whatsoever that the three-way distinction between the dual, the first-person plural inclusive and the first-person plural exclusive found in MPE mirrors the distinctions made in the relevant Melanesian languages, as Keesing (1988) describes in detail and with justification. However, it is definitely NOT the case that these distinctions were made from the start. (1996:254)

The fact that such distinctions entered Tok Pisin after the speakers returned to New Guinea and the language spread to a larger body of Austronesian language speakers is evidence of the influence of the L1s of those speakers, both at the conceptual and the morphological levels. The same distinctions did not develop in other pidgin varieties where the L1s of those speakers lacked the distinction. Singler (1993) argues from sociohistorical factors involved in Afro-American varieties that even late arrivals in a pidgin/creole formation process can influence the language. The L1s of later arrivals in the pidgin formation can become part of the composite matrix language of that pidgin and thereby may influence its structure.

Mosel (1980) discusses the controversy of Tolai influence on Tok Pisin, noting that such scholars as Wurm, Fry, and Salisbury support strong Tolai influence, whereas Mühlhäusler does not.[31] Mühlhäusler's opinion is that the origin of Tok Pisin is in Samoa, but Mosel points out that of the 6,000 Samoan plantation workers from New Guinea up until 1914, over half were from New Ireland and 20 percent from the Gazelle Peninsula area. Thus, it is not surprising that even the Samoan Plantation Pidgin was heavily influenced by the languages of New Ireland and East New Britain.

Although primarily English-based in its lexicon, Tok Pisin is not mutually intelligible with English and must be learned by English speakers like any other foreign language, though it is easier for English speakers to learn than for speakers of other languages because of the extensive English lexical content. Tok Pisin is, in fact, more different from English than the related dialects of Melanesian Pidgin English in the Solomon Islands and Vanuatu because their access to English was withdrawn when the speakers left plantations manganged by English-speaking overseers to return to the German controlled islands of New Ireland and New Britain. The structural basis for Tok Pisin (its morphosyntactic frame) is the common grammatical structure of the Austronesian languages native to most of the original speakers of this pidgin. The center for the development of Tok Pisin in New Guinea was in the islands of New Britain and New Ireland, the area of the earliest and most extensive contact with Europeans and the area from which most of the plantation laborers from New Guinea were recruited. This same area was also the possible center from which the Austronesian languages in Papua New Guinea originally spread (Capell 1969).

The Extended MLF Model for Pidgin Formation Applied to Tok Pisin

The extended matrix language frame model explains the morphosyntactic frame developed during pidgin/creole formation as will be illustrated with examples from Tok Pisin and Tigak. Myers-Scotton (1997a) suggests that there is a continuum of bilingual speech, with codeswitching at one end and language attrition at the other. Other language contact

---

[31]Mühlhäusler (1982) does acknowledge the Tolai and other Austronesian influence on the Tok Pisin spoken in the New Britain and New Ireland area.

phenomena such as convergence, second language acquisition, and pidgin/creole formation are also on this continuum.

Although pidgins and creoles have often been characterized as having the vocabulary of one language and the grammar of another, no pidgin or creole yet studied can be shown to fit that description exactly. Rather, all pidgins and creoles have both morphemes and lexical structure from more than one language. Thus, pidgins/creoles are closely related to both codeswitching and convergence on this continuum of bilingual speech since "codeswitching shows morphemes from two or more languages, and convergence shows lexical structure from more than one language" (Myers-Scotton 1998:290). A pidgin is also related to second-language learning, but with important differences. A pidgin language is learned as a second language, but unlike normal second language acquisition situations, pidgin learners do not have complete access to the target language(s). Another difference is that the speakers are not deliberately trying to acquire a single, specific language. Instead they are trying to communicate with each other in a contact situation involving multiple languages. The degree to which each language involved in the pidgin/creole development will influence the outcome depends on many factors, both linguistic and sociopolitical. The degree of influence of individual languages may also change during the life cycle of the pidgin/creole development.

The matrix language in a pidgin/creole is a COMPOSITE MATRIX LANGUAGE (CML) developed because "proficiency in at least one of the major contributing languages is problematic" (Jake and Myers-Scotton 1998). The most obvious problematic language in pidgin/creole formation in terms of a structural frame is the superstrate because most speakers involved in pidgin formation have limited access to this language, and it is the grammatical structure of the superstrate that is particularly inaccessible to them. (If the superstrate language were readily accessible to all speakers needing to communicate, it would be the language they could use, and there would be no motivation for pidgin development.) A composite matrix language is an abstract grammatical frame composed of features from more than one language (Myers-Scotton 1997b). For speakers developing a pidgin/creole, the languages most available to them are the substrate languages, their own L1s; but there are typically many substrate languages, and no single substrate may be widely known by those needing to communicate. Thus, the substrates compete with each other to provide grammatical structure, resulting in the composite frame (the composite matrix language) composed of features from more than one language (Myers-Scotton 2001). In pidgin/creole formation, then, this composite matrix language becomes one of the targets for speakers learning the pidgin.

However, another target is the superstrate. The language of those in positions of power carries prestige and the possibility of social advancement, so whatever is accessible of that language becomes a target of acquisition, too. What is available from the superstrate is the vocabulary, in particular the semantically salient content (and related early system) morphemes. The substrate speakers hear these superstrate content morphemes and can attach meaning to them in order to express their intentions. Since the grammatical structure of the superstrate is not readily available to them, the form in which the intentions are expressed takes the pattern of the substrate. Thus, the superstrate content morphemes may be reanalyzed to fit grammatical slots in the structure of the developing pidgin/creole (Myers-Scotton 2001). This view of the superstrate as a target differs from that of Bickerton (1977, 1999) and Winford (1997) of the superstrate as a missed target and the resulting pidgin/creole as the result of failed or imperfect learning of that target.

Because the speaker of a pidgin/creole is learning a second language, the process is similar to a second language acquisition process, except that the target in second language acquisition is not an inaccessible superstrate as it is in pidgin/creole formation. Thus, it is reasonable to expect processes of transfer, interference, code-mixing, convergence, and other aspects of second language acquisition to be operative in pidgin/creole development, but with a different result. Because the language being acquired (a pidgin/creole) has morphemes from more than one language, speaking that pidgin/creole is similar to codeswitching, and because the matrix language is a composite language based (primarily) on congruent aspects of the languages involved, there are characteristics of convergence.

The formulation of a composite matrix language is possible if one assumes an abstract lexical structure as formulated in the Abstract Level model (Myers-Scotton and Jake 1995) and a modular model of language production, such as the model discussed in chapter 3 (Levelt 1989). According to Levelt's model, language production occurs at three levels: the conceptual level, in which our intentions are specified; the functional level, in which lemmas supporting those intentions are selected and directions for the morphosyntactic structure are sent by the lemmas to the formulator; and the positional level, in which phonological forms are selected and positioned. Lemmas are "abstract entries in a speaker's mental lexicon...[which] include all the non-phonological aspects of an item's lexical information" (Myers-Scotton 1995:235–236). Lemmas contain the lexical-conceptual structure, the predicate-argument structure, and the morphological realization patterns for each lexeme. The different abstract levels contained in a lemma are accessed at different stages of the language production process.

During language production the information accessed at one stage can be separated and combined with information accessed at different stages from lemmas of different languages.[32] Woolford partially describes the result of this splitting and recombining of levels for Tok Pisin, stating that

> although a word may be English or German in its outer form, its meaning has often been changed to various degrees to fit native categories of meaning, and its pronunciation has of course been altered in line with indigenous phonological systems. (1979a:15)

Since the production process is carried out in stages, a bilingual speaker can access lemmas from different languages at different stages. The stage at which a particular language is accessed determines what types of morphemes from that language will occur at the surface level.

The composite matrix language of Tok Pisin

It is also true that pidgin/creole "grammars usually select unmarked options of the contact situations in which they develop" (Mufwene 1991:136); however, "the unmarked or least marked typological option in the contact situation may not correspond to the unmarked or least marked option in the lexifier" (p. 134). With a pidgin or creole, a composite matrix language will be drawn from the common morphosyntactic structures and semantic conceptions of the languages involved. Since the morphosyntactic structure of the superstrate is the least accessible aspect of that language for the speakers of the developing pidgin, the speakers incorporate the common structural aspects of their own L1s into the pidgin. In contrast, the phonological forms are the most accessible aspects of the superstrate. The accessibility of the phonological forms is one reason that most of the actual morphemes in a pidgin/creole come from the superstrate. The accessibility of the meaning associated with superstrate content morphemes provides the link to substrate morphemes with some degree of congruence at the conceptual level. Those substrate morphemes, in turn, project the morphosyntactic frame of the composite matrix language into which the superstrate morphemes are inserted.

The fact that there are usually multiple substrate languages involved in pidgin/creole formation means that these languages are in competition in terms of the morphosyntactic structure they contribute. For this reason, those structural features that are common to more substrate languages are

---

[32]A composite matrix language is also produced in cases of second-language acquisition (cf. Bolonyai 1998). A matrix language turnover is especially evident as a speaker grows more proficient in the second language (and possibly loses proficiency in the first language). This turnover process also produces a composite matrix language with features from both the L1 and L2.

more likely to be incorporated into the composite matrix language. (Examples of substrate morphosyntactic structural influence on Tok Pisin are given under "Austronesian Features of Tok Pisin" later in this chapter. For additional examples of substrate structural influences on Tok Pisin, see Crowley 1987, Dutton and Bourke 1987, Hall 1966, Mühlhäusler 1982, Reesink 1987, Rickford and McWhorter 1997, Romaine 1987, Siegel 1997, 1999, and Wolfers 1971. For examples of substrate structural influences on other jargons and pidgins/creoles, see Lumsden 1994, Siegel 1998, Silverstein 1972, and Thomason 1980.) The more homogeneous the languages in contact are, the more the common structural and conceptual features will be reinforced in the developing composite matrix language so that the resulting composite matrix language will more closely resemble those languages. Mufwene describes resulting contact languages under conditions of homogeneity and diversity.

> When the substrate languages were largely of the same typology, their common features have often prevailed over alternatives provided in the lexifier. When there was typological diversity, competition of features was more likely to be determined by factors other than convergence, e.g., salience or regularity....Variation often followed from such typological diversity. (1996:103)

Singler adds, "When the homogeneity is great enough, even elements of substrate grammar that are highly marked will be present in the pidgin" (1988:45). The Austronesian languages among whose speakers Tok Pisin developed are extremely homogeneous. This homogeneity has, indeed, allowed marked features into Tok Pisin. In fact, Mufwene (1990) observes that Melanesian pidgins and creoles have many features that are considered marked in a universal typology, but those same features are unmarked in the contact situation because of their frequency in the languages involved. The structural and conceptual similarities of Tok Pisin and its Austronesian substrate languages have often been noted (Churchill 1911, Codrington 1974, Keesing 1988, 1991, Mühlhäusler 1979). Where there is lack of homogeneity in the substrate languages, variation occurs in Tok Pisin. I will discuss these marked features and the variations caused by differences in the substrates in the following sections.

Situational factors can also affect which language supplies the grammatical structure, and this can change with time and circumstances (e.g., the particular languages involved, the relative prestige of the languages involved, or the numbers of speakers of each language). Mufwene emphasizes in his founders' principle the importance of the "vernaculars spoken by the populations that founded the colonies in which they developed"

(1996:84) as the sources of structural features of pidgins/creoles. He gives the example of Saramaccan with its mostly Kwa-like features and few Bantu-like ones because the Bantu populations were late arrivals in the colony. (As noted in the first section in this chapter, Singler (1993) expresses just the opposite view based on Afro-American features due to late arrivals on the scene.) Mufwene does acknowledge that various population mixes do account for some variations between creoles. Based on earlier changes in Tok Pisin and those currently observable, I maintain that the composite matrix language can change as a pidgin/creole develops and expands in function and structure. The composite matrix language of Tok Pisin is still changing as its use spreads into new territory and as its body of speakers, including many with very different L1s, increases in number. The linguistic repertoires of Tok Pisin speakers are also changing. The growing body of Papua New Guineans educated in English is influencing Tok Pisin structure and introducing changes in its composite matrix language. However, an acceptable standard Tok Pisin is also developing, primarily due to widespread media use. This change of the composite matrix language is also explainable under the MLF model, and the fact that such a change in the direction of English may be in progress can explain the differences developing between urban and rural Tok Pisin described by Romaine (1992).

Where there are speakers of many different first languages contributing to the formation of the pidgin/creole, the most common features from those L1s may be expected as features of the composite matrix language of the developing pidgin. The variability common in the initial phase of pidgin formation shows the influence of the various L1 substrate languages. Each speaker's native language is initially the matrix language for that speaker attempting to communicate in a contact situation. In the case of Tok Pisin, the fact that most of the speakers involved in the early stages of development were native speakers of Austronesian languages with many common structural features may have reinforced this common grammatical base as the composite matrix language. Siegel lists the following conditions under which transfer from the substrate languages may occur:

> Transfer is more likely in naturalistic settings....
> Transfer is more likely when speaking to members of one's own ethnic group....
> When corresponding features are similar, both positive and negative transfer may be more likely....
> Transfer is more successful as a communications strategy among speakers of typologically similar languages. (1999:7–8)

All four of Siegel's conditions are met in the situation under which Tok Pisin was formed and the situation in which it is currently used. I contend that Tok Pisin developed in its present form in its own territory as speakers from the same ethnic background and very similar languages communicated with each other concerning their daily affairs. Siegel lists seven substrate features (from Keesing 1988) found in Melanesian Pidgin and notes that all these features are present in most of the substrate languages. Some of these features are the verb phrase marker, transitive verb suffix, possessive constructions, and exclusive and dual number distinctions for pronouns. These features as examples of substrate constructions are each discussed below. He also lists the following four substrate features that are missing in Tok Pisin: the distinction between alienable and inalienable possession, articles, a reciprocal prefix, and adjectives following the nouns they modify. The explanation for the absence of these features is that they are marked features and are variable in the substrate languages. I do not address the reciprocal prefix here, but the other three features are explainable under the extended matrix language frame model applied to Tok Pisin in the sections that follow.

Simplification has often been cited as a characteristic of pidgins, and simplification normally involves the use of unmarked features (which are more common and therefore more likely to be understood). But the "degree of simplification will depend...on the degree to which marked features of languages they already know are shared with marked features of their interlocutors' languages" (Thomason and Kaufman 1988:192). The marked features which are likely to be incorporated into a pidgin will be the ones common to all the languages involved (p. 52). Winford calls this "substrate retention" (1997:144). Kay and Sankoff describe "contact vernaculars" (including pidgins) as "functional adaptations to particular communication situations" (1974:61) and suggest that such languages are "structurally limited" (p. 62). Because of such limitations they claim that pidgins/creoles are more likely to show universal traits than other languages. Some of the universal traits Kay and Sankoff ascribe to pidgins are "shallowness of phonology" (p. 62), "propositional qualifiers...in surface structure exterior to the propositions they qualify, or not at all" (p. 64), and "inflectional morphology [which] tends to be lacking" (p. 68). However, all these characteristics also describe Austronesian languages. Speakers from many different Austronesian languages contributed to the formation of Tok Pisin. Many features of the languages, although different in details, pattern according to a common underlying structure containing the very features described above. Therefore, "where syntactic patterns happen to be shared by some, or all, of the input languages, nothing new needs to be learned, and congruence of functions will help to ensure their retention" (Hancock 1993:187). This core of common Austronesian semantic base and syntactic structure forms the basis of the composite matrix language of Tok Pisin. This composite matrix language controls the morphosyntactic structure of the language. At points of congruence with English syntax, English reinforces the Austronesian structure. Specific features of the composite matrix language for Tok Pisin will be discussed in "Austronesian Features of Tok Pisin."

What seems simple to some people can be deceiving. Although there are many points of similarity between Austronesian languages and English (such as basic SVO word order), there are also many points of dissimilarity. These points of dissimilarity are often stumbling blocks to the native English speaker learning Tok Pisin. The high percentage of English lexical content gives many English speakers the impression that Tok Pisin is a simple language. For them L1 interference sometimes causes mistakes of interpretation resulting from incongruences, especially at the abstract conceptual level. For example, in Tok Pisin **lukim** and **painim** come from the English phonetic forms *look* and *find*. However, the meanings in Tok Pisin, 'find something' and 'look/search for something', respectively, are just the opposite of the English meanings. Example (115a) gives the correct Tok Pisin statement, and (115b) gives the most common (and incorrect) statement of a native English speaker trying to express the same meaning.

(115) a. **mi bin *painim* na *painim*, tasol mi no *lukim***
 1SG PST look and look but 1SG NEG find
 'I've been looking and looking, but I didn't find [it].'

b. *****mi bin *lukim* na *lukim*, tasol mi no *painim****

Because the phonological shape (the positional level) of the Tok Pisin forms is so similar to English forms with related meanings, the mistaken expectation of the native English speaker is that the semantics (the conceptual level) are also the same. Similarly, the native English speaker often utters (116a) thinking he/she is saying that someone is dead, when it may only mean a person is unconscious, numb, or has fainted. The correct Tok Pisin statement is (116b).

(116) a. **em i dai**

　　b. **em i dai pinis**
　　　 3SG PM die CMP
　　　 'He's dead.'

Answers to negative questions can also be confusing to expatriates speaking Tok Pisin. The Tok Pisin response is based on the Austronesian conceptual pattern of responding by expressing agreement or disagreement with the negative statement expressed in the question. The appropriate responses to (117a) are given in (117b) and (117c).

(117) a. **yu no laik pis?**
　　　 2SG NEG like/want fish
　　　 'Do you not like/want fish?'

　　b. **nogat (mi laik pis)**
　　　 no 1SG like fish
　　　 'No (I do like/want fish).'

　　c. **tru (mi no liak pis)**
　　　 yes 1SG NEG like fish
　　　 'Yes (I do not like/want fish).'

With respect to this construction, the Tok Pisin matrix language is a composite of the Austronesian level of lexical-conceptual structure realized with English phonological forms.

It is also worth noting that there are criteria other than structural ones for identifying the matrix language. Myers-Scotton discusses social and cultural factors (1993a:232) and speaker judgments (1995) which also reinforce this designation. (The designation of the matrix language, however, is ultimately based on structural criteria, such as the Morpheme Order and System Morpheme Principles stated in chapter 3.) These factors certainly apply to the composite matrix language of Tok Pisin. Even though kinship terms in Tok Pisin come primarily from English, the English morphemes are reconfigured to extend the semantic field to correspond to the Austronesian culturally determined meanings. For example, **papa** 'father' is used in Tok Pisin to refer to uncles and to cousins of the father's generation as well as to a person's biological father. This extended reference causes great confusion among many expatriates (and sometimes more than confusion, as when I became very angry with our gardener for requesting money to bury his father—his third father). Speaker judgments also support a substrate composite matrix language for Tok Pisin. Papua New Guineans quickly express their opinions that Tok Pisin is their own language—a product of Papua New Guinea. I have heard many Papua New Guineans remark that a given phrase is **olsem tok ples bilong mi** 'just like my village language'. This similarity in conceptual and morphosyntactic structure may be one reason it is so easy to codeswitch between a vernacular and Tok Pisin. Most village dwellers who speak Tok Pisin will protest that they do not know English, but they will readily converse in Tok Pisin, which is full of English phonological forms.

Constituent and morpheme types in Tok Pisin

The types of constituents defined for codeswitching situations (matrix language islands, matrix language + embedded language mixed constituents, and embedded language islands) will not occur in the formation stages of a pidgin/creole because no single language can be identified as the matrix language. Although many speakers of Tok Pisin do not know the grammatical forms of English or the semantic details of English lexemes, they do hear the vocabulary and learn a basic meaning for each form. The superstrate is the one language accessible in common (to some limited extent) to all speakers involved in pidgin genesis. Most of the morphemes in a pidgin/creole come from the superstrate, making it unlikely that a long constituent of many morphemes from a single contributing substrate language will occur in the pidgin/creole. However, since any contributing language can be an embedded language, embedded language islands (including single lexemes) can come from any of the languages involved. Because the matrix language in a pidgin/creole is a composite of multiple substrate languages (with superstrate phonological forms), individual substrate languages are also embedded languages. For this reason, what might be called mixed constituents in a developing pidgin/creole are those constituents that contain morphemes from different embedded languages (substrate or superstrate),[33] but with the controlling composite matrix language setting the grammatical frame. All the examples given throughout this book illustrate this fact and lend support to Hypothesis (4a), which states that during pidgin/creole formation most embedded language islands from individual substrate languages are single lexemes or short phrases due to the extensive use of superstrate content morphemes.

---

[33]The formula for a mixed constituent in a developing pidgin/creole might be $EL_i + EL_j$, in which i and j are any two different languages in the pidgin/creole contact situation. This formula would replace the matrix language + embedded language formula for codeswitching situations.

If the morphosyntactic structure of Tok Pisin (the composite matrix language) is primarily from the Austronesian substrate, what are the sources of the individual lexical forms? In her relexification theory Lefebvre (1997) states that a lexical entry from a substrate language is copied phonologically from the lexifier language but retains the substrate semantic and syntactic features. She implies that only the phonological form comes from the superstrate and does not explain how the superstrate phonological form is selected. Gilman (1985) espouses selection over simplification as the mechanism of producing pidgin/creole lexical forms and proposes that characteristics such as meaning, markedness, and length influence the selection of particular forms from the donor language over others. He specifies that core vocabulary, shorter forms, and unmarked forms are selected before others. These descriptions are vague, however, and there are many exceptions to them. The criterion of being unmarked is often cited as a characteristic of pidgin/creole features. What is usually implied by this characteristic is that the feature is common in the languages of the world (a typological criterion) or that it occurs frequently in a particular language (text count frequency). In the Prague School tradition a marked feature is one with a positive designation (such as [+nasal]), while in the second language acquisition literature unmarked features are those acquired first (implying that they are easier to learn). In fact, morphosyntactic features that are unmarked in the typological sense of being common among the languages involved in pidgin/creole formation are selected as features of the composite matrix language as discussed above. However, neither Gilman's selection nor Lefebvre's relexification explain how or predict which individual morpheme will come from which language. It will be pointed out below that core vocabulary, in fact, is more likely to come from the lexifier language, whereas culturally specific vocabulary comes from the substrate languages.

Other researchers have come closer to predicting which features are selected and why. Huttar (1975) reports that the linguistic substratum is of primary importance in the semantic structures of pidgins and creoles. His study involves the comparison of the meanings of morphemes in forty-three pidgins/creoles and the languages associated with them and shows the importance of a correspondence at the conceptual level between the substrate and the superstrate form used. Bock (1987) and Fay and Cutler (1977) found in psycholinguistic studies that phonetic similarity in more than one language makes a form more likely to appear in a pidgin. Both of these characteristics (semantic congruence and phonetic similarity) do contribute to the determination of the source of individual morphemes, but stating such characteristics still does not answer the questions of why and how particular morphemes are selected.

The Abstract Level and 4-M theories provide principles from which more precise predictions can be made concerning what forms will be selected or copied, and from which languages. Jake and Myers-Scotton (1998) hypothesize that content and indirectly elected system morphemes (those system morphemes required to fulfill the conceptual intent of a content morpheme) can come from any of the languages involved in the pidgin formation. The phonological shape of early system morphemes can come from the superstrate, but the morphemes will pattern structurally according to the composite matrix language. This hypothesis explains why most pidgins and creoles are heavily lexified from the superstrate language since the content morphemes of that language are the most accessible to the entire range of substrate speakers.[34] The superstrate is also the most prestigious of the languages involved (or the language of the most powerful segment of communicators in the contact situation). This position of power makes the superstrate a likely target for vocabulary. Superstrate lexemes, however, are not adopted unchanged. Many content morphemes are reanalyzed at some level of abstract lexical structure (see Myers-Scotton 2001). For example, the English lexemes *hand* and *leg* are adopted into Tok Pisin as **han** 'hand/arm' and **lek** 'foot/leg', but they are reanalyzed to fit the Austronesian semantic range including the entire arm and hand and the entire leg and foot. (The examples **han** and **lek** also illustrate how the borrowed forms are adapted in Tok Pisin according to the L1 phonological systems of the speakers. The consonant cluster in *hand* is reduced and the final obstruent in *leg* is devoiced. Winford notes that it is common to find "re-analysis of superstrate forms in terms of substrate semantic categories" (1997:146). I also noted this fact with the example of **papa** 'father/uncle' in Tok Pisin. Notice, however, that this reanalysis is not unrestricted. In the examples above involving kinship terms and body parts (and in the pronominal system discussed below) there is still some congruence in the lexical-conceptual structure. At least part of the meaning of each of these Tok Pisin lexemes is shared with the English lexeme from which the Tok Pisin form is copied. This shared semantic content supports Hypothesis (3c), which states that there will be some congruence in lexical-conceptual structure for phonetically similar forms used.

A comparison of the pronominal systems of Tok Pisin and other pidgins of the region also illustrates the fact that the composite matrix language may be

---

[34]The relexification hypothesis also claims that most of the lexemes of a pidgin/creole come from the superstrate. However, that theory does not specify what types of superstrate morphemes are used or what functions they serve in the pidgin/creole. Neither does it provide any explanation as to how a particular superstrate lexeme is chosen to be copied into the pidgin/creole.

different when languages with different structures contribute to the composite matrix language. Some speakers of South Pacific pidgins do not make all the number distinctions found in Tok Pisin. Mosel (1980:60) reports that Samoan Plantation Pidgin (which he calls "the direct predecessor of Tok Pisin") has neither the dual nor the trial forms found in Tok Pisin, whereas Bichelamar and Cape York Creole both have dual forms, but no trial. Each of these cases is a reflection of the substrate languages involved in their formation.

Although Baker (1996) admits that the number and inclusive/exclusive distinctions in the varieties of Melanesian Pidgin English spoken in Papua New Guinea reflect the same distinctions made in the Melanesian substrate languages, he maintains that these features did not originate in Papua New Guinea, but in Queensland. He argues that "pidginization and creolization are the result of...language creation" (p. 254), not substrate influences. However, in explaining this creation he continues by saying that "the earlier dual form *me two fellow*, [was] created by Melanesians working in Queensland out of *me* and the by then established numeral *two fellow*" (p. 255). His explanation is still only a descriptive statement, and the process he describes is that of speakers using morphemes from one variety and conceptual and structural patterns from another. In addition, it just happens that the conceptual and structural patterns in this case are the same as the Melanesian substrate languages of the speakers involved in that creation. Even the morphological process of suffixing a number form to a person form patterns like the Tigak trial forms given in table 4.1 of the previous chapter. Furthermore, if the distinctions found in Tok Pisin did come from Queensland Plantation English, why were they not maintained in the other varieties of Melanesian Pidgin English whose speakers were also present on the plantations in Queensland and in Cape York Creole? And why do the distinctions found in the various South Pacific pidgins parallel the distinctions found in the majority of the native languages of those speakers?

Content morphemes may also come from the substrate languages. Todd noted that such lexemes usually relate to "local culture and conditions" (1974:56). Checking through Mihalic (1971) confirms this observation for Tok Pisin. His categorized list of fish and sea products is typical. Of the sixty-seven names of fish in his list, forty-three are of Austronesian origin. The results are similar for the lists of animals, birds, trees, etc. Most of these Austronesian lexemes refer to cultural items or activities for which the lexifier language has no terms. On the other hand, in Mihalic's list of mechanical and engineering terms, all are from English. In this case, the lexemes represent cultural concepts for which the substrate languages had no terms. A sampling of Austronesian content lexemes found in Tok

Pisin is given in (118). Most of these terms in Tok Pisin are nouns, a few are adjectives, and fewer yet are verbs.

(118)
abus	'meat'	(N)
aibika, aupa	names of local greens	(N)
balus	'bird/airplane'	(N)
diwai	'wood/stick'	(N)
galip	a type of nut	(N)
garamut	'log drum'	(N)
lapun	'old/old one'	(N, Adj)
limbum	'bamboo (for floors)'	(N)
luluai	'village leader'	(N)
malolo	'rest'	(V, N)
mau	'ripe'	(Adj)
malumalu	'soft'	(Adj)
pangal	'sago palm stem'	(N)
umben	'fish net'	(N)

Three-fourths of Tok Pisin vocabulary comes from English (Ross 1992:363). The Tok Pisin variety spoken in the New Ireland/New Britain area of Papua New Guinea contains a few German content morphemes (such as **beten** 'pray' instead of **pre,** which is used in the Tok Pisin of other locations) incorporated when Germany was the superstrate power in that region. Of the remaining vocabulary, most of the Austronesian lexical items are from New Britain and New Ireland (361). Mihalic (1971:56) claims that 15 percent of Tok Pisin vocabulary is from New Britain and New Ireland.[35] He often does not identify a single language source but lists the source as being the Gazelle Peninsula. This is wise, since much of the vocabulary of Tolai (the language of the Gazelle Peninsula) and New Ireland languages are similar. (New Ireland is traditionally considered to be the origin of the Tolai people.) Many of the words attributed to Tolai or Duke of York are also found in the languages of northern New Ireland. For example, Ross (1992) lists the source for **diwai** 'tree/wood' and **liklik** 'little' as southern New Ireland. The Tigak words are *iai* and *laklik*, respectively. He gives no source for the Tok Pisin word **matmat** 'cemetery', but the same word in Tigak is *matmaat*. The difficulty of assigning a source language even extends to lexemes considered to be from English, such as

---

[35]Laycock (1970) gives slightly different figures from both Ross and Mihalic with 77 percent from English, 11 percent from Tolai, and 6 percent from other Austronesian languages. Hall attributes as much as 20 percent of Tok Pisin vocabulary to the indigenous languages, saying "the highest percentage of words from native (substratum) languages that I have come across so far is in neo-Melanesia" (1966:94).

tok 'talk', which in Tigak is *etok*. Romaine (1989b:381) gives the example of **bel** 'stomach, belly, seat of emotions' in Tok Pisin, which Mihalic also attributes to English. However, the Tolai word *bala* has the same meanings. In such cases there may not be a single source. As noted above, such similarities in phonological shape among the substrate languages and between English and the substrates only reinforce the possibility of those forms being selected by pidgin speakers.

Content morphemes from the superstrate can be reanalyzed as system morphemes in the pidgin/creole. For example, the English pronoun *he* is reanalyzed in Tok Pisin as a predicate marker **i** based on the convergence of this form with the Austronesian feature of a verb phrase subject agreement pronoun.

Indirectly elected (early system) morphemes from the superstrate may be reanalyzed according to the substrate structure also. For example, the combination of content morpheme verb and its indirectly elected verbal particle, such as English *away* in *throw away,* is reanalyzed to become part of a single Tok Pisin verb form **troawe** 'throw away'. Example (119a) illustrates the English early system past participle *been* reanalyzed as the Tok Pisin late system preverbal past tense marker following the Austronesian structural pattern shown in (119b). This example verifies Hypothesis (3b), which says that some English content and early system morphemes are reanalyzed to serve as content or early or late system morphemes in Tok Pisin and can thus fill Austronesian system morpheme slots.

(119) a. **mi   bin   slip**   [TP]
         1SG PST   sleep

   b. *naga   pon   matei*   [Tigak]
         1SG.S.AGR PERF sleep
         'I slept/was sleeping.'

Where there is not congruence between the substrate and superstrate indirectly elected morphemes, the morphemes will also not appear in the pidgin/creole. In Austronesian languages like Tigak the article is indirectly elected by the noun. It gives little semantic content such as definiteness or indefiniteness but merely serves as a noun marker. In English, articles distinguish between definite and indefinite. Thus, without the semantic congruence, articles do not appear in Tok Pisin. Instead, demonstratives and quantifiers serve the purpose of making the definite/indefinite distinction in Tok Pisin because these morphemes are semantically congruent between the two languages (see also (127) and

(128)). Except in locative expressions, the article is always used with a Tigak noun.

(120) ta   piu   tang   ian   [Tigak]
the/a dog   the/a fish

(121) a. Ø dok i   kaikai-m Ø man   [TP]
      dog PM bite-TZ   man
'A/the dog bites/bit a/the man.'

   b. *dispela* dok i   kaikai-m *wanpela* man
      this   dog PM bite-TZ   one   man
'*This* dog is biting/bit *a* man.'

Structurally assigned morphemes (late system morphemes, such as English third-person singular -*s*) from the superstrate language cannot be reanalyzed, so they do not occur in pidgins and creoles (except as part of an unanalyzed content form). I have no examples of late system English morphemes in Tok Pisin, which supports Hypothesis (3a) stating that only content and early system morphemes from English occur in Tok Pisin and Hypothesis (3d) stating that no late system morphemes from a superstrate will occur in Tok Pisin. Where there is a choice between a pattern using content morphemes and one using system morphemes, the pattern using content morphemes will be selected. In the expression 'it's raining' English normally uses a dummy pronoun construction as in the first example of (122a). Tigak also uses a construction with a dummy pronoun (122b), but both Tigak and English have alternate constructions using content morphemes. Tok Pisin uses only the content morpheme choice, avoiding the dummy pronoun construction entirely (122c).

(122) a. 'it's raining'   or   'the rain is falling'   [English]

   b. ga   langit or   ta   langit ga   puka   [Tigak]
     3SG.S.AGR rain   ART rain   3SG.S.AGR fall

   c. *em ren   but   ren i   pundaun   [TP]
     3SG rain   rain PM fall

Austronesian Features of Tok Pisin

Typical Austronesian features exemplified by Tigak in New Ireland were described in chapter 4. In this section I will demonstrate examples of these Austronesian features which are duplicated in Tok Pisin. Appendix 2 gives additional examples of many of these features from other Austronesian languages of New Ireland and New Britain.

Phonology, syllable structure, and stress

The phonemic inventory of Tok Pisin is simpler than that of many Austronesian languages in that there are fewer diphthongs in Tok Pisin. The consonant inventory, however, is closer to that of English; Tok Pisin has more consonants than most Austronesian languages. Some of these consonant phonemes may have come from English, or the set may be a combination of the consonants from a number of substrate languages. The phonemic inventory for Tok Pisin is given in (123).

(123) /a b d e f g h i j k l m n ŋ o p r s t u v w y ai au oi/

Those consonants that do not occur in all the substrate languages may still occur in Tok Pisin because different ones are missing from the different Austronesian languages. For example, /f/ does not occur in Tigak, but it does occur in the neighboring Kara language. Instead, Tigak has a bilabial fricative. In Tok Pisin /f/ only occurs word initially, and then only in a restricted set of words such as the number **faiv** 'five'. In all other environments (and at the beginning of most words) it is realized as [p]. Other consonants that only occur word initially are /h j y/. The /v/ of Tok Pisin is often realized as [b] intervocalically. For Tigak speakers who use [v] in the Tigak language, it remains [v]. However, as in Tigak, the /v/ of Tok Pisin often becomes [b] word initially for Tigaks speaking Tok Pisin. The Tok Pisin /j/ becomes [s] in all but word-initial environments. Other L1 influences are evidenced by the word-final devoicing of /b d g/, as in [ra*p*] 'rub', [ro*t*] 'road', and [do*k*] 'dog', and by the prenasalization of these obstruents in other environments, as in [ta*m*bu] 'taboo' and [si*n*daun] 'to sit'. Tigaks pronounce 'rice' as [dais], following the L1 rule r → d / #__. These pronunciation patterns are widespread, but they do vary in details according to the L1 of the Tok Pisin speaker, supporting Hypothesis (1b), which says that some variation found among Tok Pisin speakers can be explained by differences in the L1s that are transferred to the pidgin by the learners.

The syllable structure of Tok Pisin follows the basic Austronesian pattern of (C)V(C). However, there are variations in syllable structure that reflect the L1 of the speakers very closely. Consonant clusters do occur in the speech of some Tok Pisin speakers, especially those whose L1s permit such clusters and those who are highly educated in English. For example, Tigaks will pronounce Tok Pisin for 'skin' and 'store' as in (124a), whereas a speaker of a Papuan language will more likely pronounce the same words as in (124b).

(124) a. **[si.kin]** 'skin'   **[si.toa]** 'store'

      b. **[skin]** 'skin'   **[stoa]** 'store'

Stress in Tok Pisin is on the first syllable of most words, and this fact can be used to identify word boundaries. Thus, the forms **waitman** 'white man' and **dispela** 'this' < English 'this fellow' are one word each in Tok Pisin. One exception is that the grammatical predicate marker **i** is never stressed, even though it is a separate form. The stress pattern also shows that the transitive suffix **-im** < English 'him' (as in **givim** 'give') is a grammatical marker and not a true pronoun. The grammatical function of these markers follows the Austronesian substrate pattern.

Word order

The basic word order of Tok Pisin is SVO, just as in English and the Austronesian substrate languages. Although the pattern parallels English in a general sense, the specifics more closely parallel the Austronesian forms. The Tok Pisin clause follows the Austronesian word order described in Formula (38) from chapter 4. The Tok Pisin formula is given here as (125).

(125) CP_{TP} → (Comp) (SADV) SUBJ NP (SADV) VP (SADV)

The most common position for a sentence adverb is at the beginning of the clause, but it may occur in the other optional positions for emphasis. The subject NP is not normally optional in Tok Pisin as it is in Austronesian languages, being omitted only in some existential or impersonal clauses, as shown in (126).

(126) **i gat**   'there is'
      i tudak pinis 'it's already dark'

Within the verb phrase the order is also parallel between the Austronesian substrate languages and Tok Pisin. In Austronesian languages the subject-agreement pronoun indicates the beginning of the predicate, and in Tok Pisin the predicate marker **i** occupies the first slot of the VP. Capell notes that the traditional label of verbal pronoun is often used for the subject agreement morpheme in Austronesian languages. He observes that

> every verb, even if it has a noun subject expressed, must be preceded by such a marker. The pattern is reproduced in Pidgin....In this, as in so many regards, Pidgin reproduces with largely English lexemes, Austronesian forms and modes of expression. (1969:49)

Wurm also supports the Austronesian source for the Tok Pisin predicate marker. Mihalic quotes Wurm as saying "the predicate marker /i/ is derived from an Austronesian particle and its usage in Pidgin corresponds largely to that of this particle in the Austronesian languages" (Mihalic 1971:24). It is this Austronesian subject-agreement pronominal that is the model for the Tok Pisin predicate marker **i**. In each case, the subject-agreement marker and the predicate marker **i** mark the beginning of the predicate in Austronesian languages and in Tok Pisin, respectively.

(127) a. **wanpela man i sutim pik** [TP]
  one   man PM shoot pig
  ___S___   ___Predicate___
  ___S___   ___V___   ___O___

b. *tang anu gi mugi tang vogo* [Tigak]
  ART man 3SG.S.AGR spear ART pig
  ___S___   ___Predicate___
  ___S___   ___V___   ___O___
  'A man spears a pig.'

The Austronesian clause does not require an overt subject, but it does require a subject-agreement pronoun as part of the verb phrase.

(128) a. **em *i* go long haus** [TP]
  3SG PM go to house

b. *(nane) gi inang lo lui* [Tigak]
  (3SG.PRN) 3SG.S.AGR go to house
  'He is going to the house.'

In many manuscripts of early Tok Pisin transcribed by English speakers, a sentence such as (128a) was written as **he he go long haus.** This form clearly shows the pattern of an overt subject plus the verb phrase subject-agreement pronoun. In Tigak clauses this same pattern occurs, as shown in (128b). Thus, Tok Pisin is following the Austronesian composite matrix language pattern even when using what is most commonly considered to be the English morpheme *he* > **i.** This use of the semantic and phonological content of an English morpheme functioning according to the common Austronesian substrate morphological and syntactic structure is another example of the composite nature of the matrix language governing Tok Pisin. This example supports Hypothesis (1a), which states that the matrix language for Tok Pisin is a composite matrix language formed by splitting the abstract levels of language structure and recombining those levels to form a grammatical frame composed of aspects from different individual languages. Most of the lexical-conceptual structure, predicate-argument structure, and morphological patterns come from the Austronesian languages, but most of the phonological forms come from English, based on some degree of lexical-conceptual congruence between English and the Austronesian substrate.

However, another explanation for the **i** predicate marker is that it comes directly from an Austronesian language, Tolai. For several reasons Tolai is the single Austronesian language that is credited with the greatest substratal influence on Tok Pisin. First, the Tolai people are located in East New Britain surrounding the former German administration center. It is a region that had early contact with Europeans and was the first language in that region to be written and described. Second, the Tolai language group is the largest in New Britain or New Ireland. Mosel (1980:122) gives the following example from Tolai and Tok Pisin as a possible source for the Tok Pisin predicate marker.

(129) Tolai: *a tabaran i limlibur*
Tok Pisin: **tambaran i limlimbur**
'the ghost took a walk'

He does not give a morpheme-by-morpheme gloss, but the **i** patterns the same in both Tolai and Tok Pisin. Other languages in the region have the same or similar morphemes. Mosel does specify that in both Duke of York dialects (spoken on the Duke of York Islands between New Britain's Gazelle Peninsula, where Tolai is spoken, and New Ireland) the third-person singular pronoun is *i*, as it is in other related Austronesian languages of the area. Codrington (1974:568), in describing the Duke of York language, recorded the pattern of the third-person singular subject pronoun *i* following the subject and introducing the verb phrase: *"Ioane i a# wanurin* John did baptize." The corresponding Tigak pronoun is *gi*, a very similar form. It is, therefore, conceivable that the Tok Pisin predicate marker **i** was taken directly from the Austronesian phonetic form so widespread among the L1s of the early speakers of Tok Pisin. The fact that the phonological shape is so similar to English *he* could have simply reinforced the selection, again supporting the lexical-conceptual congruence hypothesis (3c), which states that there must be some congruence in lexical-conceptual structure for phonetically similar forms to be used. If the source of the Tok Pisin predicate marker **i** is the third-person subject agreement marker of the Austronesian languages, this fact supports Gross's hypothesis that if the substrate is homogeneous, it can contribute its own late system morphemes to the creole (2000:67).

The use of **limlimbur** in (129) by Tok Pisin speakers on the Gazelle Peninsula around Rabaul (home area for Tolai speakers) demonstrates the hypothesis that content morphemes may come from any contributing language (Jake and Myers-Scotton 1998). The form **limlimbur** is from Tolai. Elsewhere in Papua New Guinea the form **wokabaut** (< English *walk about*) is more commonly used instead.

The tendency cross-linguistically is for SVO languages to maintain the order of the head preceding the complement or modifier. Tok Pisin also follows this head-modifier pattern in its adverb-modifier and verb-modifier constructions, illustrated in (130) and (131).

(130) a. **longwe tru** [TP]
long.way true

b. *kongo aong* [Tigak]
far very
'very far'

(131) a. **wokabaut isi-isi** [TP]
walk easy-easy
'walk slowly'

b. *pasal ananap* [Tigak]
walk slowly
'walk slowly'

The fact that English has alternate constructions with 'walk slowly' and 'slowly walk' may reinforce this substrate pattern selection since the English construction 'walk slowly' parallels the substrate pattern.

The situation with noun phrases is not as obvious because of variability in both Tok Pisin and the Austronesian substrate languages. Although the Head-Modifier order of Tok Pisin may seem on the surface to be that of English for NPs, with the adjective preceding the head noun in most cases, this order does not prevail for all constructions (see (132) and (133)). I will claim later under "The noun phrase" that alternations in the adjective-noun order in substrate languages (see the Tolai examples in (146) and (147)) provide the pattern for the alternation in Tok Pisin. The substrate complex NP construction, as in (134), and Austronesian word classifications also may contribute to the pattern allowing two different orders in Tok Pisin.

(132) **bikpela dok** [TP]
     big   dog

Other constructions in Tok Pisin clearly reflect the alternative Austronesian substrate order with the modifying word following the head noun.

(133) Tok Pisin	Tigak		Literally
tok klia	*etok apaga*	'explanation'	'talk clear'
tok ples	*etok siva*	'native language'	'talk village'
haus kuk		'kitchen'	'house cook'
mani giaman		'counterfeit money'	'money false'
mi tasol	*naniu kisang*	'just me'	'me only'

Examples (132) and (133) show that two patterns occur in Tok Pisin: ADJ N and N ADJ. Is there an explanation for this variation within the theoretical framework of this study? I believe there is. Substrate models for the differing word orders will be given in "The noun phrase" section. Another contributing factor may be the complex noun construction found in some Austronesian languages. The Tigak formula and example are repeated in (134) and (135).

(134) $NP_{[Tigak]} \rightarrow$ article N N

(135) *na lapun ulina* or *na ulina lapun* [Tigak]
     ART old.one woman   ART woman old.one
     'old woman'   'old woman'

The fact that the Austronesian pattern allows either noun to follow the other may have contributed to the analysis of the English phonological forms that serve as [adjective + noun] as being equivalent to the [noun + noun] construction from the substrate. That is, the Tok Pisin speaker may have reanalyzed the English adjective as being a noun. Support for this notion comes from the fact that Tok Pisin speakers use many English adjective forms as nouns as in (136). Both adjectives and nouns are content morphemes activated at the conceptual level.

(136) a. **nogat, mi laik dispela waitpela**
      no,   1sg like this   white.one
      'No, I want this white one.'

   b. **wanpela waitpela pik**
      one   white   pig
      'a/one white pig'

Questions in Tok Pisin do not involve wh-movement or inversion. Like the Austronesian pattern the interrogative forms are left in place.

(137) **papa i stap *we***   [TP]
     *na tamag ga **eve***   [Tigak]
     'Where is papa?'

(138) **haus bilong *husat***   [TP]
     *ta lui te **nasi***   [Tigak]
     'Whose house?'

(139) ***hamas* dok i dai pinis**   [TP]
     ***poison** ta piu ga maat*   [Tigak]
     'How many dogs died?'

(140) **yu wokim olsem bilong *wanem***   [TP]
     *nug vili auneng ina **so***   [Tigak]
     'Why are you doing this?'

The discussion and examples above demonstrate that the word order of Tok Pisin is controlled by a composite matrix language composed of structural features of the Austronesian substrate languages. The equivalent orders include the basic SVO order of clausal constituents, the presence of a VP-initial predicate marker, the head-modifier order of verbal and adverbial constituents, the alternate adjective-noun orders, and the in situ placement of interrogative forms. Details of the order of elements in the NP and VP are given below in "The noun phrase" and "The verb phrase," respectively. These details demonstrate even more clearly the Austronesian model and the composite nature of the grammatical structure of Tok Pisin.

Word categories

Tok Pisin also uses lexemes from English according to Austronesian substrate morphological frames. As with Tigak, Tok Pisin words can be multifunctional, and alternate forms are derived by reduplication and suffixation, common Austronesian morphological patterns. Reduplication is also a means of changing meaning in Tok Pisin, just as in the Austronesian languages.

(141) Tok Pisin   Tigak
    tok[36]   etok   'talk'   N, V   (conversion)
    toktok   'story'   N   (reduplication)
                 kuskuus   'story'   N from V kuus 'say'(reduplication)
    lukluk   'stare'   V (intensive) from   (reduplication)
                                             luk 'see'
    was-im   'wash'   V (transitive)   (suffixation)
    waswas   'wash'   V (intransitive)   (reduplication)
    isi   maluak   'soft'
    isi(isi) (mal)maluak   'easy'   (reduplication)

The noun phrase

A complete noun phrase formula for Tok Pisin can be stated generally as (142). However, some Tok Pisin nouns are modified with a following adjective, as in (143b). The Tigak NP structure is repeated from (134) as (144). A different pattern is illustrated by the Tolai NP formula in (146), which more closely resembles that of Tok Pisin. (See appendix 2 for other examples of Austronesian noun phrases.)

(142) NP_{TP} → (demonstrative) (quantifier) (adjective) N (possessive)

(143) a. **dispela wanpela liklik pikinini bilong Lisum**   [TP]
      this   one   little child of   Lisum
      'this one little child of Lisum'

---

[36] Although Mihalic (1971) attributes this word to English, it is only one example of Tok Pisin lexemes which could come from an Austronesian language. The Tigak word for 'talk' is etok.

b. **banana mau**
   banana ripe
   'ripe banana'

(144) NP$_{Tigak}$ → (quantifier) article N (adjective) (demonstrative) (possessive)

(145) *sakai na natuna laklik ang i Lisum* [Tigak]
  one ART son little this GEN Lisum
  'this one little child of Lisum'

(146) NP$_{Tolai}$ → (demonstrative) article (quantifier) (adjective) N (adjective)[37]/(possessive)

(147) a. *nam ra ura tutana* [Tolai]
  DEM ART two man
  'those two men'

  b. *a tabi tutana*
   ART giant man
   'giant man'

but

  c. *a pia polapola*
   ART ground wet
   'wet ground'

The Tok Pisin NP parallels that of the Tolai NP for all elements except for the absence of an article in Tok Pisin. Austronesian articles, however, are early system morphemes that serve as noun markers. The semantic content of the Austronesian article only identifies the class of noun it marks. Thus, they show no congruence with the superstrate articles, which distinguish definite/indefinite. Instead of articles (which lack congruence), quantifiers and determiners mark the definite/indefinite distinction in Tok Pisin because this construction is congruent with both substrate and superstrate patterns. The fact that the adjective does not appear to follow the substrate pattern in which the adjective follows the noun it modifies was discussed above under "Word order."

---

[37]Only one of the Tolai adjective slots would be filled.

The plural of a Tok Pisin noun is not marked morphologically on the noun as in English, but the plural is indicated by a free form preceding the noun in the quantifier slot of (142). This plural form, **ol,** is an early system morpheme in Tok Pisin because it is indirectly elected by the content morpheme it modifies, being activated at the conceptual level. The form itself is a reanalysis of the plural pronoun **ol** < **olgeta** < English 'all together'.

(148) a. *ol dok* [TP]
    PL dog
    'dogs'

  b. *mamana piu* [Tigak]
    PL   dog
    'dogs'

(149) a. *ol diwai bilong mi* [TP]
    PL tree of   1SG
    'my trees'

  b. *maman iai ta-nig* [Tigak]
    PL   tree GEN-1SG.POS
    'my trees'

Not only is the pattern of the plural construction Austronesian, but its use is also. Once a noun is established as being plural, the plural morpheme is not stated overtly with every occurrence of that noun. It is only repeated for stylistic variation or to clarify if there is a long gap between references to that noun.

The pronominal system

A pidgin may split abstract levels and copy the lexical-conceptual level from one language (or group of languages) and the phonological form of semantically congruent morphemes from another language. Entire semantic systems can be incorporated from the substrate languages using semantically congruent phonological forms from the superstrate. The Tok Pisin pronominal system is a replica of the lexical-conceptual Austronesian system exhibited in Tigak with the complete number system (including dual and trial) and the inclusive/exclusion distinction. The morphological realizations of the forms also pattern after the Austronesian system. Compare the Tok Pisin pronoun chart in table 5.1 with the

Tigak pronouns in table 5.2. In this pronominal system the composite matrix language of Tok Pisin uses lexical-conceptual features of the substrate Austronesian languages realized by semantically congruent morphemes from another language, English. Not only are the distinctions in Tok Pisin pronouns based on the Austronesian pattern, but the fact that it uses an invariant form for both subject and object without case distinctions also follows the Austronesian morphological pattern. This combination of semantics from one language and phonological form from another is one way in which the abstract levels are split and features from two or more languages are recombined to form a composite matrix language.

Table 5.1. Tok Pisin pronouns

	Singular	Dual	Trial	Plural
1 INC		yumi(tupela)	yumitripela	yumipela
1 EXC	mi	mitupela	mitripela	mipela
2	yu	yutupela	yutripela	yupela
3	em	ol(tupela)	ol(tripela)	ol

Table 5.2. Tigak independent pronouns

	Singular	Dual	Trial	Plural
1 INC		nakarag	nakaratul	nakara
1 EXC	naniu	nameg	namemtul	namem
2	nanu	namug	namitul	nami
3	nane	nareg	naritul	nari

The use and pattern for the reflexive pronoun also illustrates the composite matrix language of Tok Pisin. The form for the Tok Pisin reflexive is **yet,** possibly copied from English 'yet' (see Mihalic 1971) but used according to the Austronesian morphosyntactic structure. Sankoff (1993) notes that the Tolai emphatic pronoun, *iat* (compare to Tigak *at*), could have been the source for Tok Pisin **yet.** The fact that a single reflexive form is used for all persons is also Austronesian.

(150) a. **mi yet mi wok-im** [TP]
    1SG REFL 1SG work/do-TZ

b. *naniu* **at** *naga vil-i* [Tigak]
   1SG   REFL 1SG.S.AGR.PST do-TZ
   'I myself did it.' / 'I did it myself.'

The verb phrase

The verb phrase and the equative clause

Just as the complement phrase structure of Tok Pisin parallels that of the Austronesian substrate, so does the VP structure. The Tigak VP formula in (151) is repeated from earlier. The Tok Pisin formula follows as (152).

(151) VP_{Tigak} → (IRR) SAGR (NEG) (PRE-V) $V_{t/\emptyset}$ (MOD) $[OBAGR]_t$
       $([PCOMP]_\emptyset)$

(152) VP_{TP} → [(FUT)] PM (NEG) (PRE-V) $V_{t/\emptyset}$ (MOD) $[OBAGR]_t$
       $([PCOMP]_\emptyset)$

The only differences in the formulae are in the labels for the first two constituents in each. In Tigak, one function of the VP-initial irrealis marker is to indicate future tense, so in this respect the two constructions are parallel. In Tok Pisin the future marker more often occurs clause initially, i.e., before the subject NP. However, since an overt subject NP is often omitted in Austronesian languages and the obligatory subject-agreement is equivalent to a clause-initial position, the position is the same in both Tok Pisin and Austronesian languages.

(153) a. *(naniu)* **vo** *nag inang amoua* [Tigak]
     1SG   IRR 1SG.S.AGR go tomorrow
     'I will go tomorrow.'

   b. **bai** em i go [TP]
     FUT 3SG PM go
     'He will go.'

From the discussion above under "Word order" it is also clear that the SAGR of Austronesian languages is the model for the predicate marker of the Tok Pisin VP. Thus, Tok Pisin patterns itself structurally according to the Austronesian substrate languages, and this structure is part of the composite matrix language structure of Tok Pisin.

There are a few conditions under which the Tok Pisin predicate marker may be omitted. When the preceding word ends with /i/ or the following word begins with /i/, the predicate marker itself is not used. (This elision is also common in Tigak, as in /gi ima/ → [gima] 'he is coming'.) The predicate marker is also omitted following the first and second-person singular pronouns, **mi** and **yu**. (Both of these conditions can be subsumed under a rule that deletes **i** whenever it occurs adjacent to another high vowel.) The last condition under which the predicate marker is omitted is in the case of a demonstrative statement, such as **em bilong yu** 'that's yours' or the name of the Papua New Guinea television network, **Em TV** 'that's TV'. However, it is never omitted in definitions.

(154) a. **dispela samting i kamputa**
 this something PM computer
 'This is a computer.'

 b. *****dispela samting Ø kamputa**

The pre-verb slot in (152) above may be filled with tense, mood, aspect (TMA) particles or with adverbs, as illustrated in (155).

(155) a. **em i** *bin* **lukim**
 3SG PM PST see
 'He saw.'

 b. **em i** *no save*[38] **kaikai-m pis**
 3SG PM NEG HAB eat-TZ fish
 'He doesn't (usually) eat fish.'

 c. **em i** *klostu* **pinis**
 3SG PM almost finish
 'He's almost finished.'

The post-verbal modifier slot in Tok Pisin can be filled by manner adverbs and by the perfective marker **pinis,** following the Austronesian pattern.

(156) a. **ol i wokabaut** *isiisi* [TP]
 3PL PM walk slowly

---

[38]The lexeme **save** < Portuguese *sabir* 'to know'.

b. *nari rig   pasal* **ananap**   [Tigak]
   3PL 3PL.S.AGR walk slowly
   'They walk slowly.'

(157) a. **em i   mek-im** *pinis* **dispela mun**   [TP]
         3SG PM make-TZ PRF   this   canoe

      b. *ga   vil   a-***kamus**-*i tang vuul*   [Tigak]
         3SG.S.AGR.PST make CS-finish-TZ ART canoe
         'He made this canoe.'

The equative clause in Tok Pisin also parallels that in Tigak, whether it is the definition type clause in (154a) and (159) or the demonstrative type that omits the PM (158).

(158) a. *ga   ro*   [Tigak]
         3SG.S.AGR good
         'It's good.'

      b. **em gutpela**   [TP]
         3SG good
         'That's good.'

(159) a. *tang ot   ga   ro*   [Tigak]
         ART thing 3SG.S.AGR good
         'The thing is good.'

      b. **em i   gutpela samthing**   [TP]
         3SG PM good   something
         'It's a good thing.'

In both Austronesian languages and in Tok Pisin, whether there is a verb or not, there is always a subject and a predicate. The Austronesian parallel for the Tok Pisin existential statements of the 'there is' type is not only structurally but also semantically based on the Austronesian substrate. Both use the verb 'to have' as the basis for this construction.

(160) a. *ga   ***togtogan*** palmit-pouak tang e-tigan-an*   [Tigak]
         3SG.S.AGR have   five-two   ART RECP-brother-unit

b. i *gat* sevenpela brata [TP]
   PM have seven   brother
   'There were seven brothers.'

Transitive and intransitive verbs

As in the Austronesian substrate, the transitivity of most verbs in Tok Pisin is indicated morphologically. Any verb with the suffix **-im** is transitive and will take an object. The transitive marker **-im** shown in (161) (and as **-m** in (155b)) can be explained in a parallel fashion to the predicate marker **i**. This suffix may be taken phonologically from the English pronoun *him,* but it patterns according to an Austronesian syntactic structure, which also uses the third-person singular object pronoun. Goulden notes, and I have also observed, that the "third-person pronoun em does not normally occur after a transitive verb" (1990:109) in Tok Pisin. In this feature also, Tok Pisin (161) patterns according to the Austronesian substrate (162) in which the object agreement pronominal is required on all cases except for the third-person singular object, which is null.

(161) a. em i   pait-*im* mi [TP]
        3SG PM   hit-TZ   1SG.OB
        'He hit/hits me.'

     b. em i   pait-*im* ∅ [TP]
        3SG PM   hit-TZ   3SG.OB
        'He hit/hits him/her/it.'

(162) a. gi   vis-i   ri[39]   tang anu [Tigak]
        3SG.S.AGR hit-TZ   3PL.OB.AGR ART   man
        'He hit the men.'

     b. gi   vis-i   ∅ [Tigak]
        3SG.S.AGR hit-TZ   3SG.OB.AGR
        'He hit him/her/it.'

Duke of York, an Austronesian language spoken on the islands between New Britain and southern New Ireland, uses pronoun objects as well, but Codrington (1974:567) wrote that "the only form that can be said to be

---

[39]Some Tigak speakers write the object agreement pronouns as separate particles from the verb except for the singular forms. Others write them as suffixes attached to the last element of the verbal construction. I follow the pattern above to show the parallelism with Tok Pisin.

suffixed to a Verb or Preposition is the Third Singular *i.*" An homophonous particle *i* was also the marker for transitive verbs and merged with the third-person pronoun, explaining why the third-person singular pronominal object is missing in some Austronesian languages, including Tigak. Both the common structure and the similar forms in English and the substrates certainly reinforced the Tok Pisin transitive form.

As with Tigak, many verbs may be used transitively or intransitively, with the transitive suffix and the object identifying the transitive ones as in (163) and (164).

(163) em i *sem*   long.wanem em i bin wok-im
      2SG PM ashamed because   3SG PM PST do-TZ

  samting   nogut
  something bad
  'He is ashamed because he did something bad.'

(164) **yu bin *sem-im* mi long pes bilong olgeta man**
      2SG PST shame-TZ 1SG in   face of   PL/all man
      'You shamed me before everyone.'

Not all transitive verbs take the transitive suffix, however. Some verbs may be used with or without it. When the transitive suffix is not used, the object is introduced by long. One of these verbs is illustrated in (165).

(165) a. **sapos yu pain-im samting, bai yu *singaut long* mi**
         if   2SG see-TZ something FUT 2SG call.out to   1SG
         'If you see something, call me.'

   b. **yu ken *singaut-im* mi**
      2SG may call-TZ   1SG
      'You may call (to/for) me.'

For a small set of transitive verbs the transitive suffix is never added, as demonstrated in (166a) below. These verbs may also be intransitive when there is no object as in (166b).

(166) a. **yu laik *pilai* futbal**
         2SG like play football (soccer)
         'Do you like to play football?'

b. em i   go ausait bilong *pilai*
   3SG PM go outside to   play
   'He went outside to play.'

The class of verbs that are always intransitive in Tok Pisin is quite small. Example (167) uses some of these intransitive verbs.

(167) yu no ken *krai* na *ranawe*
     2SG NEG may cry and runaway

     nogat, yu mas *kam* na *sindaun* na *toktok*
     no,   2SG must come and sit.down and talk
     'You can't cry and run away. No, you must come and sit down and talk.'

It can be noted with the verb **toktok** in (167) that the same Austronesian morphological pattern of reduplication of a transitive verb root (**tok(-im)**) to form an intransitive verb is used in Tok Pisin. Some of these intransitive verbs are stative verbs such as **les** 'to be tired of', **longlong** 'to be insane', and **spak** 'to be drunk'.

Woolford (1979a) argues against a passive voice in Tok Pisin. (Mihalic 1971 also expresses this view, but see Hooley 1962 for another opinion.) It is generally agreed that Austronesian languages do not have a passive construction.[40] The arguments against a passive in Tok Pisin center on the transitive-intransitive opposition of Tok Pisin verbs. Since some of the intransitive verbs have a stative (or passive-like) meaning, the passive is most often formed by the use of a transitive verb minus the transitive suffix as in (168). This use of stative verbs also has a source in the Austronesian substrate, as the Tigak example (169) shows. Examples (168a) and (169a) give the transitive form, and (168b) and (169b) give the intransitive construction of the same verb with a stative (or passive-like) meaning.

(168) a. em i   *bruk-im* diwai   [TP]
     3SG PM break-TZ stick
     'He breaks/broke the stick.'

   b. **dispela diwai i   *bruk***   [TP]
     this   stick PM break
     'This stick is broken.'

---

[40] The lack of Austronesian passives seems to be the general case. However, Tigak does have a morphological passive construction.

(169) a. *ga*   ***vuak-i*** *tang iai*   [Tigak]
3SG.S.AGR.PST break-TZ ART stick
'He broke this stick.'

b. *tang iai ga*   ***tavuak***   [Tigak]
ART stick 3SG.S.AGR be.broken
'This stick is broken.'

Serial and compound verbs

The serial verb constructions of Tok Pisin pattern like similar constructions in Austronesian languages (also see (86) in chapter 4 for another Tigak example). Example (170) shows a serial construction with the same subject as the agent of both verbs.

(170) a. **ol** *i* ***kirap*** *(i)* ***go*** *long Nonoval*   [TP]
3PL PM get.up (PM) go to Nonoval
'They get up/got up and go/went to Nonoval.'

b. *(nari) rig*   ***tatut isua***   *e Nonoval*   [Tigak]
3PL 3PL.S.AGR get.up go.down LOC Nonoval
'They get up/got up and go/went to Nonoval.'

In example (171) the object of the first verb is the subject of the second verb.

(171) a. **em** *i* ***lukim*** *simok i* ***go*** *antap*   [TP]
3SG PM see/saw smoke PM go up
'They saw the smoke rising.'

b. *(ne) ga*   ***tarei*** *tang* ***buan*** *ga*   ***aolong*** [Tigak]
3SG 3SG.S.AGR.PST see ART smoke 3SG.S.AGR.PST rise
'They saw the smoke rising.'

Serial constructions are also used to show continued action.

(172) a. **ol** *i* ***stap*** *i* ***stap*** *i* ***go*** *inap...*   [TP]
3PL PM stay PM stay PM go until
'They stay/stayed [and] stay/stayed until...'

b. *(nareg) reg-a* ***minang minang*** *gi*   *inang*   [Tigak]
3DL   3DL.S.AGR-PST stay   stay   3SG.S.AGR go

tuk...
until
'They stay/stayed [and] stay/stayed until...'

Serial constructions in Tok Pisin also follow the Austronesian semantic model to express the actions of 'bring' and 'take' by combining the verb 'to get' with 'come' and 'go', respectively.

(173) a. **man** *i* ***kis-im*** **pik** *i* ***kam***   [TP]
man PM get-TZ pig PM come
'The man is bringing/brought a pig.'

b. *tang anu gi*   ***suk ima***   *tang vogo*   [Tigak]
ART man 3SG.S.AGR get come ART pig
'The man is bringing/brought a pig.'

(174) **yu** **ken** ***kis-im*** **kaikai** *i*   ***go***   [TP]
2SG may get-TZ food PM go
'You may take [the] food.'

Some have argued that serial verb constructions in Tok Pisin are influenced by English. Todd (1984) gives the example in (175) as evidence of the English pattern.

(175) **em** *i* **bekim** **tok** *i* **spik** **yupela kam...**
3SG PM answer talk PM speak 2PL come
'He answers/answered saying: Come...'

However, there is an Austronesian counterpart for serial verbs. As demonstrated in (170)–(174), such constructions are simply conforming to a composite matrix language fashioned by the common substrate features of Austronesian languages. Givón's research also supports the Austronesian source (although indirectly). He studied the types of serial verb constructions in Tok Pisin and found that the "deictic-directional" (1987:27) type using the verbs **kam** and **go,** as in examples (173) and (174), are the most frequently used serial constructions. He also notes that Tok Pisin serial constructions are not like the Papuan languages of Kalam and Tairora to which he compared them. In his study of serial verbs in Saramaccan, McWhorter (1992) found a situation very similar to that of Tok Pisin in two respects. First, the substrate languages are typologically very similar, as is the case with the Austronesian substrate of Papua New Guinea. Second, the substrate languages provide the pattern for the serial verb constructions of the pidgin/creole.

Compound verbs are also constructed in Tok Pisin in the same ways as they are in Austronesian languages: by reduplication (**tok-tok** 'to talk', **was-was** 'to bathe') and by putting two different verbs together. In the latter case, the second verb usually gives the manner (or direction) of the action of the first verb. When the verb is transitive, sometimes the transitive suffix is used with each verb (176). In most cases, however, only one transitive suffix is applied (177). A Tigak example is given in (178).

(176) ol   i   *kar-am-ap-im* bokis bilong man i   dai pinis   [TP]
      3PL PM   cover-TZ-up-TZ box   of   man PM die PRF
      'They cover/covered the casket.'

(177) mi   *sing-aut-im* pinis
      1SG   sing-out-TZ   PRF
      'I called (out).'

(178) ritul   **ru-pisin-i-∅**   ta   motange   [Tigak]
      3TR.S.AGR   escape-leave-TZ-3SG.OB.AGR   ART   snake
      'They(3) run away from a/the snake.'

It can be seen that the verbal prepositions of such English forms as 'cover up' and 'sing out' have been realized as verbs according to the substrate pattern. In fact, they are used alone as verbs, as in (179) and (180). As verbs, they can be compounded and affixed in the same way as *ru-pisin-i* is in Tigak.

(179) em   i   aut-im   tok
      3SG PM   out-TZ   talk
      'He speaks/spoke.' (as in 'preach' or 'make announcement')

(180) mi   ap-im   han   bilong mi
      1SG   up-TZ   hand   belong 1SG
      'I raise/raised my hand.'

Tense, mood, and aspect

Only a few examples of the tense, mood, aspect, (TMA) system of Tok Pisin as compared to Tigak and other Austronesian languages of New Ireland and

New Britain will be given to demonstrate the possible Austronesian substrate source for the composite matrix language of Tok Pisin. A fuller discussion of these constructions in Tok Pisin can be found in Todd (1984). A common Austronesian characteristic is a lack of overt tense marking with context and sentential adverbs setting the temporal frame. Tok Pisin is developing more temporal and aspectual distinctions, but the Austronesian pattern was very common in the earlier stages of the pidgin and is still a widespread alternative to overt tense markers. In a discourse the time reference is often set at the beginning, and all subsequent clauses are unmarked for tense (and, thus, are often in present tense form). Tok Pisin discourses also follow this pattern. For this reason the Tok Pisin examples (170)–(173) and (175) can be translated as either present or past tense. Only in the presence of an overt tense or aspect marker is the present tense not an alternative. Because tense is not overtly marked in every clause, some linguists have proposed that "tense is one of the few innovations that can be ascribed to direct borrowing from English" (Mühlhäusler 1982:450). However, the patterns for marking tense and aspect are clearly parallel to the Austronesian patterns. For example, the past tense in Tigak is marked between the subject agreement and the verb. Although the past tense is marked morphologically as a suffix on the subject agreement pronominal in Tigak, its position is the same as the past tense marker in Tok Pisin. Other Austronesian languages do use a separate past tense marker between the subject agreement and the verb, as the Tungag example in (182) (from Fast 1988:37) shows.

(181) a. **mi *bin* go long taun** [TP]
　　　　1SG PST go to　　town
　　　　'I went to town.'

　　　b. *nag-**a***　　　inang lo　　taun [Tigak]
　　　　1SG.S.AGR-PST go　　LOC town
　　　　'I went to town.'

(182) *nem*　　　***ta*** pasal ane Vaungung [Tungag]
　　　1PL.EXC.S.AGR PST go　　to　 Vaungung
　　　'We went to Vaungung.'

Other aspect markers (such as the perfective in the Tigak example (183b)) and negation also occur between the subject pronoun and the verb in Austronesian languages (184b) and in Tok Pisin (184a), just as the past and other aspectual particles do in Tok Pisin (183a).

(183) a. **mi bin slip** [TP]
1SG PST sleep
'I slept.'

b. *nag-a* **pon** *matei* [Tigak]
1SG.S.AGR-PST PRF sleep
'I slept.'

(184) a. **mi *no* bin slip** [TP]
1SG NEG PST sleep
'I did not sleep.'

b. *nag-a* **veko** *pon matei* [Tigak]
1SG.S.AGR-PST NEG PRF sleep
'I did not sleep.'

Similarly, the position of other TMA morphemes in Tok Pisin correspond to the Austronesian order.

(185) a. **mi kaikai *pinis*** [TP]
1SG eat finish
'I ate/have eaten.'

b. *nag-a* **ngan a-kamus** [Tigak]
1SG.S.AGR-PST eat CS-finish
'I ate/have eaten.'

It is interesting that in (185a) the perfective in Tok Pisin is formed using the verb 'to finish', just as in Tigak.

(186) a. **mi bin *pinis-im* dispela wok** [TP]
1SG PST finish-TZ this work
'I finished the work.'

b. *nag-a* **kamus-i** *tang aisok* [Tigak]
1SG.S.AGR-PST finish-TZ ART work
'I finished the work.'

The future marker occurs in the same position as the irrealis marker (which also marks future) in Tigak.

(187) a. ***bai*** em i   go long situa   [TP]
         FUT 3SG PM go to   store
         'He will go to the store.'

   b. ***vo*** gi   inang lo   sitoa   [Tigak]
         IRR 3SG.S.AGR go   LOC store
         'He will go to the store.'

Several scholars (Sankoff and Laberge 1974, Sankoff 1980b, Woolford 1979a, Muysken 1981b) have discussed the variable placement of **bai** in Tok Pisin. There are two common sites for the future marker in Tok Pisin. The most common, and apparently the oldest, is the clause-initial slot shown in (187a). The second position is between the subject and the verb, shown in (189). This variation could be taken as evidence of a change in progress indicating that Tok Pisin is converging toward English syntactic structure. This explanation is possible since the pre-verbal pattern seems to be more prevalent among Tok Pisin speakers immersed in an English-speaking environment. However, there are also other possible explanations. Both patterns are heard in New Ireland (although I have no recorded incidents of Tigak native speakers placing **bai** between the subject and verb in Tok Pisin). Other Austronesian languages of New Ireland have a different morphosyntactic structure for the future. Kara, for example, indicates future tense with a particle between subject and verb as shown in (188) (from Beaumont 1989:41).

(188) mi   ***ta*** savat   [Kara]
      2SG FUT arrive
      'You will arrive.'

With this pattern available, it is not surprising to sometimes find the same order in Tok Pisin, as in (188).

(189) em ***bai*** go nau   [TP]
      3SG FUT go now
      'He will go now.'

Thus, the two patterns for the placement of a future marker found in Austronesian substrate languages (187b and 188) are reflected in the variation found in the placement of **bai** in Tok Pisin. The position in which Tok Pisin speakers place **bai** can be traced to the position of the corresponding form in the speaker's L1. Sankoff and Laberge (1974) claim that the preverbal position of **bai** is evidence of a later stage of grammaticalization. Romaine

(1987) disagrees. She claims that grammaticalization is more likely in urban creole Tok Pisin because urban creole speakers are at a more advanced stage in the development of the language. However, her data show that the preverbal pattern is more common among rural L2 speakers of Tok Pisin than among the urban L1 speakers.

It can be seen from the examples above and from the evidence of different researchers that the variation in placement of the future marker in Tok Pisin may be the influence of different composite matrix languages framing the construction. Variability in the composite matrix language may be attributed to differences in the L1s of Tok Pisin speakers. I have observed (informally) that Papua New Guineans who learned English before they learned Tok Pisin tend to follow the English pattern. From this observation I would predict that the trend will continue in that direction as English becomes more accessible to more Tok Pisin speakers. It is not unusual for such convergence to a LWC to occur as speakers use that language more regularly and in more contexts. Since the substrate pattern varies, the pattern of English can tip the balance in that direction. As Myers-Scotton (2001) proposes, there are two targets in pidgin/creole formation, not just one. The more accessible a target becomes, the more likely it will become a source for morphosyntactic structure.

Another parallel with Austronesian languages is the semantic origin for the habitual marker in Tok Pisin which uses the verb 'to know' (**save** in Tok Pisin ← Portuguese *sabir,* and *kalapang* in Tigak) for that function (cf. Comrie 1989 and Givón 1979a for discussions of the universal tendency for the habitual marker to develop from the verb 'to know').

(190) a. **em i   *save* go long Kavieng long Trinde**   [TP]
       3SG PM HAB   go   to   Kavieng on   Wednesday
       'He always/usually goes to Kavieng on Wednesday.'

   b. *ga   **kalapang** inang e   Kavieng lo   tang gaan*   [Tigak]
      3SG.S.AGR HAB   go   LOC   Kavieng LOC ART day

      potul
      three
      'He always/usually goes to Kavieng on Wednesday.'

Prepositions

The class of prepositions is small in Tok Pisin as in many Austronesian languages. Codrington observed that the Melanesian mind does not regard the locality of actions as we do; natives do not use Prepositions, therefore, as we do. It may seem to us strange that *ta na vale* should mean at once into a house or from a house, but this to the native is natural, not from indistinctness of conception, or poverty of expression, but from a different way of looking at the matter. (1974:160)[41]

The two Tok Pisin prepositions, **long** and **bilong,** fulfill most prepositional functions. **Long** satisfies all locative and directional roles, and **bilong** expresses possession.

(191) em i   go *long*   rot
     3SG PM go on/to/from road
     'He is going on/to/from the road.'

(192) **bai mi   stap *long* haus**
     FUT 1SG stay in/at house
     'I will stay in/at the house.'

(193) **pikinini *bilong* mi**
     child   belong me
     'my child'

The use of a few general purpose prepositions for all functions is a direct reflection of the Austronesian patterns of the composite matrix language. It is particularly striking that the semantic division grouping locative and directional forms together (**long** in Tok Pisin) but separating genitive forms (**bilong** in Tok Pisin) copies the Austronesian conceptual division. (See the discussion in "Prepositions" in chapter 4 on Tigak prepositions.) The conceptual parallel between **bilong** and the Austronesian genitive form does not end with possession. In Tigak, the form *ina* (from *i-na* = GEN-3SG) serves the same additional functions served by **bilong** in Tok Pisin.

(194) Part to whole
    lip *bilong* diwai   [TP]
    pakak *ina* iai   [Tigak]
    'leaf of tree'

---

[41]Codrington (1974) also noted the use of a few general prepositions in Duke of York, including *i*, which is also found in Tigak as a genitive preposition. This is another example of the numerous and widespread common features and vocabulary of Austronesian languages in the New Guinea islands.

(195) Place of origin
man *bilong* Rabaul [TP]
*tang anu **ina** Rabaul* [Tigak]
'man from Rabaul'

(196) Attribute
man *bilong* wok [TP]
*teteng **ina** aisog* [Tigak]
'one who works/hard-working person' lit., man/one of work

(197) Purpose/function
ol i mekim rop *bilong* pulim huk [TP]
*(nari) rig vili tang gaus **ina** ngaulngaul* [Tigak]
'They are making string for fishing.'

An additional parallel between the prepositional systems of Tok Pisin and the Austronesian substrate involves the use of the same preposition to indicate both instrument and accompaniment (**wantaim** in Tok Pisin ← 'one time' in English, and *pe/pa-* in Tigak).

(198) a. em   i   paitim dok *wantaim* diwai   (instrument) [TP]
       3SG PM   hit   dog with   stick

   b. ga   naki ta   piu *pana* tang iai   [Tigak]
      3SG.S.AGR hit   ART dog with   ART   stick
      'He hit the dog with a stick.'

(199) a. em   i   wokabaut *wantain* brata (accompaniment)[TP]
       3SG PM walk   with   brother

   b. ga   pasal kum   *pana* tig-om   [Tigak]
      3SG.S.AGR walk   together   with   brother-2SG
      'He walked/went with your brother.'

Possession

Austronesian languages employ two distinct possessive constructions for alienable and inalienable possession, one marked by a suffix and the other by a genitive phrase. (These constructions were discussed for Tigak in chapter 4 and for Nalik in chapter 1 under "Language shift, attrition, and death.") Briefly, the inalienable possession is marked with a possessive suffix attached to the possessed noun and coindexed to agree with the possessor in person and number.

Alienable possession is indicated with a genitive phrase using a prepositional form with the possessor as the object. This genitive phrase follows the possessed noun. Tok Pisin ((200b) and (202b)) uses this genitive phrase pattern of possession for all possessive constructions, making no distinction between alienable and inalienable possession.

(200) a. *ta   lui   te   Sam* [Tigak]
       ART house GEN Sam (Alienable)

   b. **haus bilong Sam** [TP]
     house of   Sam
     'Sam's house'

(201) a. *ta   pook ka-na* [Tigak]
       ART food GEN-3SG (Alienable)

   b. **kaikai bilong en** [TP]
     food   of   3SG
     'his food'

(202) a. *mata-g* [Tigak]
       eye-1SG.POS (Inalienable)

   b. **ai bilong mi** [TP]
     eye belong 1SG
     'my eye'

In the Tok Pisin construction, **bilong** is a late system bridge morpheme structurally assigned to connect the possessed noun to the possessor following the morphosyntactic frame of Austronesian languages. The Tok Pisin morpheme itself is copied phonologically from the English content morpheme *belong* which, because of the conceptual congruence of possession, has been reanalyzed as a possessive system morpheme. As discussed in chapter 1 with respect to Nalik, the Tok Pisin construction is now invading some of the indigenous languages of Papua New Guinea and causing those languages to converge to Tok Pisin, losing their inalienable construction as a result.

Subordinate clauses

Subordination in Tok Pisin is accomplished by introducing the subordinate clause with the appropriate subordinating conjunction. As in the Austronesian substrate languages, the morphosyntactic construction of the Tok Pisin subordinate clauses does not differ from the construction of a main clause. Compare the following Tok Pisin sentences with their Tigak counterparts. The subordinate clauses are in square brackets, and the conjunction is bolded.

(203) Conditional clause
    a. *rig   veko kaskaas akamusi tang aisog*   [Tigak]
       3PL.S.AGR NEG be.able complete ART work

       [***vouneng*** *tang vaap   rig   veko angasigiri*]
       if   ART people 3PL.S.AGR NEG help.them
       'They cannot finish the work [*if* the people don't help them].'

    b. **ol i no inap pinisim wok [*sapos* ol**   [TP]
       3PL PM NEG able finish work [if   PL

       manmeri no helapim ol]
       people   NEG help   3PL]
       'They cannot finish the work [*if* the people don't help them].'

    c. **[*sapos* ol manmeri no helapim ol] ol i**   [TP]
       [if PL people NEG help   3PL] 3PL PM

       no inap pinisim wok
       NEG able finish   work
       '[If the people don't help them], they cannot finish the work.'

The subordinate conditional clause may be fronted for emphasis in Tok Pisin (203c) just as in Tigak.

(204) Reason clause
    a. *nag   inang e Kavieng [**kula** nag   veko*   [Tigak]
       1SG.S.AGR go   LOC Kavieng because 1SG.S.AGR NEG

        pe   togoni ta   pook]
        still have   ART food
    'I am going to Kavieng [*because* I have no more food].'

  b. **mi go long Kavieng [*long   wanem* mi no**   [TP]
     1SG go to   Kavieng because   1SG NEG

     gat   kaikai]
     have food
    'I am going to Kavieng [*because* I have no more food].'

  c. **[*long   wanem* mi no   gat   kaikai] orait mi go**
     because 1SG   NEG have food all   right 1SG go

     long Kavieng
     to   Kavieng
    '[Since I don't have food], I'm going to Kavieng.'

When the reason clause is fronted in Tok Pisin (204c), the transitional **orait** (or sometimes the future marker **bai**) is inserted before the main clause. In Tigak the reason clause can be fronted with no other change in the sentence. The purpose (205) and manner (206) clauses are not normally fronted in Tigak or in Tok Pisin.

(205) Purpose clause
  a. *rig   a   ngaungaul [**ina**   ngan]*   [Tigak]
     3PL.S.AGR MA fish   [in order to eat]
    'They fish [*in order to* eat].'

  b. **ol   i   pulim huk [*bilong   kaikai]**   [TP]
     3PL PM pull   hook in.order.to eat
    'They fish [*in order to* eat].'

(206) Manner clause
  a. *gi   pasal [**malan** te   tamana   (gi*   [Tigak]
     3SG.S.AGR walk [like   of   father.his (3SG.S.AGR

     pasal)]
     walk)]
    'He walks [*like* his father (walks)].'

    b. **em i wokabaut [*olsem* papa bilong en (i**   [TP]
       3SG PM walk   like   father of   his PM

       wokabaut)]
       walk
       'He walks [*like* his father (walks)].'

(207) Time clauses
    a. *vo rig   sinug etang [**tuk** vo rig   maat]*   [Tigak]
       IRR 3PL.S.AGR sit   there [until IRR 3PL.S.AGR die]
       'They will sit there [*until* they die].'

    b. **bai ol i sindaun long hap [*inap* bai ol i**   [TP]
       FUT 3PL PM sit   at   there until FUT 3PL PM

       dai pinis]
       die PRF
       'They will sit there [*until* they die].'

A time clause introduced by **bipo** may be fronted (as may the Tigak counterpart with *kula*).

(208) a. *nug   ke   maiak [**kula** tang ulan gi*   [Tigak]
       2SG.S.AGR must fish   [before ART moon 3SG.S.AGR

       singan]
       shines]
       'You must fish [*before* the moon comes out].'

    b. **yu mas pulim huk [*bipo* mun i kamap]**   [TP]
       2SG must pull   hook before moon PM comes.up
       'You must fish [*before* the moon comes out].'

    c. **[*bipo* mun i kamap] yu mas pulim huk**
       before moon PM comes.up 2SG must pull   hook
       '[*Before* the moon comes up], you must fish.'

The introduction of quotes, both direct and indirect, is also semantically and syntactically the same in Tok Pisin and in Austronesian languages, using a form which means 'like/same as'.

(209) a. **em i tok [*olsem* yu mas kam]** [TP]
3SG PM talk same.as 2SG must come
'He said [that] you must come.'

b. *ga etok [**auneng** mug ke gima]* [Tigak]
3SG.S.AGR talk same.as 2SG.S.AGR must come
'He said [that] you must come.'

Relativization is still developing in Tok Pisin, and newer methods are entering the language as its functions expand and its base of speakers grows. Among the original means of relativization, however, is juxtaposition, following the Austronesian pattern. This is still the pattern used by New Irelanders speaking Tok Pisin regardless of the antecedent noun (see chapter 4 for Tigak relative clause constructions).

(210) a. **mi luk-im man [em i got tripela meri]** [TP]
1SG see-TZ man 3SG PM have three woman
'I see the man [who has three wives].' (Antecedent = DO)

b. *nag tare-i tang anu [ga togon potul ta* [Tigak]
1SG.S.AGR see-TZ ART man SG.S.AGR have three ART

lapan]
spouse
'I see the man [who has three wives].' (Antecedent = DO)

(211) a. **pis [mi kisim asde] i bikpela tru** [TP]
fish 1SG get yesterday PM big very
'The tuna/fish [I caught yesterday] was very big.'
(Antecedent = S)

b. *tang atul [naga ngauli ∅ nago]* [Tigak]
ART tuna [1SG.S.AGR.PST hook 3SG.OB.AGR yesterday]

ga vugvuga aong
3SG.S.AGR big very
'The tuna/fish [I caught yesterday] was very big.'
(Antecedent = S)

Discourse characteristics

The discourse characteristics of Tok Pisin are strikingly parallel to those of the substrate languages—both Austronesian and non-Austronesian. As discussed in the last section of chapter 4 for Tigak, tense as an absolute time reference is not an element of every clause in Tok Pisin as it is in English. Once the time frame is established, often with temporal adverbs, a discourse may continue indefinitely in the present (or unmarked) tense. The unmarked forms are interpreted according to the overt time references previously made, until the time reference is changed. Similarly for participant reference and plurality, once the participants are established and the number specified, the following references are primarily made with pronouns. Any nouns that are used may or may not be repeatedly marked for plurality. In a culture with a long oral tradition and only recently written languages, the memory for details is long.

The repetitions in a discourse are primarily for style. In a narrative or explanatory discourse, one event or instruction follows the other in chronological order, often connected by the coordinating conjunction **na** 'and'. There is little embedding or flashbacks. The head-to-tail linkage described for Tigak is common in Tok Pisin. An interesting discourse feature that Tok Pisin had incorporated by calquing from Austronesian languages is the formulaic ending **em tasol** meaning 'that's all'. The Tigak equivalent is *po kamus* 'finished'. I propose that such discourse characteristics are a part of the conceptual, as well as structural, aspects of a language, and as such are part of the matrix language frame. For a pidgin or creole, this matrix language is a composite matrix language as discussed throughout this work. These discourse characteristics of Tok Pisin are so strong because they are so common to the languages of Papua New Guinea, both Austronesian and non-Austronesian.

Summary of Austronesian features in Tok Pisin

The purpose of this chapter was to demonstrate the extensive influence of the Austronesian substrate languages on Tok Pisin. In particular, I have demonstrated that the variety of Tok Pisin spoken in the islands region of Papua New Guinea patterns like the Austronesian languages of that same area. Using Tigak as a typical Austronesian language, I have demonstrated the parallels in morphosyntactic structure between the two languages and the need for congruence between the substrate and superstrate in all levels of abstract structure. The following tables summarize some of the areas of Austronesian influence on Tok Pisin. Table 5.3 compares the pronominal systems in Tigak and Tok Pisin.

Table 5.3. Correspondence of Tok Pisin to Austronesian pronominal system

	Singular	Dual	Trial	Plural	
1 Inc		nakarag	nakara-tul	nakara	Tigak
		yumi(tupela)	**yumi-tripela**	**yumipela**	Tok Pisin
1 Exc	naniu	nameg	namem-tul	namem	Tigak
	mi	**mitupela**	**mi-tripela**	**mipela**	Tok Pisin
	[<me]	[tu <two]	[tri <three]		
2	nanu	namug	nami-tul	nami	Tigak
	yu	**yutupela**	**yu-tripela**	**yupela**	Tok Pisin
	[<you]				
3	nane	nareg	nari-tul	nari	Tigak
	em	**ol(tupela)**	**ol(tripela)**	**ol**	Tok Pisin
	[<him]			[<all]	

The table demonstrates that the English morphemes (shown in square brackets) selected as pronouns in Tok Pisin have some degree of lexical-conceptual congruence with the corresponding substrate forms (i.e., the same person and number). The similarity in forms within each row across the table demonstrates that the morphological realization patterns of Tok Pisin parallel those of the Austronesian substrate. The fact that each slot of the substrate pronominal system is reproduced in Tok Pisin demonstrates the lexical-conceptual congruence of the entire system with the substrate. Although the table does not show it, Tok Pisin also patterns according to the substrate at the morphological realization level because both use invariant pronominal forms for overt subjects and objects.

Other examples of the parallels in morphosyntactic structure between the Austronesian substrate and Tok Pisin are demonstrated in table 5.4, which shows the parallels in word order in a basic clause or verb phrase, and in table 5.5, which shows the parallel in word order in the noun phrase. The examples following table 5.5 are adapted from examples (9)–(12) of appendix 2. The grammatical slot in a clause or VP is in small caps in table 5.4, the actual morpheme from Tigak or Tok Pisin is given, and the example number illustrating the correspondence is in parentheses. The order in which the grammatical slots are given is the relative order in which they occur in each language, respectively.

Table 5.4. Correspondence of Tok Pisin to Austronesian VP word order

	IRR	SAGR	NEG	PRE-V	V	MOD	OBJ	COMP
Tigak	vo (212a)	gi (213a,c)	veko (214a)	kalapang (214a)	vis-i (213a,c)	ananap (215a)	ri/∅ (213a,c)	auneng... (216a)
Tok Pisin	FUT bai (212b)	PM i (213b,d)	NEG no (214b)	PRE-V save (214b)	V pait-im (215b,d)	MOD isiisi (215b)	OBJ ol/∅ (213b,d)	COMP olsem... (216b)

(212) a. ***vo*** nag inang lo sitoa [Tigak]

    b. ***bai*** mi go long situa [TP]
       IRR/FUT 1SG go to store
       'I will go to [the] store.'

(213) a. nane ***gi*** vis-i ri [Tigak]

    b. em ***i*** pait-im ol [TP]
       3SG S.AGR/PM hit-TZ 3PL.OB
       'He/she hit them.'

   or

    c. nane gi vis-i ∅ [Tigak]

    d. em i pait-im ∅ [TP]
       3SG S.AGR/PM hit-TZ 3SG.OB
       'He/she hit him/her/it.'

(214) a. nane gi ***veko kalapang*** ngan-i tang ien [Tigak]

    b. em i ***no save*** kaikai-m pis [TP]
       3SG S.AGR/PM NEG HAB eat-TZ [ART] fish
       'He does not (usually) eat fish.'

(215) a. nari rig pasal ananap [Tigak]

    b. ***ol i*** wokabaut isiisi [TP]
       3PL S.AGR/PM walk slowly
       'They walk/are walking slowly.'

(216) a. nag etok **auneng mug ke gima** [Tigak]

b. **mi tok olsem yu mas kam** [TP]
1SG talk/say like.this 2SG OBL come
'I say [that] you must come.'

Table 5.5. Correspondence of Tok Pisin to Austronesian NP word order

	DEM	QNT	ADJ	N	ADJ	DEM
Tigak (217)	—	sakai	—	na natuna	laklik	ang
Tungag (218)	mang	sikei	—	a vʌkil	lik	—
Tolai (219a)	nam	ra ura	tabi	tutana	—	—
(219b)	—	—	—	a pia	polapola	—
Tok Pisin (220a)	**dispela**	**wanpela**	**tripela**	**man**	—	—
(220b)				**banana**	**mau**	

(217) *sakai na natu-na laklik ang* [Tigak]
one ART child-3SG little this
'This one little child.'

(218) *mang sikei a vʌkil lik* [Tungag]
SPEC one ART cave little
'a certain small cave'

(219) a. *nam ra ura tabi tutana* [Tolai]
DEM ART two giant man
'those two giant men'

b. *a pia polapola*
ART ground wet
'wet ground'

(220) a. **dispela wanpela tripela man** [TP]
this one huge man
'this one giant man'

b. **banana mau**
banana ripe
'ripe banana'

The extensive morphosyntactic structuring of Tok Pisin according to the Austronesian substrate pattern is obvious from the examples presented above. Not only is the word order in table 5.4 parallel, but many morphological realization patterns are also, such as the marking of transitive verbs (examples (213) and (214)) and the null morpheme for the third-person singular object of transitive verbs (213c, d) as opposed to all other objects. Even the alternate noun-adjective and adjective-noun word orders of Tok Pisin shown in table 5.5 pattern after the same alternations found in the Austronesian substrate languages.

The contact situation from which Tok Pisin arose involved speakers of many Austronesian languages and speakers of English. The people were put together in a situation in which they had to communicate with each other, but the Austronesian languages were mutually unintelligible, and there was not a majority of speakers of any one of those languages. English was of value to them as the language of the overseers, but the substrate speakers had little access to English except for the vocabulary. Thus, English became a target of acquisition for those features of English that were available to them—phonological forms and at least some of the meaning attached to those forms. The Austronesian languages they spoke became targets for the very similar morphosyntactic structures. Thus, the speakers of the developing pidgin drew on the common morphosyntactic features of their L1s and developed a composite matrix language by which to structure the emerging contact linguistic variety using the morphemes they heard from the superstrate language.

More recently the direction of influence has changed. Tok Pisin is now effecting changes in Tigak and other Austronesian languages. In the next chapter I will demonstrate the convergence of Tigak to Tok Pisin and to English (for some speakers).

6
Convergence and Renewed Influence

One of the major claims of this study is that the vernacular languages of New Ireland and East New Britain (the Austronesian substrate) provided the morphosyntactic structure which controlled Tok Pisin during its development. Tok Pisin is now a well-established lingua franca throughout Papua New Guinea, and the number of speakers grows steadily. Today the direction of influence is shifting. Tok Pisin has become so widely used by Papua New Guineans that it is now influencing the native languages of its speakers. I gave some examples in chapter 1 of the most drastic influence of Tok Pisin on vernacular languages—replacement. The replacement of the Kuot language by Tok Pisin in New Ireland was detailed in chapter 1, as was the convergence of Nalik to Tok Pisin. These examples are not isolated. In this chapter I will discuss some of the influences of Tok Pisin that are now apparent in the Tigak language.

The renewed influence of English on Tok Pisin is also evident, especially in the contrast between the variety of Tok Pisin spoken in the urban centers as opposed to the varieties spoken in rural areas. Mühlhäusler calls this stage of renewed lexifier influence the postpidginization/postcreolization stage. He says the result of "renewed contact between a pidgin or creole and its original lexifier language is a new third system" (1982:454). The renewed influence of English on Tok Pisin is the result of a growing pidgin-speaking population educated in the English language and the more widespread access to English-language media. The changes occurring in Tok Pisin indicate that English is now becoming a source for morphosyntactic structure in Tok Pisin.

As previously defined, convergence is "the use of morphemes from a single linguistic variety, but with parts of their lexical structure coming from another source" (Myers-Scotton 1998:290). Woolford (1979b) states that convergence indicates a language shift in progress. This is true in the case of Nalik from chapter 1. However, such a shift need not go to completion in one direction, as is the case with the Sumuna language, or apparently the case with Kuot. In some cases the direction of convergence may reverse, and the signs of this reversal can indicate a turnover in the matrix language or changes in the composition of a composite matrix language. Whereas the Austronesian languages originally provided most of the grammatical frame and English most of the morphemes for Tok Pisin, today the direction of grammatical influence has reversed. Tok Pisin is now producing grammatical changes in the Austronesian vernaculars. These changes do not always result in a complete shift to another language. In this chapter I will first discuss some of the influences of Tok Pisin on Tigak, which give evidence of convergence of Tigak (and other local vernaculars) to Tok Pisin. I will then discuss the renewed English influence on Tok Pisin, which is resulting in English contributions to the morphosyntactic structure of modern Tok Pisin. I will also discuss some of the current influences that English is having directly on Tigak.

Tigak Convergence to Tok Pisin

In describing Tok Pisin in chapter 5, I discussed the details of selecting an English lexeme because of congruence at the level of lexical-conceptual structure between the English form and the speaker's intentions and of using the phonological form of that English lexeme within an Austronesian framework, exemplified by Tigak. Now the tables are turning. Tok Pisin is affecting the abstract structures of Tigak because the matrix language of Tigak/Tok Pisin codeswitch(ing) is shifting. I will differentiate the forms in Tigak using Standard Tigak (ST) and Modern Tigak (MT). By Standard Tigak I mean the traditional, conservative Tigak language described in chapter 4. By Modern Tigak I mean the Tigak spoken by (primarily) younger adult Tigaks and teenagers who are attending or have attended high school. These Tigaks are fluent in Tok Pisin and somewhat fluent in English. Many of them live in an urban center, such as Kavieng, or near enough to maintain close contacts with a town. They use Tok Pisin more than they use Tigak during a normal day's activities (or they have done so in recent years).

Convergence at different levels of abstract structure

Standard Tigak exhibits some examples of parallels with Tok Pisin at each of the different levels of abstract structure. Convergence at the lexical-conceptual level is required to express intentions, but the parallels are not always one-to-one. In chapter 5 the problem of semantic transfer from English was illustrated with the Tok Pisin lexemes **pain-im** 'to look/search for something' and **luk-im** 'to see/find something.' Native English speakers often confuse these Tok Pisin words and use them as if the meanings were reversed because of the association with the meanings of the English lexemes copied phonologically in Tok Pisin. As in English, Austronesian languages have different lexemes for these two concepts, seen in the Tigak verbs *sagul-i* 'to look/search for something' and *sivaron-i* 'to find something'. With this pair of lexemes, all three languages (English, Tok Pisin, and Tigak) are parallel conceptually. However, the phonological copies of the English content morphemes do not match the English meanings when they are incorporated into Tok Pisin. This fact is evidence that the pidgin originators were using salient phonological material from the lexifier but did not have control of the conceptual distinctions. There was congruence of meaning between the pair of English lexemes and the speakers' intentions, but a mismatch occurred between the forms and the meanings in the copying process. Lexical-conceptual congruence was also demonstrated in "Word order" in chapter 5 between the phonetically similar forms of English *he* and the third-person singular subject agreement forms of many Austronesian substrate languages (e.g., Tolai and Duke of York *i* and Tigak *gi*) that became the Tok Pisin predicate marker **i**. This congruence at the conceptual level supports Hypothesis (3c), which says that there must be some congruence in lexical-conceptual structure for phonetically similar forms used.

In the case of the Tok Pisin verb **lar-im** 'to leave something', Tigaks reanalyze this bimorphemic form (verb root plus transitive suffix) as a single unit and borrow it into Tigak as if the root were *larim*. To this reanalyzed root form Tigaks add the Tigak transitive marker as required at the morphological realization level of abstract structure to yield *larim-i* 'to leave something'. With this lexeme, the congruence occurs at the lexical-conceptual and the predicate-argument levels but not in the morphological realization pattern. Tigak has borrowed the word's meaning and predicate-argument structure as a transitive verb requiring a transitive suffix to point to an object. However, Tigak did not borrow the morphological realization pattern of the Tok Pisin word as a root plus transitive suffix. Had that been the case, the Tigak form would have been the root *lar* (as in Tok Pisin) to which the Tigak transitive suffix *-i* would be added, resulting in the form *lar-i*.

In the case of another verb, Tigaks have accepted the Tok Pisin forms at all three levels of abstract structure. They have borrowed the meanings, the morphological forms, and the predicate-argument structures of the intransitive Tok Pisin form **kuk** 'to cook' as an intransitive verb and the Tok Pisin transitive form **kukim** 'to cook something' as a complete transitive verb to which they do not add the additional transitive suffix. Thus, the surface forms *kuk* and *kukim* are used in Tigak in parallel ways as in Tok Pisin, (cf. (12)–(14) in chapter 1). As pointed out in chapter 4, there are some transitive verbs in Tigak that are semantically transitive and do not take the transitive suffix even when an overt object is given. Since this pattern is not unknown in the Tigak language, there is congruence between the two languages at all three levels.

Lexical-conceptual convergence and the loss of L1 distinctions

Because Tok Pisin so closely resembles Tigak structurally and conceptually, it is sometimes difficult to see evidence of convergence. Instead one must look at the morpheme types used and the sometimes subtle conceptual changes they reveal. For example, in Tigak the plural marker for count nouns is *(ma)mana(n)*, which also serves as an indefinite quantifier, but the indefinite quantifier for mass nouns is *rin*. In Tok Pisin the plural marker is the third-person plural pronoun **ol,** and the indefinite quantifier is **sampela.**

(221) a. *ta   mamanan ien* [ST]
　　　　ART PL　　　fish
　　　　'fish (pl) / some fish'

　　　b. *tang (rin)　bensin* [ST]
　　　　ART IND.QNT gasoline
　　　　'(some) gasoline'

(222) a. **ol pis** [TP]
　　　　PL fish
　　　　'fish (pl)'

　　　b. **sampela pis** [TP]
　　　　some　　fish
　　　　'some fish'

Young Tigaks today often transfer the semantic difference between plural and indefinite quantity in Tok Pisin to Tigak without regard for the count versus mass noun distinction. They reanalyze the quantifier in terms of the Tok Pisin semantics instead of the standard Tigak subcategorization, yielding the form in (223a) instead of the standard in (223b).

(223) a. *nug   kukim tang rin   ien*   [MT]
      2SG.S.AGR cook ART IND.QNT fish
      'Are you cooking some fish?'

    b. *nug   kukim ta mamanan ien*   [ST]
      2SG.S.AGR cook ART IND.QNT   fish
      'Are you cooking (some) fish?'

Although Tok Pisin is conceptually very close to Austronesian languages, there are also lexical-conceptual differences between Tigak and Tok Pisin. For example, Tok Pisin has only one word, **kolpela,** for the meaning 'cold', whereas Austronesian languages commonly have multiple lexemes used in different contexts as in (224). The single Tok Pisin lexeme may be the result of a selection or simplification process during pidgin formation because of lack of congruence in the languages involved in the contact situation. For example, in English the one lexeme *cold* covers all the meanings given in (224). There may also have been differences in the substrate languages in this respect. In contrast to Tok Pisin, standard Tigak has three different words used in three different culturally important contexts.

(224) *(lip)lipuk*   'cold (for sea or bath water)'   [ST]
     (mal)malakup 'cold (drinking water)'
     vutung   'to feel cold (a person)'

(225) **kolpela**   'cold'   [TP]

Many young Tigaks now use only *malmalakup* for all meanings of 'cold', converging to the lexical-conceptual pattern of Tok Pisin. Similarly, the distinction between the two different Tigak lexemes for 'hot' is being lost among younger Tigak speakers converging to Tok Pisin with its single lexeme, **hatpela** 'hot'. Examples (226) and (227) show a loss in distinctions among Tigak content morphemes. Example (227b) shows that *manaas* is taking over the meaning for *tutun* and replacing it in modern Tigak.

(226) ta   laman gi   manaas   [ST]
     ART water 3SG.S.AGR hot
     'The water is hot.' (*manaas* 'to be hot')

(227) a. ta   kuliti-na   gi   ***tutun***   [ST]
        ART skin/body-3SG 3SG.S.AGR be.hot
        'His body is hot'/'He has a fever.' (*tun* 'to be hot to touch')

     b. ta   kuliti-na   gi   ***manaas***   [MT]
        ART skin/body-3SG 3SG.S.AGR be.hot
        'His body is hot'/'He has a fever.'

An example of the loss of distinctions in late system morphemes among young Tigaks involves the locative forms. As described in chapter 4, Tigak has three locative markers. The need for a locative is established at the conceptual level, the slot is created at the lemma level and filled at the functional level, but the exact form of the locative is structurally assigned at the positional level by the class of noun that is the object of the locative preposition. Standard Tigak requires *lo* before a common place name, *e* before a proper place name, and *su* before an animate recipient.

(228) ***lo*** kono   'to/on/at [the] beach/sand'   [ST]
      e Kavieng   'to/at/in Kavieng'
      su Dinia   'to/from/for Dinia'
      su-na   'to/from/for 3SG (animate)'

Bilingual Tok Pisin/Tigak speakers for whom Tigak is still the primary language (i.e., the language determining the morphosyntactic structure of speech) have command of Tigak late system morphemes. However, those bilingual speakers for whom Tok Pisin has become the dominant language, while still using Tigak morphemes in a locative construction, use the morphemes according to the Tok Pisin conceptual structure. Tok Pisin has only one locative preposition, **long,** and it is used in all the same contexts as in (229).

(229) ***long*** **nambis**   'to/on/at/from [the] beach/sand'   [TP]
      long **Kavieng** 'to/at/in Kavieng'
      long **Dinia**   'to/from/for Dinia'
      long en   'to/from/for 3SG'

Many young Tigak speakers (primarily on the mainland of New Ireland where they are more exposed to Tok Pisin) now use the single Tigak locative *lo* in all three contexts. The actual morpheme is Tigak, but conflation of forms has occurred. Thus, the phrases in (228) become (230).

(230) **lo** *kono*   'to/on/at [the] beach/sand'   [MT]
    lo Kavieng   'to/at/in Kavieng'
    lo Dinia   'to/from/for Dinia'
    lo-*na*   'to/from/for 3SG'

In some cases these mainland Tigaks have even replaced the Tigak purpose conjunction *ina*[42] with *lo*, as in (231), based on the Tok Pisin purpose construction with **bilong** in (232). The reason for this substitution of *lo* for *ina* may be by analogous extension. Since the Tok Pisin forms **long** and **bilong** are both so similar phonologically to the Tigak locative *lo*, those speakers for whom Tok Pisin has become the dominant language may reanalyze the Tigak *lo* as the equivalent to both Tok Pisin forms and use the *lo* in all contexts analogous to the uses of Tok Pisin **long** and **bilong.**

(231) a. *gi   aisok   **ina**   marmarai tang dais*   [ST]
      3SG.S.AGR work   in.order.to buy   ART   rice
      'He works to buy rice.'

   b. *gi   aisok   **lo**   marmarai tang dais*   [MT]
      3SG.S.AGR work   in.order.to buy   ART   rice
      'He works to buy rice.'

(232) **em i   wok *bilong*   bai-m rais**   [TP]
     3SG PM work in.order.to buy-TZ rice
     'He works to buy rice.'

Another example of conceptual convergence (which is also occurring in Tok Pisin) involves the semantic range of the kinship term for 'father' discussed in chapter 5. In Tigak the form *tama-* 'father' covers uncles as well as the biological father (as does **papa** in Tok Pisin). Among English-educated Tigaks the English semantic restriction of the lexeme *papa* to only the biological father is affecting their Tigak. These Tigaks still use the form *na tama-g* 'my father' when referring to an uncle, but more often now they will specify when they mean their biological father by adding *atuman* 'true/real' to the

---

[42]The conjunction *i-na* (perhaps meaning 'for it') is actually two morphemes: the genitive preposition *i* and the third-person singular prepositional object *na*.

kinship term to yield *na tama-g atuman* 'my real father'. (In Tok Pisin the corresponding expression now is **papa stret** 'father straight/real'.)

Convergence of predicate-argument structure

Another example indicating that Tok Pisin is becoming the dominant language for some Tigaks involves the convergence to Tok Pisin in the loss of subcategorization distinctions for double object verbs. Standard Tigak has two verbs meaning 'to give', but they subcategorize for different primary objects and for different prepositions introducing the second object. These verbs are illustrated in (233).

(233) a. *tang anu ga* **lisan-i ta piu su-na ta lakek** [ST]
ART man 3SG.S.AGR.PST give-TZ ART dog LOC-3SG ART child
'The man *gave a/the dog to a/the child.*'

b. *tang anu ga* **tave-i ta lakek pa-na ta piu**
ART man 3SG.S.AGR.PST give-TZ ART child with-3SG ART dog
'The man *gave a/the child a/the dog.*'

The semantic difference between the two verbs is seen if they are translated as in (234).

(234) a. *lisan-i* 'to give something'
b. *tave-i* 'to give to someone' [ST]

The examples in (233) show that the complement of each verb as defined in (234) immediately follows the verb, and the secondary (dative) object follows the verb complement as the object in a prepositional phrase. The verb *lisan-i* subcategorizes to take a patient object with the recipient object introduced by the preposition *su-*. The verb *tave-i* subcategorizes to take a recipient object with the patient object introduced by the preposition *pa-*. In Tok Pisin three of the four possible patterns for double object constructions occur, as illustrated in (235) (see Bruyn, Muysken, and Verrips 1999 for a full discussion of double-object constructions in creoles).

(235) a. **em i giv-im dok long pikinini** [TP]
3SG PM give-TZ dog to child
'He gave/gives a/the dog to a/the child.'

b. **em i giv-im pikinini long dok**
   3SG PM give-TZ child with dog
   'He gave/gives a/the child a/the dog.'

c. **em i giv-im pikinini dok**
   3SG PM give-TZ child dog
   'He gave/gives a/the child a/the dog.'

d. *em i giv-im dok pikinini

It is not surprising to find these three patterns in Tok Pisin since all three are found among the languages involved in the formation of the pidgin, the first two in the Austronesian substrate and the third in English. Bruyn et al. quote Mühlhäusler as giving examples like (235a) and (235b) and specifying the (235a) type to be from the mainland and the (235b) type to be from the islands. In fact, both types are heard in about equal proportions on New Ireland. I have records of the type illustrated by (235c), which is modeled after one of the English double-object patterns, uttered only by non-native New Irelanders who learned Tok Pisin after learning English.

Young Tigak speakers on the mainland of New Ireland near Kavieng now mix the lexical restrictions for the two Tigak verbs. Examples (236) and (237) were heard on public transportation in Kavieng.

(236) *rig-a   **lisan-au**   pa-na   ta   **pook***   [MT]
      3PL.S.AGR-PST give-1SG.OB.AGR with-3SG ART food
      'They *gave me food.*'

(237) *vo nug   tave-i   ta   mani   su-gug*
      IRR 2SG.S.AGR give-TZ ART money to-1SG
      'Will you *give the money to me?*'

From these examples it is clear that even if these young Tigaks still know both Tigak content morphemes for the verb 'to give', they have not retained the lexical distinctions as to what type of objects each verb requires. I claim that this is convergence with Tok Pisin at the level of predicate-argument structure, in which the verb **giv-im** may take either a patient or a recipient object.

Convergence of morphological realization patterns

There are also the more noticeable aspects of convergence on the surface, at the morphological realization level. English phonemes, such as /f h j y w/ that were adopted by Tok Pisin along with the lexemes in which those phonemes occur have, in turn, been adopted into Tigak as it has borrowed Tok Pisin words and names, such as *wain* 'wine', *yist* 'yeast', *hamma* 'hammer', *James*, and *Frank*. The forms *yist* and *Frank* show that consonant clusters have also entered the language. As such clusters become more familiar, younger Tigaks are eliminating some of the epenthetical vowels common in the Tok Pisin speech of more traditional Tigaks. Thus, among younger Tigaks **sitoa** is realized as **stoa** 'store' and **kilak** is realized as **klak** 'clock'. Simplification of vowel sequences is also an influence of Tok Pisin. Tigak has twenty-one diphthongs compared to Tok Pisin's three. Some pronounced sequences in Tigak are not phonemic, but predictable. For example, a front vowel followed by the velar obstruent /k/ often requires the epenthesis of the low mid vowel /a/, as in (238). This low mid vowel is now often omitted by younger Tigaks, producing the changes indicated in (238).

(238) /gavek/ = [gaveak] → [gavek] 'no' [ST] → [MT]
/laklik/ = [lakliak] → [laklik] 'little'

The distinction between long vowels (a geminate sequence) and short vowels (a single vowel) is also no longer made or recognized by many younger Tigaks. To these speakers the words *gup* 'triggerfish' and *guup* 'dark color' are homophones, and they do not always understand the difference when they hear the words. The following exchange occurred on the beach of an island at dusk as an older man (OM) was unloading some fish from his canoe and speaking to a young nephew (YN) who was home from school in Kavieng.

(239) OM: ga gup
3SG.S.AGR.PST triggerfish
'It's triggerfish.'

YN: ong tang ias ga a-kamus
yes ART sun 3SG.S.AGR.PST CS-finish
'Yes, the sun is gone.'
[thinking the man had said *ga guup* 'it's dark']

OM: *gavek gavek nag togan-i gup a-kurul*
     no   no   1SG.S.AGR have-TZ triggerfish CS-be.full
'No, no! I've got lots of triggerfish.'

Discourse convergence

Evidence of Tok Pisin influence on Tigak at the level of discourse organization is found in the innovative use of two conjunctions. The Tok Pisin conjunction **na** can mean 'and' or 'so' as in (240) and (241).

(240) **ol man i kis-im savol *na* ol i raus-im graun** [TP]
     PL man PM get-TZ shovel and 3PL PM rouse-TZ ground
'The men got shovels *and* cleared the ground (dug a hole).'

(241) **ren i bin kam *na* mi kam bek long haus**
     rain PM PST come so 1SG come back to house
'It was raining *so* I came back to the house.'

In Tigak the coordinating conjunction is *e*, and there is a sequential conjunction *neva* ~ *ne* meaning 'then' or 'until'. Perhaps because of the phonological similarity or because the Tungag coordinating conjunction is also *na*, as in Tok Pisin, some Tigaks now use the Tok Pisin conjunction in Tigak.

(242) *karatul a ngaulngaul **na** kapseil-i akuru tang ien* [MT]
     1TR.INC.S.AGR MA fish   and catch-TZ plenty ART fish

     ***na** karatul ngan-i-ri*
     so 1TR.INC.S.AGR eat-TZ-3PL.OB.AGR
'We(3) went fishing *and* caught plenty *so* we ate them.'

In standard Tigak the first *na* in (242) would be *e* and the second *na* would be *neva* (or *ne*).

Another construction introduced by younger Tigaks is the use of *gaan* (meaning 'day' or 'time') as a subordinating conjunction meaning 'when'. A comparison of the standard Tigak construction and that of modern Tigak and Tok Pisin is given in (243)–(245). Loss of the system morphemes in the standard Tigak phrase *lo tang gaan* indicates that Tok Pisin is controlling the morphosyntactic structure of this construction.

(243) **lo tang gaan** tang vuul   gi   me sang vo nag   [ST]
      LOC ART time ART canoe 3SG.S.AGR MT arrive IRR 1SG.S.AGR

   kos
   board
   'When the canoe arrives I will get on' (lit., *at the time...*).

(244) **taim** mun   i   kam   bai   mi   kis-im   [TP]
      time canoe PM   come FUT   1SG get-TZ
      'When the canoe arrives I will get on.'

(245) **gaan** *tang vuul/ta mun*[43] *gi me sang vo nag kos*   [MT]
      'When the canoe arrives I will get on.'

Pragmatic convergence

Convergence at the pragmatic level is found in the use of questions such as 'What are you doing?' or 'Where are you going?' Tigaks would consider direct questions as being extremely impolite, even from close relatives. A traditional Tigak would not ask a direct question (using a question word) to gain information about another's activity. He would, instead, ask the question in the form of a statement, such as 'You are carving a canoe?' or 'You are going to the garden?' or make a statement such as 'I am going to the garden' in the expectation that the other would reply by saying where he/she is going. Young Tigaks are converging to the Tok Pisin convention of asking direct questions and of confronting people directly with complaints or accusations. This practice in Tok Pisin is an example of how abstract levels are split since the conceptual level in this case is from English, but the morphosyntactic patterns are from the Austronesian substratum. Today, Tigak is converging toward Tok Pisin in usage style by adopting the more direct approaches that English imparted to Tok Pisin.

Tok Pisin Convergence to English

As stated earlier English has had a renewed impact on Tok Pisin since the original formation of Melanesian Pidgin English. The fact that English was withdrawn from the population of the islands region of Papua New Guinea

---

[43]The nouns *vuul* and *mun* are used almost interchangeably in Tigak. The form *mun* (borrowed from Tok Pisin **mun**) is more common among speakers from the mainland of New Ireland.

when the German administration was in power and the fact that the Germans did not encourage the use of their language by the indigenous population gave the Austronesian languages of the indigenous population an advantage in influencing the developing pidgin. English influence was reintroduced with the Australian administration after WWI. However, the variety of Tok Pisin learned by most Papua New Guineans was learned in their own language areas and on school playgrounds where English had little power to influence an established lingua franca. The strong renewed influence of English has come from two directions. The first is the push for higher education on the part of Papua New Guineans themselves. English is the medium of this higher education (i.e., above grade 6). The second is the growth of urban centers that are dependent on (mostly) English-speaking expatriates serving in business and governmental positions. Knowing English is not only a status symbol, but also the best means of obtaining a wage-paying job in business or government. This increased use of English in those two contexts and the status that comes with English have made it the language of the elite in Papua New Guinea. The impact of English is best seen in the differences between the urban and rural varieties of Tok Pisin.

Lexical borrowing

The prestige of the language has resulted in "heavy borrowing from English," as reported by Mühlhäusler (1982:457). However, most of these loans are cultural borrowings, filling lexical gaps. All the examples Mühlhäusler gives are content morphemes, such as **eleksen** 'election' and **spika** 'speaker' (in Parliament), which have no structural influence on Tok Pisin. In hearing almost any politician or urban pastor speak it is obvious that borrowing and/or codeswitching from English are becoming more prevalent and acceptable. In one recorded sermon delivered to a Tok Pisin congregation by a Papuan New Guinean for whom Tok Pisin is at least his third language (after English), approximately 40 percent of the message was English (figured by lexeme count). Most of the recently acquired loans are still cultural loans (e.g., **satalait dis** 'satellite dish' and **vidio** 'video'), but some core vocabulary is also being replaced (e.g., **bicaus** instead of **long wanem** 'because').

Numbers and noun constructions

Other forms of borrowing by urban Tok Pisin speakers have changed some structural patterns. Two examples are in some numbers and in some NPs. Mühlhäusler (1979) gives the following examples comparing rural and urban Tok Pisin.

(246) **wanpela ten wan**   'eleven'   [Rural TP]
     eleven(pela)   'eleven'   [Urban TP]

Rural Tok Pisin speakers still follow the substrate patterns for constructing higher numerals, whereas the urban speakers are more often copying the English lexemes. Similarly, NPs that in rural Tok Pisin are often structured according to the Austronesian complex noun construction of two juxtaposed nouns (cf. (61) NP → article NN) are replaced in urban Tok Pisin by an English-like modifier plus noun construction as in (247). (These examples are also from Mühlhäusler 1979, but the differences between rural and urban speakers still hold.)

(247) Rural Tok Pisin   Urban Tok Pisin
     tok ples   **ples tok**   'local language'
     sit bet   **betsit**   'bed sheet'

Negative questions

Two other areas of convergence of urban Tok Pisin to English have been mentioned elsewhere in this study. They are the answers to negative questions and the use of overt tense and plural markers. The confusion over answers to negative questions among Tok Pisin speakers is a reflection of a changing composite matrix language in Tok Pisin. I discussed the confusion of expatriates speaking Tok Pisin with regard to responses to negative questions in chapter 5. The Tok Pisin pattern followed that of the Austronesian contributing languages in answering the negative statement within the question.

(248) a. **yu no   laik   pis**
        2SG NEG like/want fish
        'Do you not like/want fish?'

     b. **nogat (mi laik pis)**
        no   1SG like fish
        'No (I do like/want fish).'

     c. **tru (mi no liak pis)**
        yes 1SG NEG like fish
        'Yes (I do not like/want fish).'

With the growing influence of English in urban centers, some Papua New Guineans are changing to the English practice of answering the positive form of the question. From the English perspective 'no' means 'I do not want fish' and 'yes' means 'I do want fish'. Under these circumstances no one is sure of the answer to a negative question.

Tense marking and participant reference

The Tok Pisin pattern of marking tense, participants, and plurals has followed the Austronesian practices of using an overt marker when first establishing the time frame and the participants and later only when deemed necessary for understanding in the case of participant changes or long intervals between mentions. In each of these cases urban Tok Pisin is converging more to the English structure by overtly marking each clause with tense, naming participants more often, and overtly marking all occurrences of plural nouns. Loss of number distinctions is also occurring in urban Tok Pisin. The plural pronoun forms are replacing the trial forms (using **tripela**).[44] Mühlhäusler has claimed that "tense is one of the few innovations that can be ascribed to direct borrowing from English" (1982:450) in Tok Pisin. I think the evidence disproves that statement. As was demonstrated in chapter 5 with examples (121) and (175)–(180), the morphosyntactic pattern of marking tense in Tok Pisin is the same as in the Austronesian substrate languages. He is correct, however, in that the frequency of overtly marking tense is now becoming more like English among urban Tok Pisin speakers.

Tigak Convergence to English

Tense marking and participant reference

The convergence of Tok Pisin toward English in terms of tense marking is also affecting vernacular languages such as Tigak. Educated young Tigaks often use overt tense markings in each clause throughout a Tigak discourse, following the English (and the urban Tok Pisin) structure. As argued in chapter 5, the Austronesian L1s of Tok Pisin speakers determine the position of the future marker **bai**. Examples (187b) and (188) of chapter 5 illustrated the variable position of the irrealis (future) marker in two

---

[44]It can be argued that the lack of trial forms is a substrate influence since not every indigenous language of Papua New Guinea has trial pronouns. This may be true for some Tok Pisin speakers. However, I will discuss this same number loss in Tigak in the next section.

neighboring Austronesian languages of New Ireland, Tigak and Kara. In Tungag (Tigak's neighboring language in the opposite direction from Kara) there is no overt future marking except for temporal adverbs. I claim that this variation in the vernaculars of the speakers of Tok Pisin on New Ireland accounts for the variation in future marking in Tok Pisin. However, among urban Tigaks who use Tok Pisin extensively and who are exposed to and use English in their work domain, the pattern of future marking is diverging from that of Tigak (clause initial position) toward that of English (between subject and verb), as illustrated in (249).

(249) a. ***vo   gi   inang lo   sitoa***   [ST]
         IRR 3SG.S.AGR go   LOC store

   b. *gi   **vo** inang lo   stoa*   [MT]
      3SG.S.AGR IRR go   LOC store
      'He will go to the store.'

This change of position of a Tigak system morpheme (*vo*) shows convergence, indicating a matrix language turnover for those Tigaks for whom Tigak is no longer the dominant language.

Plural marking and number distinctions

Similarly, just as plural marking is becoming more frequent in urban Tok Pisin, the overt plural morpheme is used with almost half the plural nouns (46 percent by count in transcribed material) in modern Tigak compared to less than one-fifth (19 percent) in standard Tigak. Modern Tigak speakers are also following the Tok Pisin trend of losing the trial number distinction in the pronominal system and replacing it with the plural. This process is exactly parallel to that in Tok Pisin. In modern Tok Pisin the suffix **-tripela** is often dropped, and in modern Tigak the suffix *-tul* is increasingly dropped. Otherwise the trial and plural forms are identical in each language. It is difficult to determine whether this process is convergence toward English or a more universal simplification process, though the simplification appears to be convergence toward English away from the more complicated L1 system.

Possessives

The examples of convergence of Tigak to English given above could all be an indirect influence through Tok Pisin, since these changes have also occurred in urban Tok Pisin. One change evident among young Tigaks is more clearly a direct influence of English on the language. The Naliks, as discussed in chapter 1, are losing the distinction between alienable and inalienable possession. Although the Tigaks have not progressed to that point in convergence toward English, there is evidence of convergence, none the less. In describing possessive constructions in Tigak in chapter 4, example (99), repeated here as (250), showed two structurally different patterns for alienable possession.

(250) a. **ka**-na   lui
        GEN-3SG   house
        'his house'

     b. lui   **ta**-na
        house   GEN-3SG
        'his house'

Example (251) illustrates benefactive possession.

(251) ta   pook   **ka**-na
       ART   food   GEN-3SG
       'his food' (i.e., 'food for him')

The construction in (250a) is the only one found in my data corpus spoken by young educated Tigaks. It is used even in cases of clear benefactive possession, such as (252a). A friend bringing in a meal for a patient made this statement to a nurse at the local hospital where family members are responsible to supply patients' meals. The standard Tigak construction is given in (252b).

(252) a. nag   suk   ima   **ka-na**   **pook**   [MT]
        1SG.S.AGR get   come   GEN-3SG   food
        'I am bringing food for him.'

     b. nag   suk   ima   **ta**   **pook ka**-na   [ST]
        1SG.S.AGR get   come   ART   food   GEN-3SG
        'I am bringing food for him.'

This use of a standard Tigak construction in an innovative way is evidence of convergence to English at the conceptual level. The construction cannot come from Tok Pisin because Tok Pisin has no preposed possessive construction. Although the benefactive possession can be expressed in English with the prepositional phrase 'food for him', it is more often expressed by the simple possessive 'his food'. These young English-educated Tigaks no longer make the structural distinctions that express the semantic distinctions between simple possession and benefactive possession.

7
Conclusion

Papua New Guinea is a small country with the greatest linguistic diversity found in the world today, having approximately 850 languages distributed among a population of only four million. As many as five or more languages may be found within a fifty-mile radius of almost any point within the country. Because of this proximity of many languages, most Papua New Guineans speak two or more languages, making it a multilingual country in both the individual and social senses of Edwards (1994). There are advantages and disadvantages to linguistic diversity, and situations producing each change over time. Linguistic diversity builds walls. Walls help maintain ethnic identity and intragroup cohesion. They may enhance an individual's sense of security and belonging. In Papua New Guinea today this linguistic diversity that was promoted and emphasized in the tribal culture of the past is losing much of its appeal. The formerly separated and self-sufficient individual language groups have been forced into (more or less) unified administrative districts in recent centuries and into a single, self-governing nation less than thirty years ago. The needs and desires now are for education and mobility to gain economic or social advancement. Division by language is not conducive to these modern needs. Languages of wider communication are required. Two languages of wider communication are now used: English, introduced by an outside colonial power, and Tok Pisin, developed in its present form within Papua New Guinea by Papua New Guineans.

The purpose of this study was to analyze selected language contact phenomena occurring in New Ireland Province of Papua New Guinea in light of their relationships and influences on each other. In particular, I have focused on the relationship of Tok Pisin with both the superstrate (English) and the substrate (Austronesian) languages within the theoretical framework of the extended matrix language frame, Abstract Level, and 4-M models. I will summarize the findings concerning the various language contact phenomena in New Ireland in the next section. Then I will consider what this study has revealed about Tok Pisin. Finally, I will discuss the findings of this study relating to the hypotheses proposed in chapter 3.

The Interrelationships of Language Contact Phenomena in New Ireland

Many language contact phenomena are currently observable in northwestern New Ireland in Papua New Guinea. These phenomena range from lexical borrowing among monolingual speakers of a New Ireland vernacular, through codeswitching, diglossia, convergence, shift, and attrition, all the way to the ultimate attrition: language death. These phenomena are all related and begin with bilingualism and then codeswitching among bilinguals (see Myers-Scotton 1992a, 1997a, and Scotton 1986). Whether the incursions of one language into the other go beyond core content morpheme borrowing to actual language shift or even language death depends on other factors in addition to linguistic ones. Dorian comments that it is unusual for a language to die because of high prestige, but "it's fairly common for a language to become so exclusively associated with low-prestige people and their socially disfavored identities that its own potential speakers prefer to distance themselves from it and adopt some other language" (1998:3). This shift to another language is currently in progress among the Nalik and Kuot speakers of New Ireland. The former speakers of the language of Sumuna have completed the shift and lost their Sumuna language. Even among urban Tigaks in Kavieng the higher prestige and usefulness of Tok Pisin and English are resulting in a shift from the vernacular.

Referring to a phenomenon as language loss is, according to Edwards, "perhaps less accurate than language change. People are never, after all, at a point without any language" (1994:116). In fact, all New Irelanders (and all Papua New Guineans) still do have a language, and most know several languages. Tok Pisin is spoken by all school children and by the vast majority of adults. It is the primary language of wider communication for New Irelanders and serves the social function of uniting speakers of different languages in Papua New Guinea. Tok Pisin also serves the social function of distinguishing its speaker from a **bus kanaka** 'uncivilized native'. Well-educated New Irelanders also know English. It is the prestige language for many public situations. The social functions of Tok Pisin among New Irelanders make it unlikely that it will be replaced as a LWC. English will also maintain its niche as the language of the educated elite and as a means of relating to the outside (non-Papua New Guinean) world, but it is not likely to become the most widely known language of New Ireland.

More of the New Ireland vernaculars will disappear in the years to come. Knowledgeable speakers of Kuot may die out with the present adult generation. Nalik speakers will be found in the Nalik area for some generations to come, but the Nalik language will be different, more like Tok Pisin, with each new generation. Other New Ireland vernaculars, such as Tigak, Tungag, and Tiang, among others, will be maintained for the foreseeable future. Tungag and Tigak have the largest numbers of speakers of all the indigenous languages in New Ireland. These three languages are also isolated geographically on islands away from the mainland of New Ireland. Farther south on New Ireland the language groups are also more removed from the urban culture of Kavieng, so the speakers use the vernacular in the everyday life of the community. These factors reinforce language maintenance in those particular groups of speakers. As Schiffman noted, "speech communities have belief systems about their language...these beliefs are part of the social conditions that affect the maintenance and transmission of that language" (1997:211). The New Irelanders' belief systems about their languages will in the end determine which languages are maintained and for how long.

Tok Pisin: Its Development and Its Future

Pidgins and creoles are languages resulting from contact situations involving multiple languages and an immediate need to communicate. As such, they do not fit neatly into any of the traditional theories of language change and development. Because of my experience working in Papua New Guinea among speakers of an Austronesian language, I am convinced of the Austronesian influence on Tok Pisin. However, most of the substrate theories of pidgin formation have only been adequate in describing possible sources for vocabulary and individual grammatical structures rather than in explaining how the choices are made or why.

The preponderance of English word forms in Tok Pisin is obvious from first hearing the language. Although the morphosyntactic frame of Tok Pisin is

Austronesian (because the L1s of the speakers were structurally similar and, therefore, accessible to most of them), English was the prestigious superstrate language and the single language most substrate language speakers most wanted to acquire. However, they did not have access to the grammatical structures of English, only to the phonological forms of English content and early system morphemes. The English content morphemes became both content morphemes and grammatical morphemes in Tok Pisin. Content morphemes are conceptually activated, so they can be used to express speakers' intentions. Bolinger says, "words are not coined in order to extract the meanings of their elements and compile a new meaning from them. The new meaning is there FIRST" (1975:109, emphasis in the original). In order to express their intentions, the developers of Tok Pisin must have found some similarity between their intentions and the meaning of an English form. However, these English forms do not always have exactly the same meanings in Tok Pisin as the English source words.

In reference to child language learning, Clark's principle of contrast states that "any difference in FORM in a language indicates that there is a difference in MEANING. The reverse does not hold since the same form may be used to express several meanings" (1987:318, emphasis in the original). In Tok Pisin a single form often expresses more than one meaning. Where do the often multiple meanings of Tok Pisin forms come from if not from the English source? The primary alternative source is from the speakers' intentions, and a secondary source is from other languages having input into the pidgin formation. These languages are the substrate languages, the native languages of Tok Pisin speakers.

The semantic parallels between Tok Pisin and the Austronesian substrate languages are striking. Some of these parallels were discussed in chapter 5 including the pronominal system and kinship and body part terms and some problem areas for English speakers in the semantic of Tok Pisin **luk** 'find/see' and **pain** 'look for' and in answering negatively stated questions. Sometimes a concept that English expresses in a single lexeme requires two in Tok Pisin, following the conceptual pattern of the substrate languages. Cognitive concepts involving speech and thought seem especially prone to such calquing, as in (253).

(253) Tok Pisin   Tigak
    tok pilai   *etok epuk*   talk play = 'joke'
    tok tru   *etok atuman*   talk true = 'truth'
    tok ples   *etok siva*   talk village = 'native language'
    lusim tingting   *nol gavani*   lose thought = 'forget'

Similarly, a single form functions in Tok Pisin (**tasol** < English 'that's all') and in Tigak (*kisang*) as both the contrastive conjunction 'but' (254) and as a restrictive modifier 'only/just' (255).

(254) a. **em   i   gat   mani   *tasol* em   i   no   givim pe**   [TP]
       3SG PM   have money but   3SG PM NEG give   pay

   long mi
   to   1SG

   b. *nane   gi   togani ta   mani   **kisang** gi*   [Tigak]
      3SG.PRN 3SG.S.AG   have   ART   money   but   3SG.S.AGR

   veko lisani ta   pulpul su-gug
   NEG   give   ART   pay   to-1SG
   'He has money, but he did not pay me.'

(255) a. **ol   i   pilai   *tasol***   [TP]
         3PL PM play   only

   b. *nari rig   karau **kisang***   [Tigak]
      3PL 3PL.S.AGR play   only
      'They're only playing.'

These examples demonstrate that the semantic range and function of many Tok Pisin lexemes come from the Austronesian substrate languages. However, most of the phonetic forms are adopted from a lexifier (or superstrate) language because this was the prestige language and the target of acquisition to the extent that it was available to the substrate speakers. The superstrate was also the one common language available (at least to a limited extent) to all speakers for expressing their intentions. Except for the morpheme **save** 'to know' from Portuguese and **beten** 'to pray' from German, all the superstrate lexemes discussed in this study are from English phonological forms, with a few substrate Austronesian lexemes for culturally relevant terms. Thus, splitting the abstract levels and accessing some levels from one source language and other levels from different source languages contribute to the production of a composite matrix language that dictates the morphosyntactic structure of Tok Pisin.

As demonstrated in chapter 5 and illustrated in appendix 2, the features of Tok Pisin are a mixture of features from different languages. However, the mixture is not random or unprincipled. Principles extrapolated from the extended Matrix Language Frame model, the Abstract Level model, and the 4-M model combined with the sociopolitical factors of the contact situation make it predictable that the morphosyntactic frame of Tok Pisin is a composite frame based on the Austronesian substrate languages, whereas most of the phonological forms are taken from other languages, primarily the superstrate, English. In particular, the Abstract Level and 4-M models lead to the hypotheses concerning the types of morphemes available for incorporation into a pidgin/creole. The examples above have demonstrated how Tok Pisin has developed using the structural and semantic-conceptual base of its substrate Austronesian languages as a composite matrix language and lexical items from multiple languages (but mostly from English) to provide the content and system morphemes according to the hypotheses of this theoretical framework. The examples presented here are only suggestive of the range of analysis possible using these models with respect to pidgin/creole formation. However, the number and diversity of forms and structures demonstrated here to be explained by the model are an impetus for more thorough analysis with Tok Pisin and for more research in applying the model to other pidgins and creoles.

Findings and Conclusions

Much of the evidence in this section relates to more than one hypothesis, but I will summarize with the most applicable examples in each case.

Hypothesis 1: The Austronesian substrate grammatical frame is the matrix language for Tok Pisin.

   a. This matrix language for Tok Pisin is a composite matrix language formed by splitting the abstract levels of language structure and recombining those levels to form a grammatical frame composed of aspects from different individual languages. Most of the conceptual structure, predicate-argument structure, and morphological patterns come from the Austronesian languages, but most of the phonological forms come from English, based on some degree of lexical-conceptual congruence between English the Austronesian substrate.

   b. This composite matrix language is a result of compromises among the various Austronesian speakers, and the variations in Tok Pisin

Findings and Conclusions 213

reveal the differences in the substrate languages producing the pidgin.

Chapter 5 is an extensive analysis of Tok Pisin's abstract structure and the various sources for the different levels of structure under the Abstract Level model. The splitting of the lexical-conceptual abstract level is described in detail in "Constituent and morpheme types in Tok Pisin" in chapter 5 with analyses of the Tok Pisin lexemes **han, lek,** and **papa.** The previous section gives additional examples that support (1a) above. The impact of differences in the substrate languages was demonstrated with the variation found in the placement of the future marker **bai** in Tok Pisin, supporting (1b).

Hypothesis 2: The matrix language (especially a composite matrix language) need not remain unchanged in a language contact situation. Rather, the matrix language will change as the dominance of the languages in the contact situation changes.

   a. A matrix language turnover can occur with language shift from an L1 to Tok Pisin and/or English and can be seen in the changes in L1 and Tok Pisin usages and structures.

   b. Convergence is the first step in developing a composite matrix language leading to a matrix language turnover. Convergence is defined as a phenomenon in which abstract lexical structure comes from more than one variety, but all the surface forms come from a single variety.

Changes in the grammatical constructions used by bilingual speakers indicate movement in the direction of a matrix language turnover. Convergence shows the influence of abstract lexical structure from one language on monolingual speech in a different language. The effects of Tok Pisin on Nalik were described in chapter 1. Convergence was seen in the loss of Nalik inalienable possession constructions. Convergence of Tigak to Tok Pisin was illustrated in chapter 6 with the replacement of Tok Pisin semantics for Tigak plural and indefinite quantifiers, changing the morpheme types. Convergence at the lexical-conceptual level was exemplified by the loss of L1 distinctions in Tigak lexemes for 'hot' and 'cold' and for locative prepositions. Predicate-argument structure convergence was demonstrated by the loss of subcategorization differences between the two Tigak lexemes for 'to give'. Tigak convergence to English at the morphological realization level was explained by changes in the position of the irrealis marker in Tigak to the position between the subject-agreement marker and the verb, with changes in the frequency of tense marking to that approaching English, with the loss of the trial number distinction, and with the loss of the separate benefactive possession construction to a single preposed genitive. Tok Pisin convergence to English was illustrated through the increased use of overt tense marking and participant reference patterns, including plural marking of nouns. Even phonetic convergence toward English is occurring in Tigak with the introduction of new phonemes and consonant clusters and with the simplification of vowel sequences in Tigak. All these examples of convergence from chapter 6 are evidence of a composite matrix language and point to a matrix language turnover in progress because they all show that some level of abstract structure has been incorporated from another language into monolingual speech of either an L1 or of Tok Pisin.

Hypothesis 3: Content and early system morphemes can come from any language in the contact situation whether substrate or superstrate, but late system morphemes will only come from the substrate.

   a. Only content and early system morphemes from English occur in Tok Pisin.

   b. Some English content morphemes and early system morphemes are reanalyzed to serve as content or early or late system morphemes in Tok Pisin. Those reanalyzed English morphemes can thus fill Austronesian system morpheme slots.

   c. There will be some congruence in lexical-conceptual structure for phonetically similar forms used.

   d. No late system morphemes from a superstrate will occur in Tok Pisin.

   e. Late system morphemes from the homogeneous Austronesian substrate will appear in Tok Pisin if congruent enough with a superstrate form.

A look at any Tok Pisin dictionary reveals that the only English morphemes in Tok Pisin are content morphemes and some early system English morphemes such as *away* in *throw away* and the participle *been* that have been reanalyzed for their Tok Pisin function. Since English late sytem morphemes do not appear in Tok Pisin (3d), such grammatical morphemes are supplied by English content morphemes that are reanalyzed to fill those slots (3b). For example, the English content morpheme *belong* is reanalyzed as the late system bridge morpheme **bilong** in the Tok Pisin possessive construction discussed in chapters 2 and 5. (The rare exceptions to this source for late system morphemes are provided for by (3e) and are discussed below.) The necessity of some lexical-conceptual congruence of phonetically similar forms proposed in (3c) was demonstrated in chapter 5 with the Tok Pisin lexemes **han, lek,** and **papa,** which show lexical overlap with English and the Austronesian substrate languages, but not equivalence. Similarly, partial congruence was demonstrated between the English *he* and the Tok Pisin predicate marker **i.** With evidence for a substrate source for **i,** (3e) is supported by the presence of this substrate late system morpheme in Tok Pisin. The fact that some congruence between the superstrate and substrate is necessary is shown by the absence of articles in Tok Pisin. The so-called 'articles' of Austronesian languages are early system morpheme noun markers, but they lack congruence with English articles. The absence of dummy pronouns in Tok Pisin is evidence for the restriction against superstrate late system morphemes, even when there are parallel substrate patterns.

Hypothesis 4: Constituent types will change during the pidgin/creole formation and stabilization processes.

a. During pidgin/creole formation most embedded language islands from individual substrate languages are single lexemes or short phrases due to the extensive use of superstrate (or lexifier) content morphemes.

b. As the pidgin develops and stabilizes, the morphemes from the superstrate actually become morphemes of the pidgin. They are borrowed and thus completely incorporated into the pidgin itself and are no longer from an embedded language.

c. As Tok Pisin becomes a creole and as it becomes more widely used as a national language, especially among educated Papua New Guineans who know English, there will be more codeswitching between Tok Pisin and English, resulting in more mixed (matrix language + embedded language) constituents and embedded language islands (with English as the embedded language).

With three-fourths of Tok Pisin vocabulary derived from English there is little room for stretches of two or more lexemes from any given substrate language. The fact that the matrix language for Tok Pisin is a composite matrix language formed from many mutually unintelligible, though structurally similar, languages also contributes to the smaller possibility of embedded language islands of more than single lexemes from any one substrate language, giving support for (4a). The morphological adaptation of English lexemes, the frequency of their use, and the fact that bilingual speakers who know only Tok Pisin and an indigenous vernacular codeswitch between the two languages and incorporate Tok Pisin words into their vernacular is support for the claim (4b) that the superstrate morphemes of an established pidgin are actually part of the pidgin and no longer from an embedded language. The claim of (4c) is supported by the changes in Tok Pisin discussed in chapters 3 and 6. Tok Pisin is changing with its body of speakers and its extension of use. Speakers who are educated in English and those who work in businesses and government departments that require extensive use of English will continue to codeswitch, introducing more and more English words and phrases into Tok Pisin. As more Papua New Guineans in all areas of the country access English-language media, familiarity with English will promote codeswitching with Tok Pisin. Extensive codeswitching will lead to more borrowing into Tok Pisin. Finally, as Papua New Guinea develops technologically, more English lexemes and phrases (content morphemes for cultural loans) will be needed as part of the Tok Pisin lexicon because Papua New Guineans are more likely to use Tok Pisin than English when conversing among themselves about whether to get *cable TV* or how the *video recorder* works.

All the hypotheses I proposed in chapter 2 have been demonstrated in this study, as has the interrelationship of language contact phenomena. I have applied a theory that was originally developed to cover classic codeswitching to the contact phenomena observed in New Ireland. The matrix language frame and related models have been shown (within the limitations of this study) to apply to many contact situations, including pidgin/creole development. More studies are needed to continue testing these theories for applicability in other contact situations involving languages with greater differences than those encountered in New Ireland.

Em tasol.

Appendix 1

Examples of Shared Lexical Items in Austronesian Languages

Palauan (Foley and Van Valin)	Motu (Wurm and Harris)	Dobu (Capell)	Tolai (Lithgow and Claassen)	Tungag (Fast)	Tigak (Jenkins)	gloss
Content morphemes:						
	mata	mata	mata	mata	mata	'eye'
	manu	manu		mani'	manui	'bird'
	tama-na	tama-na	tama	tama	tama	'father'
ngalek (ngalek-ek 'my child')	natu				lakek	'child'
					(nalakek)	('children')
	natu			nat	natu	'son'
System morphemes:						
	toi		utul	potul	potul	'three'
			umana		(ma)mana	'plural'
	-k			-g	-g	'1SGPOSS'
				-m	-m	'2SGPOSS'
	-na	-ebe-	-na	-na	-na	'3SGPOSS'
					eve	'LOC/where'

Appendix 2

A Comparison of Austronesian Grammatical Structures

Word order within the clause:

(1)   S   V   O
    ri kʌvulik ki   *la tʌngʌ suai ani ei*   [Tungag]
    PL girl   3PL.S.AGR PRF chop remove OBJ tree
    'The girls chopped away the tree.' (Fast 1988:52)

(2)   *a tutuna i*   *gire*   *ra pap*   [Tolai]
    ART man 3SG.S.AGR   see   ART dog
    'The man saw the dog.' (Capell 1969:54)

(3)   *ga*   *na bur*   *a moro-gu...* [Nalik]
    1SG.S.AGR   FUT consecrate   ART maternal.relative-1SG
    'I will consecrate my maternal relative...' (Volker 1993:119)

(4)   *man*   *i paitim*   *dok*   [TP]
    man   PM hit   dog
    'The/a man hit the/a dog.'

Subject agreement markers: required with or without overt subject NP

	overt subject NP	SAGR	V	
(5)	rabuna rau	***ri***	tia	[Kara]
	ART people now	3PL.S.AGR	dance	
	'The people begin to dance.' (Beaumont 1989:35)			

(6) a. na va-lakek   ***reg***   inang   [Tigak]
        ART two-child   3DL.S.AGR go
        'Two boys are going.'

     b. *nareg*   ***reg***   inang
        3DL   3DL.S.AGR go
        'They(2) are going.'

     c. ∅   ***reg***   inang
                   3DL.S.AGR go
        'They(2) are going.'

(7) a. *a tarai*   ***dia***   vana   [Tolai]
        ART men   3PL.S.AGR went
        'The men went.'

     b. *diat*   ***dia***   vana
        3PL   3PL.S.AGR went
        'They went.'

     c. ∅   ***dia***   vana
                   3PL.S.AGR went
        'They went.' (Mosel 1980:121)

(8)   **em**   ***i***   **go**   [TP]
      3SG   PM   go
      'He's going.'

(Also see example (3) from Nalik.)

NP: various positioning of adjectives, quantifiers, and demonstratives

(9) *mang sikei a vʌkil lik palau* = QNT ART N ADJ INT [Tungag]
     SPEC one ART cave small very
     'a certain very small cave' (Fast 1988:31)

(10) *sakai na natuna laklik ang* = QNT ART N ADJ DEM [Tigak]
     one ART son little this
     'this one little son/child'

(11) a. *nam ra ura tutana* = DEM ART QNT N [Tolai]
        DEM ART two man
        'those two men'

     b. *a tabi tutana* = ART ADJ N
        ART giant man
        'giant man'

     c. *a pia polapola* = ART N ADJ
        ART ground wet
        'wet ground'

     d. *a ŋala na pal ~ a pal a ŋala* = ART ADJ N ~ ART N ADJ
        ART big LIG house ART house LIG big
        'big house' (Capell 1969:46–47)

(12) a. **dispela wanpela tripela man** = DEM QNT ADJ N [TP]
        this one very.big man
        'this one giant man'

     b. **banana mau** = N ADJ
        banana ripe
        'ripe banana'

Possessive NPs:

	Inalienable	Alienable	
(13) a.	*nati-gu* son-1sg 'my son'	b. *a pal kai ta tutana* ART house GEN ART man 'the man's house' (Capell 1969:46)	[Tolai]
(14) a.	*natu-g* son-1sg 'my son'	b. *ta lui ka-na* ART house GEN-3sg 'his house'	[Tigak]
(15) a.	*ngur-uria* mouth-3PL 'their mouths'	b. *kʌ-mem keva vua* GEN-1PL.EXC PL betelnut 'our betelnuts' (Fast 1988:11, 32)	[Tungag]
(16) a.	*dama-nagu* father-1sg 'my father'	b. *a vaal zunum* ART house 2sg 'your house' (Volker 1993:116)	[Nalik]
(17)	**haus bilong dispela man** house belong this man 'this man's house'	or **haus bilong en** house belong 3sg 'his/her house'	[TP]

Verbal constructions: All the languages have verbs that are unmarked for transitivity, but most also have standard patterns for marking verbs as transitive or intransitive. The intransitive form is most often unmarked morphologically, and the transitive marked with a suffix.

	Transitive	Intransitive	
(18) a.	*gi nak-i-ri* 3sg.S.AGR hit-TZ-3PL 'He hit them.'	b. *rig-a inang* 3PL.S.AGR-PST go 'They went.'	[Tigak]
c.	*reg-a polong-ani-Ø* 3DL.S.AGR-PST lie-TZ-3sg.OB 'They(2) lied about it.'		
(19) a.	*ri vil-e-Ø* 3PL.S.AGR do-TZ-3sg.OB 'They do it.'	b. *mam pi ma fafaisok* 1PL.EXC.S.AGR NEG work 'We do not work.' (Beaumont 1989:48, 46)	[Kara]

(20) a. kʌ   la rʌung-∅ a   vongo b. ki-la   rot   [Tungag]
        3SG.S.AGR PRF kill-TZ ART pig   3PL.S.AGR-PRF sleep
        'He killed the pig.'   'They slept.' (Fast 1988:27)

(21) a. *gumu-e* 'to dive for something'
     b. *gumu* 'to dive/bathe'   [Tolai]
     c. *mait-ane* 'to be sick with something'
     d. *mait* 'to be sick'
     e. *v-alir-e* 'to let someone swim'
     f. *alir* 'to float/swim' (Mosel 1980:42)

Prepositional transitive (without transitive suffix):

(22) gi   otaun eul **ani** na tama-na   [Tigak]
     3SG.S.AGR love INT for ART father-3SG
     'He loves his father very much.'

(23) ka   te   mol   **ani** ien   [Tungag]
     3SG.S.AGR PRES hungry for fish
     'He's hungry for fish.'

(24) **bai yu singaut *long* mi**   [TP]
     FUT 2SG call   to   1SG
     'Call me.'

Di-transitive:

(25) a. tang anu ga   tave-i-∅   ta lakek   [Tigak]
        ART man 3SG.S.AGR.PST give-TZ-3SG.OB.AGR ART child

        pa-na   tang ien
        with-3SG.OB   ART fish
        'A/The man gave a/the child (a) fish.'

     b. tang anu ga   lisan-i-∅   ta piu su-na
        ART man 3SG.S.AGR.PST give-TZ-3SG.OB.AGR ART dog LOC-3SG.OB

        ta lakek
        ART child
        'A/The man gave a/the dog to a/the child.'

(26) a. *a-llis   a   ien   ke   ani   ri   nnʌ-m*   [Tungag]
       CS-give ART fish DEM for ART mother-2SG
       'Give this fish to your mother.'

    b. *a-llis   a   ri   nnʌ-m   ta   ien   ke*
       CS-give ART ART mother-2SG INSTR fish DEM
       'Give your mother this fish.' (Fast 1988:52–53)

(27) a. **em i   giv-im dok long pikinini**   [TP]
       3SG PM give-TZ dog to child
       'He gave/gives a/the dog to a/the child.'

    b. **em i   giv-im pikinini long dok**
       3SG PM give-TZ child with dog
       'He gave/gives a/the child a/the dog.'

    c. **em i   giv-im pikinini dok**
       3SG PM give-TZ child dog
       'He gave/gives a/the child a/the dog.'

Tense:

Present tense is unmarked in most Austronesian languages, with Tungag being an exception.

(28) *ku-te   pasal*   [Tungag]
     2SG.S.AGR-PRES go
     'You are going.' (Beaumont 1989:38)

(29) *mi   vubokan a   so?*   [Kara]
     2PL.S.AGR want ART what
     'What do you want?' (Beaumont 1989:38)

(30) *nag   inang lo   kam   ta   lui*   [Tigak]
     1SG.S.AGR go LOC my ART house
     'I'm going to my house.'

Past tense is marked in most Austronesian languages, with Kara being an exception.

(31) ku   **ta** ago e   voi?   [Tungag]
    2SG.S.AGR PST stay LOC where
    'Where were you?' (Fast 1988: 37)

(32) u   **ga** vana   [Tolai]
    2SG.S.AGR PST go
    'You went.' (Mosel 1980:124)

(33) nag-**a**   pasal   [Tigak]
    1SG.S.AGR-PST walk
    'I walked.'

(34) ri   fangan   [Kara]
    3PL.S.AGR eat
    'They eat/ate/have eaten/had eaten.' (Beaumont 1989:40)

(35) **em i bin** go long haus   [TP]
    3SG PM PST go to   house
    'He went to the house.'

Future tense is marked variably among Austronesian languages, with Tungag being unmarked.

(36) ka   pasal   [Tungag]
    3SG.S.AGR go
    'He will go.' (Beaumont 1989:41)

(37) ga   **na** bur   a   moro-gu...   [Nalik]
    1SG.S.AGR FUT consecrate ART maternal.relative-1SG
    'I will consecrate my maternal relative...' (Volker 1993:119)

(38) mi   **ta** savat   [Kara]
    2PL.S.AGR FUT arrive
    'You will arrive.' (Beaumont 1989:41)

(39) u-**na**   vana   [Tolai]
    you-FUT go
    'You will go.'

(40) **vo** nag   inang amoua   [Tigak]
     FUT 1SG.S.AGR go   tomorrow
     'I will go tomorrow.'

(41) **bai** em i   go ~ em **bai** i go   [TP]
     FUT 3SG PM go   3SG FUT PM go
     'He will go.'

Preverbal markers:

(42) a. nʌ   **ka** an antok i-ʌ   [Tungag]
        1SG.S.AGR INT MA say   TZ-3SG.OB
        'I shall so tell him.' (Fast 1988:37)

     b. nʌ   **po** tʌv mʌlʌngʌs
        1SG.S.AGR CONT NEG clear
        'I fail to understand.' (Fast 1988:38)

(43) u   **la** vana   [Tolai]
     2SG HAB   go
     'You usually go.' (Mosel 1980:124)

(44) a. rig-a   **po** maat   [Tigak]
        3PL.S.AGR-PST PRF die
        'They have died/they are dead.'

     b. nug   **kalapang** ngek
        2SG.S.AGR HAB   cry
        'You always cry.'

     c. nag   **veko** kalapang
        1SG.S.AGR NEG   know
        'I don't know.'

(45) ri   **pi** **fele** fangan   [Kara]
     3PL.S.AGR NEG   ASP   eat
     'They are not eating/have not eaten/did not eat.' (Beaumont 1989:64)

(46) a. **em i** *stap toktok* [TP]
    3SG PM CONT talk
    'He is talking.'

  b. **em i** *save* **go**
    3SG PM HAB go
    'He always/usually goes.'

Postverbal markers:

(47) *rig-a   vil a-**kamus**-i-Ø* [Tigak]
    3PL.S.AGR-PST do CS-finish-TZ-3SG.OB
    'They finished it.'

(48) *dia   ga mat **par*** [Tolai]
    3PL.S.AGR PST die finish
    'They all died.' (Mosel 1980:125)

(49) **em i** *wokim pinis* [TP]
    3SG PM do/make finish
    'He finished it.'

Uses of reduplication: (Tolai examples below are from Mosel 1980; the Tungag examples are from Fast 1988; and the Kara examples are from Beaumont 1989.)

Transitive → Intransitive

(50) *kul* 'to buy something'   *kul-kul* 'to buy, trade,   [Tolai]
                                  go shopping'

(51) *marak* 'to please someone' *mara-marak* 'to be pleased' [Tungag]

(52) *pol* 'to lie to someone'   *pol-pol* 'to lie' [Tigak]

(53) **was** 'to wash something' **waswas** 'to bathe' [TP]

Continuative/durative/repetitive action

(54) u   *ia-ian* kauga vudu   [Tolai]
      you   RDP-eat   my   banana
      'You are eating my banana.'

(55) ri   ainʌ   ki   an   la   *tʌ-tʌun*   ani keve pok   [Tungag]
      ART   woman   3PL.S.AGR   MA   PRF RDP-bake   OB   PL   food
      'The women (went and) cooked the food.'

(56) rig   *kap-kapis* lo   tang matang   [Tigak]
      3PL.S.AGR   RDP-plant   LOC   ART   garden
      'They are planting in the garden.'

(57) ol   i   *tan-tanim*   ol   pepa   [TP]
      3PL   PM   RDP-turn   PL   paper
      'They keep on turning pages.'

Habitual action

(58) dia   *va-va*   ra   pupui   [Tolai]
      3PL.S.AGR   RDP-sleep   ART   bush
      'They sleep in the bush.'

(59) mam   pi   ma   *fa-faisok*   [Kara]
      1PL.S.AGR   NEG   RDP-work
      'We do not work.'

Distributive (Numerals)

(60) a   laptikai na   gai   ra   *lap-laptikai* na   gai   [Tolai]
      ART   six   ART month   ART   RDP-six   ART   month
      'six months'   'every six months'

(61) sikei and ponguʌ   sik-sikei and *pong-ponguʌ*   [Tungag]
      'one'   'two'   'each'   'two-by-two'

(62) *sakai* and *pouak*   ***sak-sakai*** and ***po-pouak***   [Tigak]
     'one'   'two'   'each'   'two-by-two'

(63) **wanpela**   ***wan-wan***   [TP]
     'one'   'each'

References

Alisjahbana, S. Takdir. 1984. The problem of minority languages in the overall linguistic problems of our time. In Florian Coulmas, 47–55.

Allard, Real, and Rodrigue Landry. 1992. Ethnolinguistic vitality beliefs and language maintenance and loss. In Fase, Jaspaert, and Kroon, 171–195.

Alleyne, Mervyn C. 1971. Acculturation and the culture matrix of creolization. In Hymes, 169–186.

Alleyne, Mervyn C. 1986. Substratum influences—guilty until proven innocent. In Muysken and Smith, 301–315.

Alleyne, Mervyn C. 1993. Continuity versus creativity in Afro-American language and culture. In Mufwene, 167–181.

Andersen, Roger W. 1979. Expanding Schumann's pidginization hypothesis. *Language Learning* 29:105–119.

Andersen, Roger W. 1982. Determining the linguistic attributes of language attrition. In Richard D. Lambert and Barbara F. Freed (eds.), *The loss of language skills,* 83–118. Rowley, Mass.: Newberry House.

Andersen, Roger W., ed. 1983a. *Pidginization and creolization as language acquisition.* Rowley, Mass.: Newberry House.

Andersen, Roger W. 1983b. Introduction: A language acquisition interpretation of pidginization and creolization. In Andersen, 1–56.

Andersen, Roger W. 1983c. Transfer to somewhere. In Susan M. Gass and Larry Selinker (eds.), *Language transfer and language learning,* 177–201. Rowley, Mass.: Newberry House.

Appel, René, and Pieter Muysken. 1987. *Language contact and bilingualism.* London: Edward Arnold.

Arasanyin, Olaoba F. 1995. Utility, status and languages in competition in middle belt Nigeria. *African Study Monographs* 16(4):195–223.
Backus, Albert Marie. 1996. *Two in one: Bilingual speech of Turkish immigrants in the Netherlands*. Tilburg: Tilburg University Press.
Baker, Philip. 1990. Off target? [Column]. *Journal of Pidgin and Creole Languages* 5(1):107–119.
Baker, Philip. 1993. Australian influence on Melanesian Pidgin English. *Te Reo* 36:3–67.
Baker, Philip. 1995. Some developmental influences from the historical studies of pidgins and creoles. In Jacques Arends (ed.), *The early stages of creolization*, 1–24. Amsterdam: John Benjamins.
Baker, Philip. 1996. Australian and Melanesian Pidgin English and the *fellows* in between. In Philip Baker and Anand Syea (eds.), *Changing meanings, changing functions: Papers relating to grammaticalization in contact languages* 243–258. London: University of Westminster Press.
Baker, Philip. 1997. Directionality in pidginization and creolization In Spears and Winford, 91–109.
Bakker, Peter, and Mous Maarten, eds. 1994. *Mixed languages: 15 case studies in language intertwining*. Amsterdam: Institute for Functional Research into Language and Language Use.
Baldwin, George B. 1978. *Papua New Guinea: Its economic situation and prospects for development*. Washington, D.C.: The World Bank.
Bamgbose, Ayo. 1984. Minority languages and literacy. In Coulmas, 21–28.
Bates, Elizabeth, and Brian MacWhinney. 1987. Competition, variation, and language learning. In MacWhinney, 157–193.
Beaumont, Clive H. 1972. New Ireland languages: A review. In C. Beaumont, D. T. Tryon, and S. A. Wurm (eds.), *Papers in linguistics of Melanesia*, 3:1–41. Canberra: Linguistics Circle of Canberra.
Beaumont, Clive H. 1976. Austronesian languages: New Ireland. In S. A. Wurm (ed.), *New Guinea area languages and language study, 2: Austronesian languages*, 387–397. Canberra: Linguistics Circle of Canberra.
Beaumont, Clive H. 1979. *The Tigak language of New Ireland*. Canberra: The Australian National University.
Beaumont, Clive H. 1989. The verb phrase in Tigak, Lavongai (Tungag) and Kara of New Ireland. *VICAL 1: Oceanic languages*, 33–60.
Bentahila, Abdelai, and Eirlys E. Davies. 1992. Convergence and divergence: Two cases of language shift in Morocco. In Fase, Jaspaert, and Kroon, 197–210.
Bickerton, Derek. 1977. Pidginization and creolization: Language acquisition and language universals. In Valdman, 49–60.
Bickerton, Derek. 1981. *Roots of language*. Ann Arbor: Karoma.

Bickerton, Derek. 1983. Comments on Valdman's "Creolization and second language acquisition." In Andersen, 235–240.
Bickerton, Derek. 1992. The sociohistorical matrix of creolization. *Journal of Pidgin and Creole Languages* 7(2):307–318.
Bickerton, Derek. 1999. How to acquire language without positive evidence: What acquisitionists can learn from creoles. In DeGraff, 49–74.
Blom, J. P., and J. J. Gumperz. 1972. Social meaning in linguistic structures. In John J. Gumperz and Dell H. Hymes (eds.), *Directions in sociolinguistics*, 407–434. New York: Holt, Rinehart, and Winston.
Bock, Kathryn. 1987. An effect of the accessibility of word forms on sentence structures. *Journal of Memory and Language* 26:119–137.
Bock, Kathryn, and Willem Levelt. 1994. Language production: Grammatical encoding. In Morton Ann Gernsbacher (ed.), *Handbook of psycholinguistics*, 945–984. San Diego: Academic Press.
Bolinger, D. 1975. *Aspects of language*, second edition. New York: Harcourt Brace Jovanovich.
Bolonyai, Agnes. 1998. In-between languages: Language shift/maintenance in childhood bilingualism. *International Journal of Bilingualism* 2(1):21–43.
Bolonyai, Agnes. 2000. 'Elective affinities': Language contact in the abstract lexicon and its structural consequences. *International Journal of Bilingualism* 4(1):81–106.
Braine, Martin D. S. 1987. What is learned in acquiring word classes—A step toward an acquisition theory. In MacWhinney, 65–87.
Brenzinger, Matthias, ed. 1992. *Language death: Factual and theoretical explorations with special reference to East Africa*. Berlin: Mouton de Gruyter.
Brenzinger, Matthias. 1997. Language contact and language displacement. In Coulmas, 273–284.
Brenzinger, Matthias, and Gerrit J. Dimmendaal. 1992. Social contexts of language death. In Brenzinger, 3–5.
Bresnan, Joan, ed. 1982. *The mental representation of grammatical relations*. Cambridge, Mass.: MIT Press.
Bright, William. 1997. Social factors in language change. In Coulmas, 81–91.
Bruyn, Adrienne, Peter Muysken, and Maaike Verrips. 1999. Double-object constructions in the creole languages: Development and acquisition. In DeGraff, 329–373.
Bugenhagen, Robert D. 1995. *A grammar of Mangap-Mbula: An Austronesian langauge of Papua New Guinea*. Canberra: Australian National University.

Calvet, Louis-Jean. 1986. Trade function and lingua francas. In Fishman et al., 295–302.
Campbell, Lyle, and Martha C. Muntzel. 1989. The structural consequences of language death. In Dorian, 181–196.
Capell, A. 1969. *A survey of New Guinea languages.* Sydney: Sydney University Press.
Capell, A. 1971. The Austronesian languages of Australian New Guinea. In Sebeok (ed.), *Current Trends in Linguistics 8: Linguistics in Oceania,* 240–340. The Hague: Mouton.
Chafe, Wallace L. 1970. *Meaning and the structure of language.* Chicago: The University of Chicago Press.
Chafe, Wallace L. 1984. *Cognitive constraints on information flow.* Berkeley, Calif.: Institute of Cognitive Studies.
Chaudenson, Robert. 1977. Toward the reconstruction of the source matrix of creole language. In Valdman, 259–276.
Cheshire, Jenny, and Lise-Marie Moser. 1994. English as a cultural symbol: The case of advertisements in French-speaking Switzerland. *Journal of Multilingual and Multicultural Development* 15:451–469.
Chomsky, Noam. 1973. *Language and mind.* New York: Harcourt Brace Jovanovich.
Chomsky, Noam. 1981. *Lectures on government and binding.* Dordrecht: Foris.
Chomsky, Noam. 1986. *Knowledge of language: Its nature, origin, and use.* New York: Praeger.
Chomsky, Noam. 1995. *The minimalist program.* Cambridge, Mass.: MIT Press.
Chung, Chul-Hwa, and Kyung-Ja Chung. 1998. *Modified dialect survey of the Kuot language program.* Unpublished manuscript.
Churchill, William. 1911. *Beach-la-mar: The jargon or trade speech of the Western Pacific.* Washington, D.C.: The Carnegie Institute of Washington.
Clark, Eve V. 1987. The principle of contrast: A constraint on language acquisition. In MacWhinney, 1–33.
Clark, Eve V. 1988. On the logic of contrast. *Child Language* 15:317–335.
Clark, Ross. 1979. In search of Beach-la-Mar: Towards a history of Pacific Pidgin English. *Te Reo* 22:3–63.
Clyne, Michael. 1986. Towards a systematization of language contact dynamics. In Fishman et al., 483–492.
Clyne, Michael. 1987. Constraints on code switching: how universal are they? *Linguistics* 25:739–764.
Clyne, Michael. 1997. Multilingualism. In Coulmas, 257–270.

Codrington, Robert. 1974 [1885]. *The Melanesian languages.* Amsterdam: Philo Press.
Comrie, Bernard. 1989. *Language universals and linguistic typology,* second edition. Chicago: The University of Chicago Press.
Cooper, Robert L. 1989. *Language planning and social change.* New York: Cambridge University Press.
Coulmas, Florian, ed. 1984a. *Linguistic minorities and literacy.* New York: Mouton.
Coulmas, Florian. 1984b. In Coulmas, ix–x.
Coulmas, Florian. 1984c. Linguistic minorities and literacy. In Coulmas, 5–20.
Coulmas, Florian. 1992. *Language and economy.* Oxford: Blackwell.
Coulmas, Florian, ed. 1997. *The handbook of sociolinguistics.* Oxford: Blackwell.
Craig, Colette Grinevald. 1997. Language contact and language degeneration. In Coulmas, 257–270.
Crowley, Terry. 1987. Serial verbs and preposition in Bislama. In Verhaar, 57–89.
Cruse, D. A. 1986. *Lexical semantics.* Cambridge: Cambridge University Press.
DeCamp, David. 1971. Introduction: The study of pidgin and creole languages. In Hymes, 13–39.
DeCamp, David. 1977. The development of pidgin and creole studies. In Valdman, 3–20.
DeCamp, David, and Ian F. Hancock, eds. 1974. *Pidgins and creoles: Current trends and prospects.* Washington, D.C.: Georgetown University Press.
DeGraff, Michael, ed. 1999a. *Language creation and language change: Creolization, diachrony, and development.* Cambridge, Mass.: MIT Press.
DeGraff, Michael. 1999b. Creolization, language change, and language acquisition: A prolegomenon. In DeGraff, 1–46.
DeGraff, Michael. 1999c. Creolization, language change, and language acquisition: An epilogue. In DeGraff, 473–543.
Dell, Gary S. 1986. A spreading-activation theory of retrieval in sentence production. *Psychological Review* 93(3):283–321.
Di Pietro, Robert J. 1978. Code-switching as a verbal strategy among bilinguals. In Paradis, 275–282.
Di Sciullo, Anne-Marie, Peter Muysken, and Rajendra Singh. 1986. Government and code-mixing. *Journal of Linguistics* 22:1–24.
Dodson, C. J. 1986. Bilingualism and a sense of 'peopleness'. In Fishman et al., 387–393.
Dorian, Nancy C. 1981. *Language death: The life cycle of a Scottish Gaelic dialect.* Philadelphia: University of Pennsylvania Press.

Dorian, Nancy C. 1982. Language loss and maintenance in language contact situations. In Richard D. Lambert and Barbara F. Freed (eds.), *The loss of language skills,* 44–59. Rowley, Mass.: Newberry House.

Dorian, Nancy C. 1983. Natural second language acquisition from the perspective of the study of language death. In Andersen, 158–167.

Dorian, Nancy C. 1986. Gathering language data in terminal speech communities. In Fishman et al., 387–393.

Dorian, Nancy C., ed. 1989. *Investigating obsolescence: Studies in language contraction and death.* Cambridge: Cambridge University Press.

Dorian, Nancy C. 1998. Western language ideologies and small-language prospects. In Grenoble and Whaley, 3–21.

Durán, Richard P., ed. 1981. *Latino language and communicative behavior.* Norwood, N.J.: Ablex.

Dutton, Tom, and R. Michael Bourke. 1987. Taim in Tok Pisin: An interesting variation in use from the Southern Highlands of Papua New Guinea. In Verhaar, 251–262.

Dyen, Isidore. 1971. The Austronesian languages and Proto-Austronesian. In Sebeok, 5–54.

Eastman, Carol M. 1983. *Language planning, an introduction.* San Francisco: Chandler and Sharp.

Eastman, Carol M. 1984. Language, identity and change. In Edwards, 259–276.

Edwards, John. 1984. *Linguistic minorities: Policies and pluralism.* London: Academic Press.

Edwards, John. 1992. Sociopolitical aspects of language maintenance and loss: towards a typology of minority language situations. In Fase, Jaspaert, and Kroon, 37–54.

Edwards, John. 1994 *Multilingualism.* New York: Routledge.

Eersel, Christian. 1971. Prestige in choice of language and linguistic form. In Hymes, 317–322.

Fase, Willem, K. Jaspaert, and S. Kroon, eds. 1992. *Maintenance and loss of minority languages.* Amsterdam: John Benjamins.

Fast, Leslie. 1988. *Tungak grammar essentials.* Unpublished manuscript.

Fay, David, and Anne Cutler. 1977. Malapropisms and the structure of the mental lexicon. *Linguistic Inquiry* 8(3):505–520.

Ferguson, Charles A. 1959. Diglossia. *Word* 15(2):325–340.

Ferguson, Charles A. 1971. Absence of copula and the notion of simplification: a study of normal speech, baby talk, foreigner talk, and pidgins. In Hymes, 141–150.

Ferguson, Charles A. 1991. Diglossia revisited. *Southwest Journal of Linguistics* 10(1):214–234.

Ferguson, Charles A., and Charles E. DeBose. 1977. Simplified registers, broken language, and pidginization. In Valdman, 99–125.
Fischer, John L. 1958. Social influences on the choice of a linguistic variant. *Word* 14:47–56.
Fishman, Joshua A. 1967. Bilingualism with and without diglossia; diglossia with and without bilingualism. *Journal of Social Issues* 23(2):29–38.
Fishman, Joshua A. 1972a. *Language and nationalism.* Rowley, Mass.: Newberry House.
Fishman, Joshua A. 1972b. Societal bilingualism: Stable and transitional. In Joshua A. Fishman (ed.), *The sociology of language: An interdisciplinary social science approach to language in society,* 91–108. Rowley, Mass.: Newberry House.
Fishman, Joshua A. 1997. Language and ethnicity. In Coulmas, 327–341.
Fishman, Joshua A., Andrée Tabouret-Keller, Michael Clyne, Bh. Krishnamurti, Mohamed Abdulaziz, eds. 1986. *The Fergusonian impact 2: Sociolinguistics and the sociology of language.* Berlin: Mouton de Gruyter.
Fodor, Janet Dean, and Stephen Crain. 1987. Simplicity and generality of rules in language acquisition. In MacWhinney, 35–63.
Fodor, Jerry A. 1975. *The language of thought.* New York: Thomas Y. Crowel Company.
Fodor, Jerry A. 1983. *The modularity of mind.* Cambridge, Mass.: MIT Press.
Fodor, J. A., T. G. Bever, and M. F. Garrett. 1974. *The psychology of language.* New York: McGraw-Hill Book Company.
Foley, William A., and Robert D. Van Valin. 1985. Information packaging in the clause. In Timothy Shopen, *Language typology and syntactic description 1: Clause structure,* 282–364. Cambridge: Cambridge University Press.
Ford, Marilyn. 1982. Sentence planning units: Implications for the speaker's representation of meaningful relations underlying sentences. In Joan Bresnan, 797–827.
Ford, Marilyn, Joan Bresnan, and Ronald M. Kaplan. 1982. A competence-based theory of syntactic closure. In Joan Bresnan, 727–796.
Ford, Marilyn, and Virginia M. Holmes. 1978. Planning units and syntax in sentence production. *Cognition* 6:35–53.
Francescato, Giuseppe. 1986. Bilingualism and diglossia in their relationship. In Fishman et al., 387–393.
Fromkin, Victoria A. 1968. Speculations on performance models. *Journal of Linguistics* 4:47–68.

Fromkin, Victoria A. 1971. The non-anomalous nature of anomalous utterances. *Language* 47:27–52.
Fromkin, Victoria A., ed. 1973. *Speech errors as linguistic evidence.* The Hague: Mouton.
Fry, D. B. 1973. The linguistic evidence of speech errors. In Fromkin, 157–163.
Gal, Susan. 1988. The political economy of code choice. In Monica Heller, (ed.), *Code-switching: Anthropological and sociolinguistic perspectives,* 245–254. Berlin: Mouton de Gruyter.
Gal, Susan. 1989. Lexical innovation and loss: The use and value of restricted Hungarian. In Dorian, 313–331.
Garfield, Jay L., ed. 1987a. *Modularity in knowledge representation and natural-language understanding.* Cambridge, Mass.: MIT Press.
Garfield, Jay L. 1987b. Introduction: Carving the mind at its joints. In Jay L. Garfield (ed.), *Modularity in knowledge representation and natural-language understanding,* 1–13. Cambridge, Mass.: MIT Press.
Garrett, M. F. 1975. The analysis of sentence production. In Gordon H. Bower (ed.), *The psychology of learning and motivation,* 133–177. New York: Academic Press.
Garrett, M. F. 1980. Levels of processing in sentence production. In B. Butterworth (ed.), *Language production, Vol. 1: Speech and talk,* 177–220. London: Academic Press.
Gass, Susan M., and Larry Selinker, eds. 1983. *Language transfer in language learning.* Rowley, Mass.: Newberry House.
Gilbert, Glenn G., ed. 1980. *Pidgin and creole languages: selected essays by Hugo Schuchardt.* New York: Cambridge University Press.
Gilbert, Glenn G. 1986. The language bioprogram hypothesis: Déjà vu? In Muysken and Smith, 15–24.
Giles, H., R. Y. Bourhis, and D. M. Taylor. 1977. Toward a theory of language on ethnic group relations. In Howard Giles (ed.), *Language, ethnicity and intergroup relations,* 307–348. New York: Academic Press.
Giles, Howard, and Patricia Johnson. 1987. Ethnolinguistic identity theory: A social psychological approach to language maintenance. *International Journal of the Sociology of Language* 68:69–99.
Gilman, Charles. 1985. *Pidgin languages: Form selection or simplification?* Bloomington: Indiana University Linguistics Club.
Givón, Talmy. 1979a. *On understanding grammar.* New York: Academic Press.
Givón, Talmy. 1979b. Prolegomena to any sane creology. In Hancock, 3–35.

Givón, Talmy. 1987. Verb serialization in Tok Pisin and Kalam: A comparative study of temporal packaging. In Verhaar, 19–55.
Goodman, Morris. 1993. African substratum: Some cautionary words. In Mufwene, 64–73.
Goulden, Rick J. 1990. *The Melanesian content in Tok Pisin.* Canberra: Australian National University.
Grenoble, Lenore A., and Lindsay J. Whaley, eds. 1998a. *Endangered languages: Language loss and community response.* Cambridge: Cambridge University Press.
Grenoble, Lenore A., and Lindsay J. Whaley, eds. 1998b. Toward a typology of language endangerment. In Grenoble and Whaley, 22–54.
Grice, H. P. 1957. Meaning. *Philosophical Review* 66:377–388.
Grice, H. P. 1968. Utterer's meaning, sentence-meaning, and word-meaning. *Foundations of Language* 4:225–242.
Grimshaw, Allen D. 1971. Some social forces and some social functions of pidgin and creole languages. In Dell Hymes, 169–186.
Grosjean, François. 1989. Neurolinguists, beware! The bilingual is not two monolinguals in one person. *Brain and Language* 36:3–15.
Gross, Steven. 2000. When two become one: Creating a composite grammar in creole formation. *International Journal of Bilingualism* 4(1):59–80.
Gumperz, John J. 1964. Linguistic and social interaction in two communities. In Gumperz and Hymes, 137–153.
Gumperz, John J. 1982. *Discourse strategies.* Cambridge: Cambridge University Press.
Gumperz, John, and Dell Hymes. 1972. *Directions in sociolinguistics.* New York: Holt, Rinehart, and Winston.
Gumperz, John J., and Robert Wilson. 1971. Convergence and creolization: A case study from the Indo-Aryan/Dravidian border. In Hymes, 151–168.
Hall, Robert A., Jr. 1943. *Melanesian Pidgin English: Grammar, texts, vocabulary.* Baltimore: Linguistic Society of America.
Hall, Robert A., Jr. 1966. *Pidgin and creole languages.* Ithaca, N.Y.: Cornell University Press.
Halmari, Helena. 1997. *Government and codeswitching: Explaining American Finnish.* Amsterdam: John Benjamins.
Hancock, Ian F. 1977a. Recovering pidgin genesis: Approaches and problems. In Valdman, 277–294.
Hancock, Ian F. 1977b. Appendix: Repertory of pidgin and creole languages. In Valdman, 362–391.

Hancock, Ian F., ed. 1979a. *Readings in creole studies*. Ghent: E Story-Scientia.
Hancock, Ian F. 1979b. On the origin of the term *pidgin*. In Hancock, 81–86.
Hancock, Ian F. 1993. Creole language provenance and the African component. In Mufwene, 182–191.
Harris, Alice C., and Lyle Campbell. 1995. *Historical syntax in cross-linguistic perspective*. Cambridge: Cambridge University Press.
Hatch, Evelyn. 1983. Simplified input and second language acquisition. In Andersen, 64–86.
Haugen, Einer. 1953. *The Norwegian language in America*. Philadelphia: University of Pennsylvania Press.
Haugen, Einer. 1973. Bilingualism, language contact, and immigrant languages in the United States: A research report 1956–1970. In Thomas A. Sebeok (ed.), *Current trends in linguistics* 10, 505–591. The Hague: Mouton.
Hesseling, Dirk Christiaan. 1979. How did creoles originate? In T. L. Markey and Paul T. Roberge (eds.), *On the origin and formation of creoles: a miscellany of articles,* 62–69. Ann Arbor, Mich.: Karoma.
Hill, Jane H., and Kenneth C. Hill. 1986. *Speaking Mexicano: Dynamics of syncretic language in central Mexico*. Tucson: The University of Arizona Press.
Hill, Kenneth C., ed. 1979. *The genesis of language*. Ann Arbor: Karoma.
Hock, Hans Henrich. 1991. *Principles of historical linguistics,* second edition. Berlin: Mouton de Gruyter.
Holm, John A. 1986. Substrate diffusion. In Muysken and Smith, 259–278.
Holm, John A. 1988a. *Pidgins and creoles, 1: Theory and structure*. Cambridge: Cambridge University Press.
Holm, John A. 1988b. *Pidgins and creoles, 2: Reference survey*. Cambridge: Cambridge University Press.
Hooley, Bruce A. 1962. Transformations in Neo-melanesian. *Oceania* 33:116–127.
Hornstein, Norbert. 1987. Levels of meaning. In Jay L. Garfield (ed.), *Modularity in knowledge representation and natural-language understanding,* 133–150. Cambridge, Mass.: MIT Press.
Huddleston, Mark. 1980. Which language for literacy? *Notes on Literacy* 30:9–13.
Huttar, George L. 1975. Sources of creole semantic structures. *Language* 51:684–695.
Hymes, Dell, ed. 1971a. *Pidginization and creolization of languages*. Cambridge: Cambridge University Press.

Hymes, Dell. 1971b. General conceptions of process: Introduction. In Hymes, 65–90.
Jackendoff, Ray. 1990. *Semantic structures.* Cambridge, Mass.: MIT Press.
Jake, Janice L. 1994. Intrasentential code switching and pronouns: On the categorial status of functional elements. *Linguistics* 32:271–298.
Jake, Janice L. 1998. Constructing interlanguage: Building a composite matrix language. *Linguistics* 26(2):333–382.
Jake, Janice L., and Carol Myers-Scotton. 1997a. Codeswitching and compromise strategies: Implication for lexical structure. *International Journal of Bilingualism* 1(1):25–39.
Jake, Janice L., and Carol Myers-Scotton. 1997b. *Categorizing morphemes: An election-based classification explains what you get.* Notes from paper presented at the Second Language Research Forum '97.
Jake, Janice L., and Carol Myers-Scotton. 1998. *How to build a creole: Splitting and recombining lexical structure.* Abstract of paper presented at Society for Pidgin and Creole Linguistics meeting, January 1998.
Jenkins, Charles, and Sue Jenkins. 1996a. *Tigak dictionary.* Unpublished manuscript.
Jenkins, Charles, and Sue Jenkins. 1996b. *Tigak area survey data.* Unpublished corpus.
Jenkins, Sue. 1996. *Tigak grammar essentials.* Unpublished manuscript.
Jenkins, Sue. 1998. *Island Tigak phonology essentials.* Unpublished manuscript.
Johnson-Laird, P. N. 1975. Meaning and the mental lexicon. In Alan Kennedy and Alan Wilkes, (eds.), *Studies in long term memory,* 123–142. London: John Wiley and Sons.
Kapanga, André. 1998. Impact of language variation and accommodation theory on language maintenance: an analysis of Shaba Swahili. In Grenoble and Whaley, 261–288.
Kay, Paul, and Gillian Sankoff. 1974. A language-universals approach to pidgins and creoles. In David DeCamp and Ian F. Hancock (eds.), *Pidgins and creoles: Current trends and prospects,* 61–72. Washington, D.C.: Georgetown University Press.
Keesing, Roger M. 1988. *Melanesian Pidgin and the Oceanic substrate.* Stanford, Calif.: Stanford University Press.
Keesing, Roger M. 1991. Substrates, calquing and grammaticalization in Melanesian Pidgin. In Elizabeth Closs Traugott and Bernd Heine (eds.), *Approaches to grammaticalization 1,* 315–342. Amsterdam: John Benjamins.
Kelman, Herbert C. 1972. Language as aid and barrier to involvement in the national system. In Joshua A. Fishman (ed.), *Advances in the sociology of language 2,* 185–212. The Hague: Mouton.

Kempen, Gerard. 1977. Conceptualizing and formulating in sentence production. In Rosenberg, 259–274.

Kempen, Gerard, and Edward Hoenkamp. 1987. An incremental procedural grammar for sentence formation. *Cognitive Science* 11:201–258.

Kempen, Gerard, and Pieter Huijbers. 1983. The lexification process in sentence production and naming: Indirect election of words. *Cognition* 14:185–209.

Kennedy, Alan, and Alan Wilkes, eds. 1975. *Studies in long term memory*. London: John Wiley and Sons.

King, Ruth. 1989. On the social meaning of linguistic variability in language death situations: Variation in Newfoundland French. In Dorian, 139–148.

Kloss, Heinz. 1966. Types of multilingual communities: A discussion of ten variables. *Sociological Inquiry* 36(2):135–145.

Knab, Tim. 1980. When is a language really dead: The case of Pochutec. *International Journal of American Linguistics* 46(3):230–233.

Koefoed, Geert. 1979. Some remarks on the baby talk theory and the relexification theory. In Hancock, 37–54.

Kulick, Don. 1992. *Language shift and cultural reproduction: Socialization, self, and syncretism in a Papua New Guinean village*. New York: Cambridge University Press.

Kulick, Don, and Christopher Stroud. 1987. Code-switching in Gapun: Social and linguistic aspects of language use in a language shifting community. In Verhaar, 205–234.

Labov, William. 1966. *The social stratification of English in New York City*. Washington, D.C.: Center for Applied Linguistics.

Labov, William. 1972. On the mechanism of linguistic change. In John J. Gumperz and Dell Hymes (eds.), *Directions in sociolinguistics*, 512–538. New York: Holt, Rinehart, and Winston.

Lambert, Richard D., and Barbara F. Freed, eds. 1982. *The loss of language skills*. Rowley, Mass.: Newberry House.

Lass, Roger. 1984. *Phonology: An introduction to basic concepts*. Cambridge: Cambridge University Press.

Laver, John D. 1973. The detection and correction of slips of the tongue. In Fromkin, 132-143.

Laycock, Donald C. 1970. *Materials in New Guinea Pidgin (coastal and lowlands)*. Canberra: The Australian National University.

Lefebvre, Claire. 1986. Relexification in creole genesis revisited: the case of Haitian Creole. In Muysken and Smith, 279–300.

Lefebvre, Claire. 1993. The role of relexification and syntactic reanalysis in Haitian Creole: Methodological aspects of a research program. In Mufwene, 254–279.

Lefebvre, Claire. 1996. The tense, mood, and aspect system of Haitian Creole and the problem of transmission of grammar in creole genesis. *Journal of Pidgin and Creole Languages* 11(2):231–311.

Lefebvre, Claire. 1997. Relexification in creole genesis: The case of demonstrative terms in Haitian Creole. *Journal of Pidgin and Creole Langauges* 12(12):181–206.

Lehmann, Winfred P. 1973. *Historical linguistics: An introduction,* second edition. New York: Holt, Rinehart and Winston.

Le Page, Robert. 1977. Processes of pidginization and creolization. In Valdman, 222–255.

Levelt, Willem J. M. 1981. The speaker's linearization problem. *Philosophical Transactions Royal Society London* R295:305–315.

Levelt, Willem J. M. 1989. *Speaking: From intention to articulation.* Cambridge, Mass.: The MIT Press.

Levelt, W. J. M. and G. Kempen. 1975. Syntactic and semantic aspects of remembering sentences: a review of some recent Continental research. In Alan Kennedy and Alan Wilkes (eds.), *Studies in long term memory,* 201–216. London: John Wiley and Sons.

Li Wei. 1994. *Three generations, two languages, one family: Language choice and language shift in a Chinese community in Britain.* Bristol, Penn.: Multilingual Matters.

Lieberson, Stanley, Guy Dalto, and Mary Ellen Johnson. 1975. The course of mother-tongue diversity in nations. *American Journal of Sociology* 81(1):34–61.

Lincoln, P. C. 1979. Dual-lingualism: Passive bilingualism in action. *Te Reo* 22:65–82.

Lipski, John M. 1978. Code-switching and the problem of bilingual competence. In Paradis, 250–264.

Lithgow, David, and Oren Claassen. 1968. *Languages of the New Ireland District.* Port Moresby, Papua New Guinea: Department of Information and Extension Services.

Litteral, Robert. 1987. Tok Pisin: The language of modernization. In Verhaar, 375–385.

Litteral, Robert. 1995a. *Four decades of language policy in Papua New Guinea: The move towards the vernacular.* Unpublished manuscript.

Litteral, Robert. 1995b. *Language development in Papua New Guinea: Cheaper by the hundreds.* Unpublished manuscript.

Lumsden, John S. 1994. Possession: Substratum semantics in Haitian Creole. *Journal of Pidgin and Creole Languages* 9(1):25–49.

Lumsden, John S. 1999. Language acquisition and creolization. In DeGraff, 129–157.

Lynch, John. 1987. The future of Tok Pisin: Social, political, and educational dimensions. In Verhaar, 387–397.

Lynch, John, Malcolm Ross, and Terry Crowley. 2000. *The Oceanic languages*. London: Curzon Press.

Mackey, William F. 1986. The polyglossic spectrum. In Fishman et al., 237–243.

Macnamara, John. 1967. The bilingual's linguistic performance—a psychological overview. *Journal of Social Issues* 23(2):58–77.

MacWhinney, Brian, ed. 1987a. *Mechanisms of language acquisition*. Hillsdale, N.J.: Lawrence Erlbaum Associates.

MacWhinney, Brian, ed. 1987b. The competition model. In MacWhinney, 249–308.

Makkai, Valerie Becker. 1978. Bilingual phonology: Systematic or autonomous? In Paradis, 47–52.

Marshall, John C. 1984. Multiple perspectives on modularity. *Cognition* 17:209–242.

Marslen-Wilson, William, and Lorraine Komisarjevsky Tyler. 1987. Against modularity. In Garfield, 37–62.

McClure, Erica. 1981. Formal and functional aspects of the code-switched discourse of bilingual children. In Durán, 69–94.

McWhorter, John H. 1992. Substratal influence in Saramaccan serial verb constructions. *Journal of Pidgin and Creole Languages* 7(1):1–53.

Meijer, Guus, and Pieter Muysken. 1977. On the beginnings of pidgin and creole studies: Schuchardt and Hesseling. In Valdman, 21–45.

Meisel, Jürgen. 1983. Strategies of second language acquisition: More than one kind of simplification. In Andersen, 120–157.

Mihalic, F. 1971. *The Jacaranda dictionary and grammar of Melanesian Pidgin*. Brisbane: Jacaranda Press.

Milroy, Leslie, and Pieter Muysken, eds. 1995a. *One speaker, two languages*. Cambridge: Cambridge University Press.

Milroy, Leslie, and Pieter Muysken. 1995b. Introduction. In Lesley Milroy and Pieter Muysken (eds.), *One speaker, two languages*, 1–14. Cambridge: Cambridge University Press.

Mintz, Sidney W. 1971. The socio-historical background to pidginization and creolization. In Hymes, 481–496.

Mithun, Marianne. 1992. The substratum in grammar and discourse. In Ernst Hakon Jahr (ed.), *Language contact*, 103–115. Berlin: Mouton de Gruyter.

Mosel, Ulrike. 1980. *Tolai and Tok Pisin: The influence of the substratum on the development of New Guinea Pidgin*. Canberra: Linguistics Circle of Canberra.

Mous, Maarten. 1994. Ma'a or Mbugu. In Peter Bakker and Maarten Mous (eds.), *Mixed languages: 15 case studies in language intertwining*, 175–200. Amsterdam: IPOTT.
Mufwene, Salikoko S. 1986. The universalist and substrate hypotheses complement one another. In Muysken and Smith, 129–162.
Mufwene, Salikoko S. 1990. Transfer and the substrate hypothesis in creolistics. *Studies in Second Language Acquisition* 12:1–23.
Mufwene, Salikoko S. 1991. Pidgins, creoles, typology, and markedness. In Francis Byrne and Thom Huebner (eds.), *Development and structures of creole languages,* 123–143. Amsterdam: John Benjamins.
Mufwene, Salikoko S, ed. 1993. *Africanisms in Afro-American varieties.* Athens: The University of Georgia Press.
Mufwene, Salikoko S. 1996. The founder principle in creole genesis. *Diachronica* 73(1):83–134.
Mufwene, Salikoko S. 1997. Jargons, pidgins, creoles, and koines: What are they? In Spears and Winford, 35–70.
Mufwene, Salikoko S. 1999. On the language bioprogram hypothesis: Hints from Tazie. In DeGraff, 95–127.
Mühlhäusler, Peter. 1979. *Growth and structure of the lexicon of New Guinea Pidgin.* Canberra: Australian National University.
Mühlhäusler, Peter. 1980. Structural expansion and the process of creolization. In Albert Valdman and Arnold Highfield (eds.), *Theoretical orientations in creole studies,* 19–55. New York: Academic Press.
Mühlhäusler, Peter. 1981. The development of the category of number in Tok Pisin. In Pieter Muysken (ed.), *Generative studies on creole languages,* 35–84. Dordrecht: Foris Publications.
Mühlhäusler, Peter. 1982. Tok Pisin in Papua New Guinea. In Richard W. Bailey and Manfred Görlach (eds.), *English as a world language,* 439–466. Ann Arbor: University of Michigan Press.
Mühlhäusler, Peter. 1987a. Tok Pisin: Model or special case? In Verhaar, 171–185.
Mühlhäusler, Peter. 1987b. On the origins of the predicate marker in Tok Pisin. In Verhaar, 235–249.
Mühlhäusler, Peter. 1990. "Reducing" Pacific languages to writing. In John E. Joseph and Talbot J. Taylor (eds.), *Ideologies of language,* 189–205. London: Routledge.
Mushakoji, Kinhide. 1984. Foreword. In Coulmas, 1–4.
Muysken, Pieter, ed. 1981a. *Generative studies on creole languages.* Dordrecht: Foris Publications.
Muysken, Pieter. 1981b. Creole tense/mood/aspect systems: The unmarked case? In Pieter Muysken, 181–199.

Muysken, Pieter. 1981c. Half-way between Quechua and Spanish: The case for relexification. In A. R. Highfield and A. Valdman (eds.), *Historicity and variation in creole studies*, 52–78. Ann Arbor, Mich.: Karoma.

Muysken, Pieter, and Norval Smith, eds. 1986a. *Substrata versus universals in creole genesis*. Amsterdam: John Benjamins.

Muysken, Pieter, and Norval Smith. 1986b. Introduction: Problems in the identification of substratum features in the creole languages. In Muysken and Smith, 1–13.

Myers-Scotton, Carol. 1992a. Codeswitching as a mechanism of deep borrowing, language shift, and language death. In Brenzinger, 31–58.

Myers-Scotton, Carol. 1992b. Comparing codeswitching and borrowing. In Carol M. Eastman (ed.), *Codeswitching*, 19–39. Clevedon: Multilingual Matters.

Myers-Scotton, Carol. 1993a. *Duelling languages: Grammatical structure in codeswitching*. Oxford: Clarendon Press.

Myers-Scotton, Carol. 1993b. *Social motivations for codeswitching*. Oxford: Clarendon Press.

Myers-Scotton, Carol. 1993c. Elite closure as a powerful language strategy: The African case. *International Journal of the Sociology of Language* 103:149–163.

Myers-Scotton, Carol. 1995. A lexically based model of code-switching. In Lesley Milroy and Pieter Muysken (eds.), *One speaker, two languages*, 233–256. Cambridge: Cambridge University Press.

Myers-Scotton, Carol. 1997a. Code-switching. In Coulmas, 217–237.

Myers-Scotton, Carol. 1997b. 'Matrix language recognition' and 'morpheme sorting' as possible structural strategies in pidgin/creole formation. In Spears and Winford, 151–174.

Myers-Scotton, Carol. 1998. A way to dusty death: The matrix language turnover hypothesis. In Grenoble and Whaley, 289–316.

Myers-Scotton, Carol. 1999. Putting it all together: The matrix language and more. In Bernt Brendemoen, Elizabeth Lanza, and Else Ryen (eds.), *Language encounters in time and space*, 13–28. Oslo: Novus Press.

Myers-Scotton, Carol. 2001. Implications of abstract grammatical structure: Two targets in creole formation. *The Journal of Pidgin and Creole Languages* 16:2.

Myers-Scotton, Carol, and Janice Jake. 1995. Matching lemmas in a bilingual language production model: Evidence from intrasentential codeswitching. *Linguistics* 33:981–1024.

Myers-Scotton, Carol, and Janice Jake. 2000a. Explaining aspects of codeswitching and their implications. In Janet Nicole (ed.), *One mind, two languages: Bilingual language processing*, 91–125. Oxford: Blackwell.

Myers-Scotton, Carol, and Janice Jake. 2000b. Four types of morphemes: Evidence from aphasia, codeswitching, and second language acquisition. *Linguistics* 38:6.
Naro, Anthony J. 1978. A study on the origins of pidginization. *Language* 54:314–347.
Naro, Anthony J. 1983. Comments on "Simplified input and second language acquisition." In Andersen, 109–112.
Nekitel, Otto. 1985. *Sociolinguistic aspects of Abu'*. Ph.D. dissertation. The Australian National University.
Nelde, Peter Hans. 1986. Language contact versus language conflict. In Fishman et al., 469–482.
Nelde, Peter Hans. 1997. Language conflict. In Coulmas, 285–300.
Nivens, Richard J. 2002. *Borrowing versus code-switching.* Publications in Sociolinguistics 8. Dallas, Tex.: SIL International.
Nooteboom, S. G. 1973. The tongue slips into patterns. In Fromkin, 144–151.
O'Connell, Daniel C. 1977. One of many units: The sentence. In Rosenberg, 307–314.
Odlin, Terence. 1992. Transferability and the linguistic substrate. *Second Language Research* 8(3):171–202.
Osgood, Charles E., and J. Kathryn Bock. 1977. Salience and sentencing: Some production principles. In Rosenberg, 89–140.
Ozolins, Uldis. 1993. *The politics of language in Australia.* New York: Cambridge University Press.
Paradis, Michel, ed. 1978a. *Aspects of bilingualism.* Columbia, S.C.: Hornbeam Press.
Paradis, Michel. 1978b. The stratification of bilingualism. In Paradis, 165–175.
Paulston, Christina Bratt. 1986. Social factors in language maintenance and language shift. In Fishman et al., 469–482.
Paulston, Christina Bratt. 1994. *Linguistic minorities in multilingual settings: Implications for language policies.* Philadelphia: John Benjamins.
Pfaff, Carol W. 1979. Constraints on language mixing: Intrasentential code-switching and borrowing in Spanish/English. *Language* 55:291–318.
Pinker, Steven. 1982. A theory on the acquisition of lexical interpretive grammars. In Joan Bresnan (ed.), *The mental representation of grammatical relations,* 655–726. Cambridge, Mass.: MIT Press.
Pool, Jonathan. 1972. National development and language diversity. In Joshua A. Fishman (ed.), *Advances in the sociology of language* 2, 213–230. The Hague: Mouton.

Poplack, Shana. 1980. Sometimes I start a sentence in Spanish *y termino en español:* Toward a typology of codeswitching. *Linguistics* 18:7–8, 581–618.
Poplack, Shana. 1981. Syntactic structure and the social function of codeswitching. In Durán, 169–184.
Poplack, Shana, and Marjory Meechan. 1998. Introduction: How languages fit together in codemixing. *International Journal of Bilingualism* 2(2):127–138.
Poplack, Shana, David Sankoff, and Christopher Miller. 1988. The social correlates and linguistic processes of lexical borrowing and assimilation. *Linguistics* 26:47–104.
Rabin, Chaim. 1986. Language revival and language death. In Fishman et al., 403–415.
Radford, Andrew. 1988. *Transformational grammar: A first course.* Cambridge: Cambridge University Press.
Rappaport, Malka, and Beth Levin. 1998. What to do with θ-roles. In Wendy Wilkins (ed.), *Syntax and semantics, thematic relations* 21, 7–36. New York: Academic Press.
Reesink, Ger P. 1987. Mother tongue and Tok Pisin. In Verhaar, 289–306.
Rickford, John R. and John McWhorter. 1997. Language contact and language generation. In Coulmas, 238–256.
Rizzi, Luigi. 1999. Broadening the empirical basis of universal grammar models: A commentary. In Michael DeGraff, 453–472. Cambridge, Mass.: MIT Press.
Roberts, Ian. 1999. Verb movement and markedness. In DeGraff, 287–327.
Romaine, Suzanne. 1981. The transparency principle. *Lingua* 55:277–300.
Romaine, Suzanne. 1987. Change and variation in the use of *bai* in young children's creolized Tok Pisin in Morobe Province. In Verhaar, 187–203.
Romaine, Suzanne. 1988. *Pidgin and creole languages.* London: Longman.
Romaine, Suzanne. 1989a. *Bilingualism.* Oxford: Basil Blackwell.
Romaine, Suzanne. 1989b. Pidgins, creoles, immigrant, and dying languages. In Dorian, 369–383.
Romaine, Suzanne. 1992. *Language, education and development: Urban and rural Tok Pisin in Papua New Guinea.* Oxford: Clarendon Press.
Rosenberg, Sheldon, ed. 1977a. *Sentence production: Developments in research and theory.* Hillsdale, N.J.: Lawrence Erlbaum Associates.
Rosenberg, Sheldon. 1977b. Semantic constraints on sentence production: An experimental approach. In Rosenberg, 195–228.
Ross, Malcolm D. 1988. *Proto Oceanic and the Austronesian languages of Western Melanesia.* Canberra: The Australian National University.

Ross, Malcolm D. 1992. The sources of Austronesian lexical items in Tok Pisin. In Tom Dutton, Malcolm Ross, and Darrell Tryon (eds.), *The language game: Papers in memory of Donald C. Laycock,* 361–384. Canberra: Pacific Linguistics, C-110.

Samar, Reza Ghafar, and Marjory Meechan. 1998. The Null Theory of code-switching versus the Nonce Borrowing Hypothesis: Testing the fit in Persian-English bilingual discourse. *International Journal of Bilingualism* 2(2):203–219.

Samarin, William J. 1971. Salient and substantive pidginization. In Hymes, 117–140.

Sankoff, Gillian. 1979. The genesis of a language. In Kenneth C. Hill (ed.), *The genesis of a language,* 23–47. Ann Arbor: Karoma Publishers.

Sankoff, Gillian. 1980a. Variation, pidgins and creoles. In Albert Valdman and Arnold Highfield (eds.), *Theoretical orientations in creole studies,* 139–164. New York: Academic Press.

Sankoff, Gillian. 1980b. *The social life of language.* Philadelphia: University of Pennsylvania Press.

Sankoff, Gillian. 1983. Comments on Valdman's "Creolization and second language acquisition." In Andersen, 241–245.

Sankoff, Gillian. 1993. Focus in Tok Pisin. In Francis Byrne and Donald Winford (eds.), *Focus and grammatical relations in creole languages,* 117–140. Amsterdam: John Benjamins.

Sankoff, Gillian and Penelope Brown. 1976. The origin of syntax in discourse: A case study of Tok Pisin relatives. *Language* 52:631–666.

Sankoff, Gillian, and Suzanne Laberge. 1974. On the acquisition of native speakers by a language. In David DeCamp and Ian F. Hancock (eds.), *Pidgins and creoles: Current trends and prospects,* 73–84. Washington, D.C.: Georgetown University Press.

Sasse, Hans-Jürgen. 1992a. Theory of language death. In Brenzinger, 7–30.

Sasse, Hans-Jürgen. 1992b. Language decay and contact-induced change: Similarities and differences. In Brenzinger, 59–80.

Schiffman, Harold F. 1993. The balance of power in multiglossic languages: implications for language shift. *International Journal of the Sociology of Language* 103:115–148.

Schiffman, Harold F. 1997. Diglossia as a sociolinguistic situation. In Coulmas, 205–216.

Schlesinger, I. M. 1977. Components of a production model. In Rosenberg, 169–193.

Schmitt, Elena. 2000a. Overt and covert codeswitching in immigrant children from Russia. *International Journal of Bilingualism* 4(1):9–28.

Schmitt, Elena. 2000b. *The lost word: Language attrition among children.* Unpublished manuscript.
Schumann, John H. 1976. Second language acquisition: The pidginization hypothesis. *Language Learning* 26(2):391–408.
Schumann, John H. 1978. The relationship of pidginization, creolization and decreolization to second language acquisition. *Language Learning* 28:367–379.
Scotton, Carol Myers. 1976. Strategies of neutrality: Language choice in uncertain situations. *Language* 52:919–941.
Scotton, Carol Myers. 1986. Diglossia and code switching. In Fishman et al., 403–415.
Sebba, Mark. 1998. A congruence approach to the syntax of codeswitching. *International Journal of Bilingualism* 2(2):1–19.
Sebeok, Thomas A., ed. 1971. *Current trends in linguistics 8: Linguistics in Oceania.* The Hague: Mouton.
Seuren, Pieter A. M., and Herman Wekker. 1986. Semantic transparency as a factor in creole genesis. In Muysken and Smith, 57–70.
Shaffer, Douglas. 1978. The place of code-switching in linguistic contacts. In Paradis, 265–274.
Siegel, Jeff. 1997. Mixing, leveling, and pidgin/creole develpoment. In Spears and Winford, 111–149.
Siegel, Jeff. 1998. *Substrate reinforcement and the development of Hawai'i Creole English.* Paper from the Symposium on Language Contact and Change. Australian Linguistics Institute.
Siegel, Jeff. 1999. Transfer constraints and substrate influence in Melanesian Pidgin. *Journal of Pidgin and Creole Languages* 14(1):1–44.
Silverstein, Michael. 1972. Chinook Jargon: Language contact and the problem of multi-level generative systems. *Language* 48:378–406; 596–625.
Singler, John Victor. 1988. The homogeneity of the substrate as a factor in pidgin/creole genesis. *Language* 64(1):27–51.
Singler, John Victor. 1992. Nativization and pidgin/creole genesis: A reply to Bickerton. *Journal of Pidgin and Creole Languages* 7(2):319–333.
Singler, John Victor. 1993. African influence upon Afro-American language varieties: A consideration of sociohistorical factors. In Mufwene, 235–253.
Slobin, Dan I. 1983. What the natives have in mind. In Andersen, 246–253.
Smith, David M. 1972. Some implications for the social status of pidgins. In David M. Smith and Roger W. Shuy (eds.), *Sociolinguistics*

in cross-cultural analysis, 47–56. Washington, D.C.: Georgetown University Press.
Smith, Michael Sharwood. 1983. On first language loss in the second language acquirer: Problems of transfer. In Susan M. Gass and Larry Selinker (eds.), *Language transfer and language learning,* 222–231. Rowley, Mass.: Newberry House.
Souter, G. 1963. *New Guinea: The last unknown.* Sydney: Angus and Robertson.
Spears, Arthur K., and Donald Winford, eds. 1997. *The structure and status of pidgins and creoles.* Amsterdam: John Benjamins.
Stoller, Paul. 1979. Social interaction and the development of stabilized pidgins. In Hancock, 69–79.
Tabouret-Keller, Andrée. 1997. Language and identity. In Coulmas, 315–326.
Talmy, Leonard. 1985. Lexicalization patterns: Semantic structures in lexical form. In Timothy Shopen (ed.), *Language typology and syntactic description 3: Grammatical categories and the lexicon,* 57–149. Cambridge: Cambridge University Press.
Taylor, Douglas. 1956. Language contact in the West Indies. *Word* 12:399–414.
Thomason, Sarah Grey. 1980. On interpreting 'The Indian Interpreter'. *Language in Society* 9:167–193.
Thomason, Sarah Grey. 1993. On identifying the sources of creole structure. In Mufwene, 280–295.
Thomason, Sarah Grey. 1997. A typology of contact languages. In Spears and Winford, 71–88.
Thomason, Sarah G. 2001. *Language contact: An Introduction.* Washington, D.C.: Georgetwon University Press.
Thomason, Sarah Grey, and Terrence Kaufman. 1988. *Language contact, creolization, and genetic linguistics.* Berkeley: University of California Press.
Todd, Loreto. 1974. *Pidgins and creoles.* London: Routledge & Kegan Paul.
Todd, Loreto. 1984. *Modern Englishes: Pidgins and creoles.* Oxford: Blackwell.
Traugott, Elizabeth Closs. 1977. Pidginization, creolization, and language change. In Valdman, 99–125.
Treffers-Daller, Jeanine. 1993. *Mixing two languages: French-Dutch contact in a comparative perspective.* Berlin: Mouton de Gruyter.
Unknown. 1911. *A ro na papasa Markus qa kalaqi. Das evangelium nach S. Markus im dialekt von Neu Mecklenburg Nord.* Sidney: Samuel E. Lees.

Unknown. 1921. *A buk ina iqai we a buk ina gain we a kaimatan lotu patakai. Pana etok Nusa tana papar Omo.* Rabaul: Methodist Missionary Society of Australia.

Valdés, Guadalupe. 1981. Codeswitching as deliberate verbal strategy: A microanalysis of direct and indirect requests among bilingual speakers. In Durán, 95–107.

Valdman, Albert, ed. 1977. *Pidgin and creole linguistics.* Bloomington: Indiana University Press.

Valdman, Albert. 1983. Creolization and second language acquisition. In Andersen, 212–234.

Valdman, Albert, and Arnold Highfield, eds. 1980. *Theoretical orientations in creole studies.* New York: Academic Press.

Verhaar, John W. M., ed. 1987. *Melanesian Pidgin and Tok Pisin.* Amsterdam: John Benjamins.

Volker, Craig. 1993. Changing language patterns in a Papua New Guinean society. *Annals of the Gifu University for Education and Languages* 25:107–123.

Volker, Craig. 1998. *The Nalik language of New Ireland, Papua New Guinea.* New York: Peter Lang Publishing.

Voorhoeve, Jan. 1971. A note on reduction and expansion in grammar. In Hymes, 189.

Waiko, John Dademo. 1993. *A short history of Papua New Guinea.* Melbourne: Oxford University Press.

Waters, Glenys. 1997. *On the brink: A survey and evaluation of vernacular education and language programming at the provincial level within Papua New Guinea.* Unpublished manuscript.

Weinreich, Uriel. 1953. *Languages in contact.* The Hague: Mouton.

Whinnom, Keith. 1971. Linguistic hybridization and the "special case" of pidgins and creoles. In Hymes, 91–115.

Whinnom, Keith. 1977a. The context and origins of lingua franca. In Jorgen M. Meisel (ed.), *Langues en contact—pidgins—creoles,* 3–18. Tübingen: TBL Verlag Guntar Narr.

Whinnom, Keith. 1977b. Lingua franca: Historical problems. In Valdman, 295–310.

Williams, Colin H. 1984. More than tongue can tell: Ethnic separatism. In Edwards, 179–219.

Williams, Colin H. 1991. Conclusion: Sound language planning is holistic in nature. In Colin H. Williams (ed.), *Linguistic minorities, society and territory,* 315–322. Philadelphia: Multilingual Matters.

Winford, Donald. 1997. Column: Creole formation in the context of contact linguistics. *Journal of Pidgin and Creole Languages* 12(1):131–151.

Winford, Donald. 2003. *An introduction to contact linguistics.* Malden, Mass.: Blackwell.

Wolfers, Edward. 1971. A report on Neo-Melanesian. In Hymes, 169–186.

Woolard, Kathryn A. 1989. Language convergence and language death as social processes. In Dorian, 355–368.

Woolford, Helen B. 1979a. *Aspects of Tok Pisin grammar.* Canberra: The Australian National University.

Woolford, Helen B. 1979b. The developing complementizer system of Tok Pisin: Syntactic change in progress. In Kenneth C. Hill (ed.), *The genesis of language,* 108–124. Ann Arbor: Karoma Publishers.

Wurm, S. A. 1975. Language distributuion in the New Guinea area. In S. A. Wurm (ed.), *New Guinea area languages and language study* 1, 3–38. Canberra: Linguistics Circle of Canberra.

Wurm, S. A. 1980. Standardization and instrumentationalism in Tok Pisin. In Albert Valdman and Arnold Highfield (eds.), *Theoretical orientations in creole studies,* 237–244. New York: Academic Press.

Wurm, S. A. 1986. Remarks on a case of language decay and revival. In Fishman et al., 533–541.

Wurm, S. A., and J. B. Harris. 1963. *Police Motu.* Canberra: The Australian National University.

SIL International
Publications in Language Use and Education

1. **Reading is for Knowing,** by Patricia M. Davis, 2004.
2. **"And I, in My Turn, Will Pass It On": Knowledge Transmission among the Kayopó,** by Isabel I. Murphy, 2004.
3. *Namel Manmeri* **'The In-Between People': Language and Culture Maintenance and Mother-Tongue Education in the Highlands of Papua New Guinea,** by Dennis L. Malone, 2004.

Publications in Sociolinguistics

8. **Borrowing Versus Code-Switching in West Tarangan (Indonesia),** by Richard J. Nivens, 2002.
7. **The Dynamics of Sango Language Spread,** by Mark E. Karan, 2001.
6. **K'iche': A Study in the Sociology of Language,** by M. Paul Lweis, 2001.
5. **The Same but Different: Language Use and Attitudes in Four Communities of Burkina Faso,** by Stuart Showalter, 2000.
4. **Ashéninka Stories of Change,** by Ronald James Anderson, 2000.
3. **Assessing Ethnolinguistic Vitality: Theory and Practice,** M. Paul Lewis and Gloria Kindell, eds., 1999.
2. **The Early Days of Sociolinguistics: Memories and Reflections,** Christina Bratt Paulston and G. Richard Tucker, eds., 1997.
1. **North Sulawesi Language Survey,** Scott Merrifield and Martinus Selsa, 1996.

For further information or a full listing of SIL publications contact:

International Academic Bookstore
SIL International
7500 W. Camp Wisdom Road
Dallas, TX 75236-5699

Voice: 972-708-7404
Fax: 972-708-7363
Email: academic_books@sil.org
Internet: http://www.ethnologue.com

www.ingramcontent.com/pod-product-compliance
Lightning Source LLC
Chambersburg PA
CBHW070243230426
43664CB00014B/2392